The Promise of Justice

The Promise of Justice

Essays on *Brown v. Board of Education*

EDITED BY

MAC A. STEWART

 THE OHIO STATE UNIVERSITY PRESS • COLUMBUS

Library of Congress Cataloging-in-Publication Data
The promise of justice : essays on Brown v. Board of Education / edited by Mac A.
Stewart.
    p. cm.
  Includes bibliographical references and index.
  ISBN-13: 978-0-8142-1087-1 (cloth : alk. paper)
  1. Brown, Oliver, 1918—Trials, litigation, etc. 2. Topeka (Kan.). Board of Education—
Trials, litigation, etc. 3. Segregation in education—Law and legislation—United States.
4. Race discrimination—Law and legislation—United States. 5. United States—Race
relations. I. Stewart, Mac A.
  KF4155.A2P76 2008
  344.73'0798—dc22

                                              2007050227

This book is available in the following editions:
Cloth (ISBN 978-0-8142-1087-1)
CD-ROM (ISBN 978-0-8142-9167-2)

Cover design by Jenny Poff
Type set in Bitstream Aldine
Printed by Thomson-Shore, Inc.

♾ The paper used in this publication meets the minimum requirements of the American National Standard for Information Sciences—Permanence of Paper for Printed
Library Materials. ANSI Z39.48-1992.

9 8 7 6 5 4 3 2 1

I dedicate this book to my wife, Tena, for her love, patience, and support during my graduate studies and throughout my professional career, and to our sons, Bruce and Justin.

Contents

FOREWORD AND ACKNOWLEDGMENTS

I have titled this collection of essays that consider the fifty-year legacy of *Brown v. Board of Education of Topeka, Kansas* as "The Promise of Justice" partly because of the prophetic overtones of this phrase, although I believe that normally we are wise to be suspicious when writers, especially political writers, use prophetic or apocalyptic language. To describe ordinary events with extraordinary language exaggerates the events and eventually diminishes the language. For example, the words "vision" and "visionary" once were reserved for high purposes, as in: "Lincoln had a *vision* of the Union enduring and, for all its citizens, free." Now, it is usual to hear "vision" in more commonplace contexts: "Young man, what is your *vision* for this entry-level job as an insurance salesman?"

In times when some of our strongest language has been thus denatured, it is therefore all the more remarkable that some language retains its historical power to rouse audiences and move them emotionally. Many decades after the death of Martin Luther King Jr., his greatest speeches—"I have a dream," "I have been to the mountain"—retain their force among new generations of listeners. Surely part of the reason for this continuing power is the historical context of King's words. Like Israel in Egypt in the Old Testament Book of Exodus, Black people in America's South, though emancipated by federal proclamation, were still in legal bondage. Jim Crow legislation constricted every part of their lives, determining where they could live, where they could work, whom they could marry, whether they could vote, and where they could send their children for education. Within the historical context, it is no exaggeration, it seems to me, to refer to the Supreme Court's 1954 decision in the case of *Brown v. the Board of Education of Topeka, Kansas* as bringing "the promise of justice."

Professor Manning Marable, in the opening essay in this collection, correctly says that "the *Brown* decision of 1954 set the legal framework for the emergence of what would become a mass Black Freedom movement to overturn legal segregation in all public accommodations and institutions, which was achieved a decade later with the passage of the 1964 Civil Rights Act." *Brown* had established, in the words of Chief Justice Earl Warren's decision, "that in the field of public education, the doctrine of 'separate but equal' has no place. Separate educational facilities are inherently unequal." By the time of the passage of the Civil Rights Act of 1964, it was becoming settled jurisprudence that "separate . . . is inherently unequal" applied to all public services, institutions, and facilities.

But of course, before 1954 it was inescapable common knowledge among blacks and whites, those in the South and those in the North, that separate *meant* unequal. That, of course, was the point of keeping whites and blacks apart. In my all-black elementary school in rural Georgia, we knew that when the students at the local white school received new textbooks, trucks filled with their discarded books would soon be arriving at our school, to replace our long outdated texts with others only slightly out of date. There was no question in our minds that separate meant "less than equal" for us. The wonder to me now is that we accepted this condition as the way the world worked. Although we objected to the segregated environment of the 1950s and earlier, mass protests against it were rare.

Within the separate world legislated for American Blacks, hierarchies and support structures developed to make life possible. Some Blacks flourished by providing for community needs that were invisible for outsiders. A leading example was Madam C. J. Walker, the Indianapolis entrepreneur who catered to the beauty needs of the Black community. Others founded businesses and generated personal fortunes in similar ways. As the financial leaders of Black society, they felt an obligation to give back to the community by supporting local and national efforts to make life better for African Americans. Separation from the majority community and power structure helped to foster solidarity within the African American towns, churches, and civic clubs. As a rule, we accepted "separate and unequal" and learned to make it work. *Brown* showed us that the world could be different—that at least under law, we might be entitled to equal justice, in education and in many other parts of life as well.

The authors of the essays included here share the point of view that *Brown v. Board of Education* reiterated in a very specific way the general promise of justice for all made by the Founding Fathers in the Constitution. Standing on the steps of the Lincoln Memorial in 1963, a decade after *Brown,* Martin Luther King referred to the Constitution as a "promissory note to which every American was to fall heir. This note was the promise that all men, yes, black men as well as white men, would be guaranteed the unalienable rights of life, liberty, and the pursuit of happiness. It is obvious today that America has defaulted on this promissory note as far as her citizens of color are concerned." The Emancipation Proclamation of 1862 renewed that promise, and ninety years later, so did the Supreme Court in *Brown.*

The opening essay in this anthology, by Manning Marable, defines "The Promise of *Brown*" with a dual focus: first, on the legal framework established by *Brown* and the policies and actions, notably affirmative action, made newly possible within that framework; and second, on heroic persons, like Judge Robert Carter, one of the principal attorneys who argued and won in *Brown.* Recognizing that the promise has not yet been fulfilled, Marable concludes that the example of men like "Robert Carter, Charles Hamilton Houston, and Thurgood Marshall set into bold relief for us the political courage and selfless dedication that will be required to achieve that final victory over structural racism . . . in today's America. . . . It is our living legacy to fulfill the long deferred promise of *Brown.*" Samuel DuBois Cook, author of the second essay, turns to philosophers (among them Aristotle, John Rawls, Reinhold Niebuhr, and Paul Tillich) and legal authorities to probe the meaning of "equality" and "justice" as these ideals relate to the U.S. Constitution and "the Human Person." The triumph of *Brown,* and thus the promise of *Brown,* is that by the decision in this case, "Gone is the idea of 'partial,' fragmentary, limited, relative equality (of Blacks) in comparison to whites. Equality is truly constitutionalized." The decision in *Brown,* Cook writes, "has nudged America in the noble direction of justice and equality for us all both as citizens and as human beings."

Harvard sociologist Charles V. Willie measures the impact of *Brown* and concludes: "*Brown,* as an innovation in public education, was not a failure. *Brown* has not failed us; but the law enforcement process in our democratic nation failed *Brown.*" Willie stresses that *Brown* "was an equity case and should be remembered as such because excellence and equity ought always to be kept together. We need both because equity is a correction for the excesses of individualism and excellence is a correction for the excesses of collectivism in a society." C. U. Smith painstakingly traces judicial history as the context for *Brown* and brings the issue forward to the present time. He includes much recent information that is discouraging in view of the promise of *Brown,* then concludes with the affirmation of actions promoting educational diversity provided by the Supreme Court in *Grutter v. Bollinger:* in the words of Justice Sandra Day O'Connor, "The Equal Protection Clause does not prohibit the Law School's narrowly tailored use of race in its admissions decisions to further a compelling interest in obtaining the educational benefits that flow from a diverse student body."

The next four essays—by Lester Monts, Ralph K. Frasier, Judge Robert Duncan, and William and Adia Harvey—are included in order to add the personal testimony of eyewitnesses to the weighty arguments and histories of the previous scholars. These witnesses include one of the plaintiffs in a court action subsequent to *Brown,* the case of *Frasier, et al. v. the Board of Trustees of the University of North Carolina et al.,* as well as the presiding federal judge in the case of *Penick v. Columbus Board of Education,* one of the last desegregation cases involving a large urban school district. These accounts present details to instruct and remind audiences who did not see, and therefore may not otherwise be aware of, the injustices that *Brown* was intended to correct. These accounts also bring the dialogue forward, with comments on "a decidedly post-segregationist world, but one that still wrestled with issues of integration" (in the words of Adia M. Harvey). Because some forces still actively oppose realizing the promise of *Brown,* we believe it is important to keep alive the memory of the injustice and inequality which that promise was expected to redress.

The focus of the last five essays in this collection shifts perceptibly to the legacy of *Brown,* with a secondary theme in each of these five that depends on the difference in meaning between "desegregation" and "integration." Professor john a. powell cites Martin Luther King on this distinction:

The word *segregation* represents a system that is prohibitive, it denies the Negro equal access to schools, parks, libraries and the like. *Desegregation* is eliminative and negative, for it simply removes these legal and social prohibitions. *Integration* is creative, and is therefore more profound and far-reaching than desegregation. . . . As America pursues the important task of respecting the "letter of the law," i.e., compliance with desegregation decisions, she must equally be concerned with the "spirit of the law," i.e., commitment to the democratic dream of integration. (emphasis in original)

powell argues first that for full understanding, *Brown,* the judgment released in 1954, requires *Brown II,* released a year later, with its famous prescription that desegregation should proceed "with all deliberate speed." Further, powell argues that the Supreme Court underestimated the degree of change necessary for compliance with *Brown,* and finally, that the "profound vision of *Brown*" requires a radical shift in the meaning of "whiteness" and an understanding of how whites are injured by segregation and "white space." In his final section, powell discusses variant *mis*understandings of *integration,* which is not simply desegregation or assimilation: "*Brown* and *Brown II* can more aptly be seen as a profound vision of integration and a multiracial and multiethnic democracy. It is the vision of a society without a superior class." In this vision, for powell, is the promise of *Brown.*

Deborah Jones Merritt also focuses on *Brown's* legacy, pointing out the downside that "judicial power can serve the interests of elites by helping to marginalize more democratic forms of policy making," with consequences for integration that, she argues, the courts themselves will not solve. Philip T. K. Daniel traces the aftermath of *Brown* through local desegregation decisions such as *Griffin v. County School Board of Prince Edward County, Alexander v. Holmes County Board of Education,* and others, concluding that "the circle of racial segregation in schools has completed itself based on the more recent Supreme Court cases weakening the welfare of African-American and other students of color. . . ." Vincene Verdun traces a history of Supreme Court actions and omissions that, in her view, led to "a separate and unequal America." She cites such factors as the lack of a clear mandate in *Brown,* the Court's failure to include suburban school districts in the remedy for state-supported segregation of urban schools, the requirement of intent to demonstrate discrimination, and the failure to recognize benign discrimination. Finally, Janine Hancock Jones and Charles R. Hancock survey the educational landscape as it stood fifty years after *Brown* to answer the question "Where are we now?" Sadly, they conclude that, if asked "to rate the current level of success of *Brown v. Board of Education,*" they "would assign a grade of C+ at this point in our nation's history."

The essays in this collection all attempt to come to terms with the decision in *Brown* in light of the experience of the fifty years that followed. Most of these essays first appeared in a special issue, published in January 2005, of *The Negro Educational Review.* The essays by Robert Duncan, Lester Monts, and john powell are printed here for the first time and add significantly to the perspectives in the original group. For example, Robert Duncan was the federal judge in *Penick, et al., v. Columbus Board of Education,* one of the last desegregation cases involving a large urban school district to be litigated. The case was argued from April to June 1976, but its consequences continued to reach his court through 1985 and beyond. A goal for many of the authors in this volume was to assess the positive differences that *Brown* has made. I agree with most of the contributors that since 1954 much good has been accomplished in response to *Brown,* but that as I write in 2006, it would be inaccurate to assert that equal justice has been achieved.

I am pleased to acknowledge the encouragement and very practical assistance of those who have helped in the preparation of this volume. The project originated with the members of the editorial board of *The Negro Educational Review* (*NER*), when Dr. F. C. Richardson was chairman and Dr. C. U. Smith was managing editor. Members of my staff at the Office of Minority Affairs were instrumental in the preparation of the manuscript, first for the *NER* special issue (volume 6, no. 1, January 2005), and again for this enlarged volume. We appreciate the permission granted by *NER* to reproduce those essays in this volume. I am grateful also to Ellen Banks, Dr. Thomas Minnick, Sarah Sunderhaus, Edie Waugh, and Gregory Williams.

CHAPTER 1

The Promise of *Brown*

*Desegregation, Affirmative Action
and the Struggle for Racial Equality*

MANNING MARABLE

It was a brilliantly sunny, warm, early Friday afternoon in mid-September, the kind of memorable moment one yearns for in the bleakness of a New York City winter. Classes at Columbia University had just started, and hundreds of students were clustered along the steps and sidewalks, sunbathing and leisurely enjoying their noisy conversations. I hurriedly navigated my way through these human obstacle courses, embarrassed at being uncharacteristically late for my lunch appointment. Finally I could peer through the throng, seeing at the corner of Amsterdam Avenue and West 116 Street, Columbia's Law School. Crossing against the light, I searched frantically for my guest. Cool as a cucumber, eighty-six-year-old Federal Judge Robert Carter was already there, patiently waiting for me to arrive. "Not to worry," Judge Carter smiled warmly, shaking my hand firmly. "It's a lovely day."

It's not often that a historian has a lunch date with African American history. But lunch with Robert Carter, the original attorney of the *Brown v. Board of Education* decision, was exactly that.

Carter is remarkably youthful in appearance, still physically trim, dapper in dress, and his mental dexterity is as extraordinarily sharp as it was in legendary court battles a half century ago. Yet for one who has accomplished so much in a celebrated career of public service and social justice advocacy, Carter's manner is remarkably modest. His deep interest in African American history and especially the experiences of struggle by blacks during Reconstruction, he explained over lunch, had helped to motivate him toward pursuing a law degree at Howard University. It was at Howard on November 8, 1938, while as a student, that Carter witnessed the incomparable civil rights attorney, Charles Hamilton Houston, rehearse the arguments he would successfully employ before the Supreme Court the next day, in what would be called the *Gaines* case. Hamilton's victory in *Gaines* over the all-white law school of the University of Missouri would pave the road toward the ultimate triumph over all segregated education many years later.

After military service during World War II, Carter joined the NAACP Legal Defense and Education Fund (LDF), and quickly rose as second-in-command to the LDF's charismatic and capable leader, attorney Thurgood Marshall. Judge Carter talked fondly about his early experiences on the LDF staff back in the 1940s and 1950s. I reminded him that for a time the offices of Thurgood Marshall and Dr. W. E. B. Du Bois were adjacent to each other, much to Du Bois's displeasure. Carter laughed aloud, recalling Marshall's habit of caucusing with his talented legal assistants at the end of a hard workday in boisterous, smoke-filled bull sessions around his office at late hours. The constant noise, and not infrequent earthy language, Carter carefully explained, irritated the proper scholar. Carter's small office was right down the hall on the same floor, so he was an intimate witness to the sometimes tense relationship between these two icons of black history.

Today, Robert Carter is best known as one of the principal attorneys who won famous *Brown v. Board of Education* case, which along with four other cases, culminated in the U.S. Supreme Court's 1954 decision outlawing legal racial segregation in public schools. But the political story behind this remarkable civil rights achievement is too little appreciated.

In 1896, in the *Plessy v. Ferguson* decision, the Supreme Court had declared that racially segregated schools were constitutional, provided that all-black schools were "separate but equal" to white schools. In practical terms, however, the separate-but-equal standard created and perpetuated gross inequalities in the educational access of African Americans, especially in the Jim Crow South. The NAACP's attorneys, first led by Houston, and subsequently by Marshall, launched a series of successful legal challenges against unequal access in higher education over a quarter century. These early cases did not challenge the principle of "separate but equal" head on. But they nevertheless laid the foundation for a direct assault on the legality of Jim Crow Education. It was not until 1950 that Marshall and the NAACP leader Walter White were sufficiently confident that racial segregation could be successfully assaulted in education cases before the high court.

As Marshall's chief lieutenant, Carter was central in mapping the entire legal strategy. It was Carter who contacted social scientists Kenneth and Mamie Clark, whose studies establishing the destructive psychological effects of racial exclusion on black children provided an important rationale for their legal argument to outlaw separate schools. Carter and his colleagues argued that the *Plessy* standard was unconstitutional because it denied equality under the law to Negroes as stipulated in the Fourteenth Amendment. But hedging their bets, just in case the Supreme Court refused to overturn the *Plessy* precedent, they also pointed out that even *Plessy* mandated fully "equal" educational facilities for Negroes. The only way to accomplish this was to integrate all public schools.

On May 17, 1954, in a surprisingly unanimous decision, the Supreme Court ruled in favor of the LDF, the NAACP, and the plaintiffs in *Brown* and the other cases. Supreme Court Chief Justice Earl Warren, in his decision, declared: "Does segregation of children in public schools solely on the basis of race, even though the physical facilities and other tangible factors may be equal, deprive children of the minority group of equal educational opportunities? We believe it does. . . . We conclude, unanimously, that in the field of public education, the doctrine of 'separate but equal' has no place. Separate educational facilities are inherently unequal." The *Brown* decision of 1954 set the legal framework for the emergence of what would become a mass Black Freedom movement to overturn legal racial segregation in all public accommodations and institutions, which was achieved a decade later with the passage of the 1964 Civil Rights Act.

A half-century has now passed since the Supreme Court rendered the *Brown* decision. How far have we come toward the realization of *Brown's* promise of racial equality and social justice?

If measured by the words we use in academic discourse and popular culture, the separate-but-equal doctrine has given way to the mantras of "diversity" and "multiculturalism."

Who *isn't* for diversity? No one opposed the widespread view that diversity enhances and enriches our society. Even the generals at the Pentagon and former members of the Joint Chiefs of Staff submitted *amicus* briefs in the 2003 Supreme Court cases of *Grutter v. Bollinger* and *Gratz v. Bollinger* on behalf of affirmative action. Even neoconservatives like Ben Wattenberg,[1] whom I've debated, declare that "we are all multiculturalists now."

But if we all value diversity, why are half of our prisons filled with young black men? If diversity is our greatest strength, why are Latino and black jobless rates still 2 to 2.5 times that for whites? If we all value diversity in our workplaces, why are our residential districts in America still so heavily segregated by race?

My own personal story about the legacy of the *Brown* decision, and the pursuit of diversity within America's flawed democracy, begins with my memories about life as a black boy, growing up in Dayton, Ohio in the 1950s and 1960s. I am a child of the *Brown* decision, and my own personal journey symbolizes the successes and failures of legal desegregation.

As I grew up, I could never forget, not even for a single moment, that I was black. Regardless of our incomes, education, and material successes, despite our relatively privileged social status as middle-class African Americans, we still lived in a world apart from whites. The barrier of race isolated us from opportunities in thousands of ways, even in a midwestern town where formal, legal segregation did not exist. My father attempted to obtain a mortgage to purchase a house to start a nursery school business, and over a two-year period was denied credit at every bank in Dayton. Negroes were confined largely to the city's ghetto on the west side; they were usually not allowed to purchase homes or even to rent apartments in many quarters of the city. Even as a child growing up in the 1950s, I could vividly comprehend that as Negroes we lived in a separate, unequal world.

Yet within that segregated world apart, we found joy and laughter; we found music and dignity within our souls. We prayed to the Lord in our own houses of worship; we celebrated our own heroes during "Black History Month" every February; when we sang our national anthem, it was James Weldon Johnson's "Lift Ev'ry Voice and Sing." We were the orphans of American democracy: part of the household, but never members of the family. The principles and policies of democracy, the core values and ideals in which Negroes deeply believed, were never fully extended to us. But our tenuous status as permanent outsiders gave us a peculiar insight into the nature and unequal reality of white power.

1. Ben Wattenberg is a Senior Fellow at the American Enterprise Institute, a conservative think tank, and moderator of a weekly PBS television program.

Within that pervasive veil of race stood another bastion of power and violence called poverty, which had definable features I began to understand. Even as a boy, I gradually deciphered the burden of social inequality in its different manifestations: the unemployed who clustered along Fifth Street desperately seeking a day's wages, while affluent whites drove by, deciding which man would be hired; the factory workers living in our neighborhood who came home filthy and tired; the middle-aged black women standing at the bus stop, leaving their own children to travel across town to care for the children of well-to-do households. Traveling to the South, I watched in silence as our family automobile slowly passed a work gang along the side of a country road. The men wore black and white coarse garments and were roughly chained together at their ankles. Guards with guns supervised their labor. It was a shocking scene I never forgot. Diversity, I learned, meant more than color; it was also about "class."

The first real lessons in my political education of diversity occurred in the early 1960s with the eruption of the Civil Rights Movement, America's "Second Reconstruction." On television, along with millions of other Americans, I witnessed a series of unprecedented and powerful confrontations: the "sit-in" movement, initiated in February 1960 by a group of college students in North Carolina, which escalated in hundreds of nonviolent protests across the South; the "Freedom Rides," led by the Congress of Racial Equality, which challenged segregation in public transportation facilities throughout the heart of Dixie; the nonviolent demonstrations of thousands of men, women, and children in the streets of Birmingham during spring 1963, mobilizing dissent in the "Citadel of Segregation." We closely followed these dramatic events and were inspired to act in our own small community. We staged modest protest demonstrations in white-owned department stores and businesses in our downtown, demanding an end to racial segregation in hiring policies. Banks were pressured to extend credit and capital to blacks. The local newspapers and television stations, which had carefully ignored any coverage of the African American community, gradually lifted the information blockade on blackness. The "iron curtain" that had separated capitalist democracies from communist countries in Europe was less pervasive than the racial curtain that separated the disadvantaged African American community from comfortable white enclaves of affluence and privilege.

What I began to learn in the relatively idealistic days of the early 1960s was that the meaning and impact of "race" could be changed. As oppressed people mobilized themselves in nonviolent civil disobedi-ence, as they registered new voters and organized Freedom Schools in shanties and churches across the rural South, the political definition of what blackness could be was sharply transformed. As the struggle for power grew more intense, as Negroes boldly asserted themselves as never before, millions of white Americans were pressured and forced to reex-amine their racist stereotypes and prejudices. Over time, most whites began to modify their language, their public behavior, and their treat-ment of black people in daily life. I observed these changes in daily life from my practical experiences. The schedules of public buses, which had never been routed through parts of the black suburban community, were changed, permitting us to travel downtown when I was a teenager. School curricula slowly began to reflect more multicultural themes and a new recognition of black history and culture. Blacks were hired in the police department and were elected to the city council. The Black Free-dom Movement had permitted Negroes to perceive themselves as real actors in their own history. The boundaries of what whites had defined as blackness were radically reinterpreted and renegotiated. In short, race was not fixed, grounded in biological or genetic differences, or created through "cultural deprivation"; it was the logical consequence of struc-tural power, structural privilege, and anti-black violence. As Negroes challenged and overthrew the institutions of racial inequality, the actual relationship between black and white was sharply altered. Young people of color today must learn this lesson—that through direct action and struggle, constructive change in racism is possible. We do not have to become the passive victims of racism and intolerance.

Desegregation led to the unprecedented numbers of African American students who entered white academic institutions during the period of Civil Rights and Black Power. In 1960, there were barely 200,000 African Americans enrolled in college, and three-fourths of that number attended historically black universities and colleges. By 1970, 417,000 black Amer-icans between ages 18–24 were attending college. Three-fourths of them were now at predominantly white institutions. Five years later, 666,000 African Americans age 18–24 were enrolled in college, more than one out of every five blacks in their age group. Similar gains occurred at every level of education. The percentage of all African Americans completing four years of high school more than doubled in only fifteen years, from 20 percent in 1960 to 43 percent in 1975. The total number of African Americans under age thirty-five who held college degrees more than tripled in these same years from 96,200 in 1960 up to 341,000 by 1975.

White Americans today need to be reminded that these unprecedented increases in educational access for black Americans were made possible, in large degree, by liberal public policies such as affirmative action, race-based minority scholarship programs, and race-based recruitment efforts to identify promising African American high school students and to offer them "need blind" admissions packages, which made it financially possible for them to attend college. These impressive gains were not a result of voluntary actions. One should also keep in mind that the architects of these race-based affirmative action policies were frequently Republicans, from Earl Warren to Richard M. Nixon. There was a general political consensus between both major parties at the time that "compensation" was due African Americans as a result of the legacy of legal racial segregation, which had only been outlawed officially by Congress in 1964. As the language of the 1968 Kerner Commission made clear, Americans' racial dilemma was perceived almost exclusively within a black-white, bipolar template: "Our Nation is moving toward two societies, one black, one white—separate and unequal."

As black popular culture also in the 1970s and 1980s began to have a truly major impact on white middle American cultural institutions and social behavior, the majority of whites did *not* overtly oppose affirmative action-type reforms that addressed blacks' historic disadvantages. One measure of how "liberal" the racial consensus was during these years was the national debate over the *Bakke* decision of 1978. In a narrow five to four decision, the U.S. Supreme Court overturned the University of California at Davis's admissions program, which set aside a specific number, or quota, for minority applicants to be admitted. Writing for the majority, Associate Justice Lewis Powell rejected racial quotas, but strongly reaffirmed that the racial diversity of a student body comprised "a compelling state interest." As a necessary remedy for past discrimination, race could be legitimately used as a factor in awarding college scholarships and in other educational programs. At the time of the *Bakke* ruling, most African Americans saw this as a retreat from racial justice. Associate Justice Thurgood Marshall, in a vigorous dissent, angrily declared: "It must be remembered that, during most of the past two hundred years, the Constitution as interpreted by this Court did not prohibit the most ingenious and pervasive forms of discrimination against the Negro. Now, when a State acts to remedy the effects of that legacy of discrimination, I cannot believe that this same Constitution stands as a barrier." Sadly, the nation has moved so far to the extreme ideological right in the past quarter century that progressives and civil rights activists now find themselves fighting desperately just to maintain the *Bakke* standard from being entirely erased.

Despite the conservative retrenchment of the Reagan years, black progress, especially in higher education, still continued. Beginning in the late 1980s, both universities and corporations began to promote what I have previously termed "corporate multiculturalism"—celebrating everyone while criticizing no one. "Diversity" became an institutional mantra, a value worthy of corporate and even the U.S. military's endorsement and support. Schools like Columbia doubled their budgets to recruit blacks, Latinos, and American Indians into their graduate schools. The Mellon Foundation initiated a massive, race-based fellowship program, identifying talented black and Latino undergraduate students and encouraging them to enter doctoral programs. By the late 1990s, over one thousand Mellon Fellows at more than three dozen institutions had received hundreds of millions of dollars for summer stipends, travel expenses, tuition support, and debt forgiveness. Between 1989 and 2002, the number of African Americans receiving professional degrees rose by 70 percent. Between 1990 and 2000, black enrollments in law schools jumped 50 percent. Blacks earning Ph.D.s doubled in the decade, with 1,656 new doctorates produced in 2000.

Beginning in the early 1990s, the modern assault against black progress in higher education was simultaneously political, economic, cultural, and ideological. There was a dedicated, concerted effort by conservatives to literally turn the discourse of civil rights upside down; in effect, to rewrite the American public's memory about what had actually transpired in the 1950s and 1960s. Dr. Martin Luther King Jr.'s image and words were cynically manipulated to provide a posthumous endorsement for outlawing affirmative action programs. An important turning point occurred in California in November 1996, with the passage of Proposition 209, the so-called "California Civil Rights Initiative." Winning by a margin of 54 to 46 percent, the initiative outlawed the use of "race, sex, color, ethnicity, or national origin" in many aspects of public life. Thousands of black and Latino voters, confused by the language of the initiative, failed to understand that affirmative action would be outlawed in California, and voted for it. On the day of the referendum, the *Los Angeles Times* exit polls indicated that a clear majority of California voters supported affirmative action programs. Yet these same voters, confused or not, approved Proposition 209 and made it state law. All of this was made possible because the lessons and history of the Civil Rights Movement have been largely erased from the national consciousness. As Ward

Connerly, the Negro conservative who led the campaign for Proposition 209, explained: "The past is a ghost that can destroy our future. It is dangerous to dwell upon it. To focus on America's mistakes is to disregard its virtues."

White moderates and liberals who had long defended race-based affirmative action programs waffled and largely collapsed before the conservative onslaught. Setting the tone was President William Jefferson Clinton, who in his reelection campaign of 1996 declared that he had "done more to eliminate affirmative action programs I didn't think were fair and tighten others up than my predecessors have since affirmative action has been around." Clinton's failure to frame the issue of affirmative action around issues of U.S. racial history and the need to implement measures of compensatory justice for historically oppressed minorities would prove decisive. In 1996, the U.S. Court of Appeals for the Fifth Circuit in the *Hopwood v. State of Texas* decision outlawed the use of race as a factor in admissions to universities. Initiative 200 in Washington State in 1998 followed California in outlawing affirmative action enforcement. As a direct consequence, in the first year of Proposition 209's enforcement, the number of African American first-year undergraduates enrolling at the Berkeley campus fell from 258 to 95, a 63 percent decline. At the University of California at Los Angeles, the drop was from 211 black students down to 125 students.

In June 2003, the U.S. Supreme Court decided two lawsuits involving affirmative action programs at the University of Michigan at Ann Arbor. The more important of the two decisions, *Grutter v. Bollinger,* declared that there was a compelling state interest in fostering programs enhancing "diversity," and that the quality of education was enriched by having individuals from different racial and ethnic backgrounds as part of a university environment. Therefore, the court declared in its narrow five to four ruling, the use of race as a factor was acceptable, so long as it was not applied as a quota. In effect, the Lewis Powell standard set in *Bakke* was deemed still constitutional. The initial response from the academic community was that *Grutter* represented a clear victory for the forces of affirmative action and "diversity." They unfortunately ignored the full weight of the majority's opinion on the high court: that universities had to consider prospective students henceforth "as individuals" and not to reject or admit them through any programs based primarily or exclusively on racial categories. This part of the ruling was quickly interpreted to mean that all programs within a college or university should not be based primarily or exclusively on racial categories.

From late 2003 through March 2004, in a relatively brief period of time, hundreds of U.S. universities and colleges shut down or significantly transformed their minority-oriented programs. The list is truly stunning: at Yale University, a summer preregistration program for pre-freshmen, "Cultural Connections," was opened to white participation; at Princeton University, all "race-exclusive programs" were halted, including its Junner Summer Institute that annually brought African American and Latino college students to the Woodrow Wilson School of Public and International Affairs; at Boulder, the University of Colorado's "Summer Minority Access to Research Training Program" was renamed and opened to whites; at the California Institute of Technology, its campus visit program designed for blacks, Latinos, and American Indians was opened to whites and Asian Americans; at Indiana University, its nine-week "Summer Minority Research Fellowship" originally designed "to get minority high school and college students interested in medical research by matching them with mentors" was restructured to recruit Asian Americans and whites; at Saint Louis University, a scholarship program annually awarding $10,000 each to thirty African American students was "disbanded" and substituted with the new "Martin Luther King Jr." scholarships, reduced to $8,000 per student, and accepting applications without consideration of race; and at Williams College in Massachusetts, a pre-doctoral fellowship program, which for more than a decade awarded annually two to five general dissertation stipends to black and Latino advanced graduate students, with the original purpose of increasing minority professors, has been radically opened to anyone regardless of color who is deemed "underrepresented," such as "women in physics departments," or "white applicants in Asian Studies." *Grutter* was no victory. It marked a cruel defeat that will reduce the opportunities for education advancement for thousands of Latino and African American students in the coming years, all in the name of "diversity." African Americans increasingly now ask themselves, "why did *Brown's* promise fail?"

We also must be frank about the weaknesses of affirmative action as a strategy for achieving compensatory justice. Affirmative action policies first were crafted in reaction to the struggles and demands of the Civil Rights Movement. The central issue, in the language of the day, was the status of the Negro in American society. Groups who were not originally part of the national debate over segregation, or who entered the country after the passage of the Civil Rights Act of 1964, materially benefited in real terms from blacks' sacrifices. By 2000, the overwhelming number of beneficiaries of affirmative action programs, however, was non-black. In a recent conversation, legal scholar Lani Guinier estimated that 73 percent of the beneficiaries of minority-oriented, affirmative action programs at Harvard University were non-black. Affirmative action was a beneficial reform that could have worked well long-term only if "race" stood still. It doesn't. Race is a dynamic, changing social relationship grounded in structural inequality. As the human composition of American society's social order has shifted, the lived reality of structural racism has also changed in everyday existence.

Affirmative action, secondly, never in any meaningful way addressed the economic foundations of structural racism. As political scientist Ronald Walters has observed, affirmative action was essentially "paycheck equality." It gave millions of mostly middle-class, better educated African Americans opportunities for career advancement. It did not fundamentally alter the racial inequality in wealth ownership within U.S. society. The average African American household today owns only 12 percent of the net wealth held by the average white household. One-third of all black families actually have a *negative* net wealth. The growing problem of inequality, to be sure, is not an exclusively racial issue in itself. Researchers Stacie Carney and William G. Gale in 2001 estimated that fully one-fourth of all U.S. households have virtually no financial assets; 20 percent have no savings or checking accounts; and about one-half of all American families have under $5,000 in total financial assets. The argument that the majority of Americans are comfortably part of an affluent middle class is flat-out wrong. But the racial element has never been incidental in the structural arrangements of U.S. society. The lack of assets accumulation has been severely crippling to the development of all kinds of African American institutions and communities as a whole. Affirmative action as an approach to racial reform did not address the necessary transfer of wealth needed to materially develop black communities. Only reparations could begin to address this.

What remains of the promise of *Brown?* Separate-but-equal has given way to what I have termed in my writings the "New Racial Domain" of color-blind, structural racism. In the place of legal segregation and the discrimination of Jim Crow laws, we now have a new regime of racial domination, centered on three deadly institutional processes: mass unemployment, mass incarceration, and mass disfranchisement. All three combine to create the new enslavement of the African American people for the twenty-first century.

The modern cycle of racial destruction starts with chronic, mass unemployment and poverty. Real incomes for the working poor actually fell significantly during Clinton's second term in office. After the 1996 welfare act, the social safety net was largely pulled apart. The Bush administration took power, and chronic joblessness spread to black workers in the manufacturing sector. By early 2004, in cities such as New York, fully one-half of all black male adults were now outside of the paid labor force. By January 2004, the number of families on public assistance had declined to two million, down from five million families on welfare in 1995. New regulations and restrictions intimidate thousands of poor people from requesting public assistance.

Mass unemployment inevitably feeds mass incarceration. About one-third of all prisoners were unemployed at the time of their arrests, and others averaged less than $20,000 annual incomes in the year prior to their incarceration. When the Attica prison insurrections occurred in upstate New York in 1971, there were only 12,500 prisoners in New York State's correctional facilities, and about 300,000 prisoners nationwide. By 2001, New York State held over 71,000 women and men in its prisons; nationally, 2.1 million were imprisoned. Today about five million Americans are arrested annually, and roughly one in five Americans possesses a criminal record. Mandatory-minimum sentencing laws adopted in the 1980s and 1990s in many states stripped judges of their discretionary powers in sentencing, imposing draconian terms on first-time and non-violent offenders. Parole has been made more restrictive as well, and in 1995 Pell grant subsidies supporting educational programs for prisoners were ended. Those fortunate enough to successfully navigate the criminal justice bureaucracy and emerge from incarceration discover that both the federal and state governments explicitly prohibit the employment of convicted ex-felons in hundreds of vocations. The cycle of unemployment starts again.

In seven states, former prisoners convicted of a felony lose their voting rights for life. In the majority of states, individuals on parole and probation cannot vote. About 15 percent of all African-American males nationally are either permanently or currently disfranchised. In Mississippi, one-third of all black men are unable to vote for the remainder of their lives. In Florida, 818,000 residents cannot vote for life. Even temporary disfranchisement fosters a disruption of civic engagement and involvement in public affairs. This can lead to "civil death," the destruction of the capacity for collective agency and resistance. This process of depolitization undermines even grassroots, non-electoral-oriented organizing. The deadly triangle of the New Racial Domain constantly and continuously grows unchecked.

Not too far in the distance lies the social consequence of these policies: an unequal, two-tiered, uncivil society, characterized by a governing hierarchy of middle- to upper-class "citizens" who own nearly all
property and financial assets, and a vast subaltern of quasi- or subcitizens
encumbered beneath the cruel weight of permanent unemployment,
discriminatory courts and sentencing procedures, dehumanized prisons,
voting disfranchisement, residential segregation, and the elimination of
most public services for the poor. The later group is virtually excluded
from any influence in national public policy. Institutions that once provided space for upward mobility and resistance for working people such
as unions have been largely dismantled. Integral to all of this is racism,
sometimes openly vicious and unambiguous, but much more frequently
presented in race neutral, color-blind language.

How do we fulfill the promise of *Brown* by building resistance to
the New Racial Domain? It should be no surprise that the resistance
is already occurring, on the ground, in thousands of venues. In local
neighborhoods, people fighting against police brutality and mandatory-
minimum sentencing laws, and for prisoners' rights; in the fight for a
living wage, to expand unionization and worker's rights; in the struggles
of working women for day care for their children, health care, public
transportation, and decent housing. These practical struggles of daily life
are really the core of what constitutes day-to-day resistance. Building
capacities of hope and resistance on the ground develops our ability to
challenge the New Racial Domain in more fundamental, direct ways.

The recently successful "Immigrant Worker Freedom Ride," high-
lighting the plight of undocumented workers who enter the U.S., represents an excellent model that links the oppressive situation of new
immigrants with the historic struggles of the Civil Rights Movement
forty years ago to overthrow Jim Crow. White activists who believe in
racial justice need to learn more about the historic Black Freedom Movement, and the successful models of resistance—from selective buying
campaigns or economic boycotts, to rent strikes, to civil disobedience—
which that movement established.

In conclusion: in measuring the shortcomings of *Brown*'s victory and
legacy, we must remember that Robert Carter never underestimated the
enormous difficulty of achieving racial fairness through the desegregation
of public schools, or the pervasiveness of racial discrimination. Reflect-
ing on the ambiguous legality of the *Brown* decision in 1994, Carter
wrote that "for most black children, *Brown*'s constitutional guarantee of
equal educational opportunity has been an abstraction, having no effect

whatever on the educational offerings black children are given or the deteriorating schools they attend." Carter's point, I believe, is that behind the formal structures of racial exclusion lies an even more powerful dynamic of economic and class oppression, which still places underfunded, urban school districts at an enormous disadvantage in comparison to suburban white schools.

As historian James T. Patterson recently noted in his excellent history of the *Brown* decision and its legacy, by 1998–1999 the vast majority of America's urban school districts were as racially segregated as they had been a half century earlier. That school year, 90 percent of all public school students in Detroit and Chicago were either African American or Latino. Today, roughly 70 percent of all black children still attend public schools where less than half the student population is white. The promise of equality in *Brown* still remains unfulfilled.

Yet the examples of Robert Carter, Charles Hamilton Houston, and Thurgood Marshall set into bold relief for us the political courage and selfless dedication that will be required to achieve that final victory over structural racism and the New Racial Domain in today's America. These principled advocates of civil rights effectively used the courts and the political process to force this nation to implement its own constitutional democratic principles on behalf of all its citizens. That same willingness to directly challenge the institutions of racialized inequality must inform the building of a new democratic movement for social and racial justice in our own time. It is our living legacy to fulfill the long deferred promise of *Brown*.

CHAPTER 2

What are the Ultimate Meaning and Significance of *Brown v. Board of Education?*

A Note on Justice, Constitutionalism, and the Human Person

SAMUEL DUBOIS COOK

Introduction

Much of the country has participated in the fiftieth anniversary celebration of *Brown v. Board of Education,* a decision handed down by the
Supreme Court on May 17, 1954. This historic, landmark, controversial,
and revolutionary case nullified and reversed so much of the content,
character, and spirit of American constitutional history, jurisprudence,
and moral philosophy on the status, rights, and privileges of blacks and
helped to catalyze, mobilize, and energize the Civil Rights Movement
and the Black Revolution. It was fraught with deep and heavy symbolism
and significance—moral, social, constitutional, political, and cultural. It
is not easy to grasp the full dimensions of the "radical" and "revolutionary" decision. A completely new legal era, with fresh ethical and
constitutional presuppositions and juristic vision, integrity, and higher
possibilities, was born. The crowning jewel or element was the discovery
or rediscovery and application of the great, precious, basic, and perennial
ideal and sense of justice in the context of the African-American journey. Equality is the cornerstone of the edifice of justice. A distinguished

professor of constitutional law and law school dean, Gene R. Nichol, makes the following observation on the uniqueness and far-reaching significance of *Brown:*

> *Brown* is surely the most central, defining, culture-altering decision ever handed down by a U.S. court. It not only bolstered an unfolding, muscular civil rights movement; it provided direct lineage for the historic Civil Rights Act of 1964 and the Voting Rights Act of 1965. It initiated a framework of constitutional equality that has dealt steady blows to formal, legal discrimination across an impressive array of fronts in our national life. . . . The Supreme Court's powerful rejection of state-imposed racial apartheid helped change the nation (Nichol 2004).

Justice and the Human Person

Justice is one of the most precious, primordial, luminous, unique, and universal claims of the human person. It is, the ancients taught us, one of the most basic and perennial values of civilization and indeed the rational, moral, and natural order and structure of being. Whatever the definition, no one wants to be treated unjustly. Justice may be defined, for example, in Aristotelian terms as the disposition to give each person his due or proportion, or according to contemporary philosopher, John Rawls, as "fairness," or in an endless variety of other ways, but whatever definition is offered, each person wants "justice." There are aristocratic and democratic as well as oligarchic and hierarchical conceptions of justice. Ultimately, the moral claim to justice is generally rooted in the doctrine of the intrinsic dignity and value of the human person, each and every person—an inheritance of his/her common humanity. This is the democratic and humanistic ideal of justice.

Equality is a regulative principle of justice, and so is liberty or freedom. A higher and more creative justice is always a more equal and inclusive justice. Thus Reinhold Niebuhr asserts in *Moral Man and Immoral Society* that the "conclusion which has been forced upon [us] again and again is that equality, or to be a little more qualified, that equal justice is the most rational ultimate objective for society" (Niebuhr, 234). Equal justice entails both formal and material conditions.

"The whole world," asserted Emil Brunner, "is crying out for justice. All suffering is bitter, but unjust suffering is doubly bitter. The suffering which is fate unites men; unjust suffering breeds strife" (Brunner, 4).

Injustice not only divides but tragically polarizes and corrupts groups, societies, and cultures.

1. Blacks in the Constitutional System and Framework

The institution of slavery reduced blacks to property, chattel, and things. Blacks were deprived of their humanity or at least their essential humanity. One is reminded of Paul Tillich's compelling assertion that a "wrong, unjust, power relation may destroy life" (Tillich, 56). Or, again, justice demands that every person be treated "as a person. Justice is always violated if men are dealt with as if they were things. . . . It contradicts the justice of being, the intrinsic claim of every person to be considered a person" (Tillich, 60).

In a discussion of "African Americans in the Constitution," Walton and Smith observe that

> As far as we can tell from the records of the federal convention, slavery was not the subject of much debate at that gathering. Certainly its morality was never at issue, although there were several passionate opponents of slavery present including the venerable Benjamin Franklin, president of the Pennsylvania Society for Promoting the Abolition of Slavery. But neither Franklin nor any other delegate proposed abolition at Philadelphia, knowing that to do so would destroy any possibility of union. Hence, slavery was simply just another of the issues (such as how the small and large states were to be represented in the Congress) that had to be compromised to accomplish the objective of forming the union.
>
> Slavery is dealt with explicitly in four places in the Constitution, although the words slave and slavery are never used. It was James Madison, generally considered the "Father of the Constitution," who insisted that all explicit references to slavery be excluded. Madison is also the author of the most important and infamous of the clauses dealing with slavery—the so-called three-fifths compromise (Walton and Smith, 10).

Significantly, both the South and the North, in the 3/5 Compromise, used and exploited slaves to increase their power, advantage, and regional self-interest: the South in terms of representation and the North in terms of taxation. Slaves, of course, were completely excluded from voting and other forms of participation in the political process. They were not persons, but things; not subjects but objects, not moral and political agents but helpless, exploited victims deprived of all constitutional protection and all human rights and civil liberties.

2. *Dred Scott v. Sanford,* 1857: Constitutional Degradation and Moral Scandal

The famous and infamous Dred Scott decision was monumental for historical and substantive reasons. Historically, the Dred Scott decision is important "because the case marks the first time in the seventy-year history of the Court that it squarely addressed the rights of the African people in the United States" (Walton and Smith, 205). C. Herman Pritchett called the Dred Scott decision "disastrous" and "plunged the Court to its lowest depths" (Pritchett, 50–51 and 141).

Speaking for a unanimous Court, Mr. Chief Justice Roger B. Taney declared that a person of African descent, whether a slave or not, belonged to "a subordinate and inferior class of beings," and was not, under the Constitution, included "in the people," and was not and could not be a citizen of a state or of the United States. The Court went on to maintain that persons of African descent had no rights that whites were bound to respect. Black rights depended on the arbitrary and capricious whims, desires, and decisions of whites. Whatever rights whites gave blacks, they could take away at will. Persons of African heritage "had for more than a century before," concluded the august and majestic Supreme Court of the United States, "been regarded as beings of an inferior order, and altogether unfit to associate with the white race, either in social or political relations; and so far inferior, that they had no rights which the white man was bound to respect; and that the Negro might justly and lawfully be reduced to slavery for his benefit. . . ." (*Dred Scott v. Sanford*)

Thus, under the Dred Scott decision, the Constitution of the United States did not confer any rights, privileges, or immunities on black people. Justice was not a matter of constitutionalism but simply a matter and function of power—naked power. Here was Plato's Thrasymachus presiding over American justice. Justice is the interests of the strong or the ruling or dominant class. Might is right in pious, religious, righteous, and democratic America? Herein lies justification by the Supreme Court of the United States of the unbridled "tyranny of the majority" as well as "white supremacy."

3. The Civil War and the Emasculation of the Civil War Amendments

It has been well said that the infamous Dred Scott decision was overruled by the Civil War. It was. However, it is equally true that the Fourteenth Amendment, designed to confer full citizenship on Negroes, and the Fifteenth Amendment, designed to guarantee them the basic right of suffrage, as well as several crucial Reconstruction laws passed to ensure equal protection for blacks, were, in a series of critical cases, during Reconstruction and in the post-Reconstruction era, in effect, reduced to shambles and nullified by the Supreme Court and the Southern "Redeemers," with the complicity of the North. "Practically all relevant decisions of the Supreme Court during Reconstruction and to the end of the century," asserted Rayford W. Logan, "nullified or curtailed rights of Negroes which many of the Reconstruction 'Radicals' thought they had written into laws and into the Constitution" (Logan, 97).

Of special significance was the Supreme Court's declaration, in the *Civil Rights Cases* of 1883, that the Civil Rights Act of 1875 was unconstitutional. What a terrible blow to the haunting and bitter cry of Negroes for the security, affirmation, comfort, and embrace of the equal protection clause of the Fourteenth Amendment. The law banned racial discrimination in public accommodations such as public conveyances, hotels, and theaters and required equality in jury service. Oddly, the Supreme Court, in its narrow, myopic interpretation of law, proclaimed that the equal protection clause of the Fourteenth Amendment did not prohibit racial discrimination by private businesses or individuals. It prohibited racial discrimination only by states. Incredibly, the country had to wait until the Civil Rights Act of 1964 to achieve in public facilities and accommodations what was intended by the Civil Rights Act of 1875. How different history might have been!

4. *Plessy v. Ferguson* and the Separate but Equal Doctrine, 1896

Plessy v. Ferguson, 1896, involved segregation in transportation. It was an historic, landmark case which established and affected patterns of race relations and indeed human relations over the total institutional and social landscape of the South for generations. The Supreme Court declared, in

Plessy v. Ferguson, that racial segregation did not violate the equal protection clause of the Fourteenth Amendment. Separate but equal facilities are constitutionally permissible for blacks and whites. The key, of course, was "separate." The "equal" was never enforced or taken seriously. No standard of equality was even considered across racial lines. "Thus, the doctrine of equality in *Plessy* was a lie. *African Americans in violation of the Court's own decision were relegated to separate and unequal schools and other facilities"* (Walton and Smith, 210; emphasis in original).

Amazingly and incredibly, lo and behold, in *Cumming v. Richmond County Board of Education,* 1899, "the Court found no denial of the equal protection of the laws in the failure of a county to provide a high school for sixty colored children, although a high school was maintained for white children. It seemed to the Court an adequate answer that the county did not have money enough to build a high school for colored children" (Cushman, 147).

What about the social, psychological, and ethical dimensions, implications, and consequences of enforced, legalized racial segregation? Does it impose a "badge of inferiority" on the segregated blacks? In the *Plessy* case, the authoritative answer of the Supreme Court is in the negative—unless blacks self-apply the "badge of inferiority," which, of course, they are free to do. The objective assumption to the contrary is fallacious, contended the Court. "We consider," said the Court, "the underlying fallacy of the plaintiff's argument to consist in the assumption that the enforced separation of the two races stamps the colored race with a badge of inferiority. If this is so, it is not by reason of anything found in the act, but solely because the colored race chooses to put that construction upon it. . . ." Oh, what tortuous, insensitive, and inhumane sentiments and "reasoning"!

If African Americans are demeaned, humiliated, degraded, insulted, and deeply hurt and pained to be legally forced to be separated or isolated from other human beings merely because of their race or the color of their skin, or if they are treated as outcasts, pariahs, or untouchables; if they are constantly offended and insulted by "colored" water fountains and other public facilities or excluded from them altogether, they have only themselves to blame for their inner feelings, wounded pride and sense of self, hurts, attitudes, and perceptions—so suggested the Supreme Court. Blame the victims for their self-torture, low self-esteem, and lack of self-respect and sense of self-worth and dignity. They are responsible. The choice is theirs. They impose such a construction or interpretation on their enforced Jim Crow experiences.

However, in an eloquent, powerful, and prophetic dissent in *Plessy v. Ferguson*, Mr. Justice John M. Harlan asserted that our "Constitution is color-blind, and neither knows nor tolerates classes among citizens." Incidentally, in recent decades and years, many individuals have pointed out the terribly negative, destructive, and harmful consequences that enforced racial Jim Crow segregation and isolation have on the segregator as well as the segregated. Especially perceptive and eloquent from this perspective were Benjamin Elijah Mays and Martin Luther King Jr.

The deep meaning and continuing legacy of *Plessy v. Ferguson* are the justification and sanctification of grave racial inequities, racism, and other terrible injustices in the whole enterprise and process of the American social order, institutions, culture, and life.

5. Progress toward Justice and Equality and *Brown v. Board of Education*

While we must reject the illusion of the inevitability of progress, we must recognize and celebrate progressive social and historical changes in the direction of justice and equality when they occur. In the 1930s and 1940s, a variety of events interacted and coalesced to undermine, erode, and overturn the substance and spirit of *Plessy v. Ferguson* with its "separate but equal" dogma and invigorate the movement for full equality for blacks. Economic, political, social, international, and constitutional changes took place. World War II had a far-reaching impact on the American landscape. Of special relevance was its transformative impact on the racial climate and status-undermining, neutralizing, eroding, and assaulting racial segregation and discrimination. A variety of social and institutional forces, impulses, and vitalities conspired to alter the racial climate and accelerate social and racial change in the status quo.

World War II had a galvanizing impact on the black struggle for first-class citizenship and the quest for full equality and justice. As John Hope Franklin and Alfred A. Moss Jr. asserted:

> Among the numerous adjustments the American people had to make at the end of World War II was adaptation to a new position of African Americans in the United States. This new status arose not merely because a substantial portion of the gains made during the war were retained but also because of the intensification of the drive, in several quarters, to achieve equality for blacks.

The war had created a climate in which substantial gains could be made, but the very nature of the emergency imposed certain restraints that could no longer be justified after 1945. Black organizations, notably the NAACP, began to press more vigorously for full equality. They were effectively assisted by numerous groups, many of them new, in various parts of the country, including political organizations and civic, labor, and religious groups. The courts, chiefly but not exclusively the federal ones, increasingly took cognizance of racial questions and rather frequently ruled in favor of equality. The executive branch of the federal government, moreover, sensitive to both domestic and foreign pressures, exerted considerable influence in eradicating the gap between creed and practice in American democracy. The interaction of these forces created a better place for African Americans as the nation moved into the second half of the twentieth century. (Franklin and Moss, 461)

President Harry S. Truman, in several ways, contributed mightily to the movement for full equality of blacks and the end to racial segregation and discrimination. Of special significance was the impressive fact that he, as no president before him, used the Oval Office as a "bully pit" and instrument of moral authority and suasion, to modify the racial climate in the country and call the nation to the higher vision of justice and equality for blacks. His words and commitment established a new racial environment, challenge, and atmosphere.

More specifically, in 1946, Truman appointed a distinguished interracial committee to look into the status of the civil rights of blacks and to make recommendations for improvement. The group's groundbreaking report, "To Secure These Rights," forcefully denounced inequalities in civil rights and recommended the elimination of segregation and discrimination from American life based on race, color, creed, or national origin. The report generated a national discussion on race and equality. Truman also issued an executive order desegregating and integrating the armed services. Also, in 1948, he issued an executive order requiring fair employment by the federal government without discrimination based on race, color, religion, or national origin.

The migration of Negroes from the South to northern and western cities gave them new political clout and the ability to influence the political process, even holding the "balance of power" in hotly contested presidential elections. In 1944, the Supreme Court nullified the "white primary" in *Smith v. Allwright,* which ushered in a new era of black political power in the South—a development which changed the national political landscape.

In 1947, Jackie Robinson desegregated modern baseball and contributed much to the development of black pride, consciousness, self-assertion, hope, optimism, and resolve to enter the mainstream of American life and culture on terms of equality.

Against this broad background of social and historic change in terms of justice and equality for blacks, enter *Brown v. Board of Education,* with a new normative dimension.

6. Pre-*Brown* Attacks on "Separate But Equal" Dogma in Education

However, there were more direct legal processes and judicial decisions which had provided a framework for the *Brown* case. For quite some time, there had been assaults on the grave inequalities in educational opportunities—including the salaries of black teachers. But there had been a steady, persistent, and successful attack on the inequalities and inequities of educational opportunities for learning. Attacks had centered on graduate and professional schools in states which, by law, required the segregation of the races under the illusion of the "separate but equal" dogma of *Plessy v. Ferguson.* Several cases whittled away at the unequal educational opportunities under Jim Crow.

In *Missouri ex rel. Gaines v. Canada,* in 1938, the Supreme Court nullified Missouri's policy of denying blacks admission to its law school, while offering to pay for their out-of-state legal education. The Court ruled that equal education had to be provided within the state. In *McLaurin v. Oklahoma State Board of Regents,* the Court ruled that it was unconstitutional for the state of Oklahoma to segregate black students in its graduate schools. A pivotal case was *Sweatt v. Painter,* in 1939, which held that the law school established for blacks was "inherently inferior" to the law school of the University of Texas which was established and maintained for whites, and ordered the admission of blacks to the University of Texas Law School. The Court not only looked at the faculty and administration but also at significant "intangibles" such as prominent and well-connected alumni, community status, tradition, and prestige.

7. *Brown v. Board of Education:* A New Day and a New Norm

The NAACP, which had spearheaded the movement for equality of opportunity in education, changed strategy and decided to meet the constitutional issue of justice and equality head-on. Significantly, the NAACP "decided to attack the very principle of segregation as unconstitutional and a clear contravention of the 'basic ethical concepts of our Judaeo-Christian tradition'" (Franklin and Moss, 412). In 1952, the NAACP decided to test the very constitutionality of segregated public schools. Five cases, representing considerable diversity, were brought before the Supreme Court. Involved were South Carolina, Virginia, Kansas, Delaware, and the District of Columbia.

Chief Justice Earl Warren spoke for a unanimous Court. He emphasized the importance of public education in a democratic society. He faced the critical question directly: "Does segregation of children in public schools solely on the basis of race, even though the facilities be equal, deprive children of the minority group of equal educational opportunity?" His answer was in the affirmative. He concluded: "Separate educational facilities are inherently unequal. Therefore, we hold that the plaintiffs and others similarly situated for whom the actions have been brought are, by reason of the segregation complained of, deprived of the equal protection of the laws guaranteed by the 14th Amendment."

Thus, according to the *Brown* case, the constitutional imperative of the Fourteenth Amendment is that of genuine, full, "real" equality. When Chief Justice Warren turned to *Boiling v. Sharpe,* which involved the District of Columbia, which presented a somewhat different legal problem, he referred to "our American ideal of fairness."

Brown v. Board of Education has been criticized on a number of grounds. "The harsh truth is," asserted Judge Loren Miller, "that the first *Brown* decision was a great decision; the second *Brown* decision was a great mistake" (Miller, 351). But its emphasis on equality is of monumental significance and enduring relevance. It deals with the heart of justice— equality of blacks both as citizens and as human beings. The Court said compellingly and unequivocally that the segregation of black children in public schools is unconstitutional because it deprives them "of the equal protection of the laws guaranteed by the 14th Amendment." No wonder it helped to catalyze, energize, and mobilize the Civil Rights Movement and the Black Revolution. It brings to the fore the eternal quest for justice whose heart and soul are equality. It will continue to haunt the conscience and ethical consciousness of America.

Conclusion: Justice, Equality, and Constitutionalism

The *Brown* case makes justice and equality or "equal justice" the centerpiece and cornerstone of American constitutionalism in reference to blacks as citizens and human beings. Central is substantial, meaningful, and full equality. Gone is the idea of "partial," fragmentary, limited, relative equality in comparison to whites. Equality is truly constitutionalized. The constitutional ground is level—no gradations, classifications, distinctions, hierarchy, superior or inferior, subordination or elevation categories of citizens and human beings under the American Constitution. The rights of whites and blacks are equal and on the same level. Involved is what Walton and Smith call "universal freedom" or the "universalization of freedom" (Walton and Smith, 29–32). Thanks to the decision, the timely ideal of equal justice under the law took on new meaning, vitality, relevance, symbolism, and urgency.

The *Brown* decision can be, in part at least, redemptive of one of the country's greatest and most tragic failures—the terrible racist injustices inflicted on black people. "We failed catastrophically only on one point in our relation to the Negro race," observed Reinhold Niebuhr. "This 'American dilemma' is on the way to being resolved, and one of the instruments of its resolution has proved to be the constitutional insistence on equality as a criterion of justice" (Stone, ed., 197).

Ultimately, *Brown v. Board of Education* was about simple justice. Justice is one of civilization's and humankind's highest values and deepest yearnings. "Justice is the first virtue of social institutions, as truth is of systems of thought" (Rawls, 3). "Being first virtues of human activities, truth and justice are uncompromising" (Rawls, 4). "To establish justice in a sinful world," said Niebuhr, "is the whole sad duty of the political order" (Davis and Good, 180). The *Brown* decision could advance, in a profound and compelling way, what Daniel Webster called "the great work of humans on earth, achieving justice" (Gene R. Nichol).

Inspired by the *Brown* decision and other forces, Congress passed the first civil rights legislation in almost a century in 1957. It dealt primarily with the right to vote, but also created the U.S. Commission on Civil Rights. Another Civil Rights Act was passed in 1960, again dealing essentially with voting. The great Civil Rights Act of 1964, in effect, reinstituted the 14th Amendment, and the Voting Rights Act of 1965, in effect, reinstituted the Fifteenth Amendment. Congress also passed the Fair Housing Act of 1968.

This progressive Congressional legislation moved the country toward the justice and equality of the *Brown* case.

Martin Luther King Jr. spoke eloquently and profoundly about the Beloved Community uniting justice and love. Paul Tillich said that "creative justice is a form of reuniting love" (Tillich, 66). "Justice was defined as the form in which power of being actualizes itself in the encounter of power with power. Justice is immanent in power, since there is no power of being without its adequate form" (Tillich, 67). *Brown v. Board of Education,* in meaning, symbolism, vitality, and creative power has nudged America in the noble direction of justice and equality for us all both as citizens and as human beings. It endows American idealism and humanism with new and enlarged ethical meaning, material content, depth, direction, and energy.

America desperately needs, in the depths of its being and throughout its institutions and culture, a heightened, inclusive, and exciting, renewed and reinvigorating moral vision, humanistic commitment, consistent and overall strategy, and political will to bring the spirit and content of justice and equality to bear upon blacks and other disadvantaged or minority groups to ensure their fair treatment and opportunity as both citizens and human beings. Such would transcend and redeem national self-alienation.

References

Brunner, E. 1945. *Justice and the Social Order,* trans. by Mary Hottinger. New York and London: Harper & Brothers.

Cushman, R. 1947. *Leading Constitutional Decisions,* 8th ed. New York: F. S. Crofts.

Davis, H., and R. Good, eds. 1960. *Reinhold Niebuhr on Politics.* New York: Charles Scribner's Sons.

Franklin, J. H., and A. A. Moss Jr., 1994, 7th ed. *From Slavery to Freedom: A History of African Americans.* New York: McGraw-Hill, Inc.

Logan, R. 1997. *The Betrayal of the Negro.* New York: Da Capo Press.

Miller, L. 1966. *The Petitioners: The Story of the Supreme Court of the United States and the Negro.* New York: Pantheon Books, A Division of Random House.

Niebuhr, R. 1932. *Moral Man and Immoral Society: A Study in Ethics and Politics,* New York: Charles Scribner's Sons.

Nichol, G. 2004. "A Great Decision Rescued the Court." *The News & Observer,* May 9.

Pritchett, C. H. 1959. *The American Constitution.* New York: McGraw-Hill Book Company, Inc.

Rawls, J. 1971. *A Theory of Justice.* Cambridge, MA: Harvard University Press.

Stone, R. H., ed., 1968. *Reinhold Niebuhr: Faith and Politics.* New York: George Braziller.

Tillich, P. 1960. *Love, Power, and Justice: Ontological Analyses and Ethical Applications.* New York: Oxford University Press.

Walton, H., Jr., and R. C. Smith. 2003. *American Politics and the African American Quest for Universal Freedom,* 2nd ed. New York: Addison Wesley Longman, Inc.

CHAPTER 3

The Continuing Spirit of the *Brown* Decision of the Supreme Court

CHARLES V. WILLIE

Richard Kluger, author *of Simple Justice* (1975), is correct in stating that *Brown* deserves "a high place in the literature of liberty" (Kluger 1975, x). Historian John Hope Franklin has written that "Perhaps no public question in the United States in the twentieth century aroused more interest at home and abroad than the debate about the constitutionality of segregated public schools" (Franklin 1974, 421).

 Brown, indeed, became both an exhilarating and a troubling experience for citizens of a nation-state whose government is guided by a Constitution. The Declaration of Independence, adopted unanimously July 4, 1776 by the Second Continental Congress, declared that "all . . . are created equal." And the Preamble to the Constitution of the United States, ratified in 1789, indicated that this nation was founded "to create a more perfect union," "to establish justice . . . [and] to promote the general welfare . . ." (Harvard Classics 1938, 150–55). And the Fourteenth Amendment proscribes all state-imposed discrimination against any citizen of the United States. *Brown* was exhilarating to citizens of this nation who recognized it as a way of achieving these goals mentioned above. *Brown* was troubling to citizens who classified it as judicial activism that ignored the authority of the legislative and executive branches of government. They pointed out that the Constitution empowered three separate but interdependent units of government to serve as checks and balances on each unit (Harvard Classics 1938, 180–98).

Actually, the *Brown v. Board of Education* decision of the U.S. Supreme Court descended upon this nation as a way of checking the pervasive injustice rendered by public educational institutions on people of color, particularly African Americans. The injustices resulted from laws, regulations, and other public policies promulgated or facilitated by actions of legislative and executive branches of government. Thus, *Brown* was a legitimate limitation on discriminatory activities facilitated by policies of government that violated the Constitution.

In 1896, the Supreme Court in its *Plessy v. Ferguson* decision permitted public agencies to separate people of different races, if the separate accommodations were equal. In the *Brown* decision, the Court rejected the *Plessy* opinion because the segregated public accommodations for black people and white people were unequal. The National Association for the Advancement of Colored People (NAACP) fashioned a litigation strategy beginning in 1938 designed to demonstrate in courts of law that separate educational facilities and policies in local communities for black and white populations were never equal. The *Brown* decision in 1954 was the outcome of several court cases argued by NAACP lawyers.

I, personally, experienced the inequality of secondary schools in Dallas, Texas, the city of my birth where I grew up. Before 1940, all blacks in this big city attended one high school, Booker T. Washington High School located in North Dallas. From East Dallas, West Dallas, and South Dallas came black students to matriculate in this single high school reserved exclusively for them. Parenthetically, may I say, the black students used public transportation to go to and from Booker T. Washington High School; and the price for this transportation to maintain segregation was assumed by black students and their parents. In effect, we were forced to cooperate in our own oppression. There is a limit to the capacity of any school, including a segregated school for black people, to accommodate one more student. Booker T. Washington High School was so crowded that it had to operate in double sessions, half of the student body attending school in the morning and half attending in the afternoon.

Thus, the Dallas Independent School District decided to erect a new high school in South Dallas for black students. Students like me who lived in Oak Cliff in the western sector of Dallas were reassigned to the new school in South Dallas. We still had to travel to school by bus or trolley car and personally pay for the cost of transportation.

There were two high schools—Sunset and Addison—in Oak Cliff where I and my family resided. But the little Willie boys and girl in the 1930s, 1940s, and 1950s could not enroll in these nearby schools in this western sector of Dallas because all high schools in Oak Cliff were reserved for whites. Although these schools were nearer to my home than was Lincoln High School in South Dallas, to which I was assigned in the 1940s, I was prevented from attending Sunset or Addison because school segregation was an official policy of the Dallas Board of Education.

What was unique about the new Lincoln High School for blacks is that it was erected for blacks. In the past, when practicable, new schools were erected for whites, old abandoned white schools were reassigned for blacks. The new Lincoln High School for blacks in South Dallas was a new development in Dallas school construction policy.

White citizens in Dallas were so enraged over the fact that a new building near one of their neighborhoods would be occupied first by blacks rather than whites that they went to court and obtained an injunction in the late 1930s that prevented Lincoln High School from opening at the beginning of the school year. Whites in Dallas also threatened to blow up the new Lincoln High School building if it was not reassigned to them but did not follow through on this threat.

Eventually, blacks obtained a just decision. The court injunction against occupancy was lifted and black students and their teachers marched into Lincoln High School the second semester of the school year singing "God Bless America" (Willie 1978, 84). It is interesting and ironic that blacks chose to sing this song during their victory march into the new high school that was built to perpetuate racial segregation. My big brother was in that group, singing this song. Eventually, I attended Lincoln High School too, from 1940 to 1944.

Let me share with you one more story about the atrocious desegregation-resistance by whites and their attempt to continue segregation after the *Brown* decision. In her book entitled *The Long Shadow of Little Rock* (1962), Daisy Bates tells about the courageous behavior of Elizabeth Eckford, one of the black students who integrated Little Rock's Central High School in 1957. On what was to be the first day of class, Elizabeth boarded a city bus alone en route to school. She got off the bus a block away from the school building, saw a large crowd, but proceeded to walk toward the front entrance of the school. The crowd shouted and moved in closer; some spat at her. Someone yelled, "Lynch her, lynch her!" Elizabeth said afterwards, "I wasn't too scared because all the time I kept thinking they [the soldiers in the National Guard surrounding the school] would protect me." When she finally reached the front entrance to the school, Elizabeth discovered that soldiers in the National Guard were there with guns and bayonets—not to protect her but to keep her out of Central High School in Little Rock, Arkansas. Then, she became nearly hysterical and ran toward a bench at the bus stop. There, she was befriended by only one white man and one white woman as the angry crowd of white people surged closer shouting in a hostile way. Eventually a city bus came; she boarded the bus and narrowly escaped.

Historian James Patterson reports that Elizabeth Eckford as well as eight other black children who had been assigned to desegregate Central High School were prevented from entering the school by the Arkansas National Guard. The Little Rock Nine, as they were called, who had been admitted to the school by the Little Rock School Board as a token experience in desegregation, had to wait several days before action was taken to uphold *Brown* as the law of the land.

After a federal court judge enjoined the governor of Arkansas from preventing the Little Rock Nine from enrolling in Central High School, the President of the United States, Dwight Eisenhower, federalized the Arkansas National Guard and withdrew its members from Central High School and sent in army troops to protect the nine black children assigned to that school nearly two weeks after the opening day of school (Patterson 2001, 110–11).

What many people did not realize is that resistance to the court order of *Brown v. Board of Education* placed the continued existence of the United States as a democratic nation in jeopardy. Racial discrimination has no place in a just society. It is prohibited by the Fourteenth Amendment of the Constitution and the Civil Rights Act of 1964. Philosopher John Rawls tells us that it is "the idea of society as a fair system of social cooperation between [free and equal] citizens" that has a prominent place in a democratic nation-state (Rawls 2001, 97). "The principle of justice," according to Rawls, "protects the rights and liberties of . . . [all] members by the constraints to which all . . . are subject" (Rawls 2001, 164). I believe that *Brown* saved this nation from splitting apart because it represented an overlapping consensus regarding *excellence,* commonly found among dominant people of power, with an overlapping consensus of *equity,* frequently advocated by subdominant people of power in this nation. The truth is that the adaptations emphasized by both groups are appropriate since equity and excellence complement each other. One without the other is incomplete. The search for excellence relies upon the social process of exclusion, while the search for equity relies upon the social process of inclusion. Inclusion and exclusion complement each other. Social contracts in public education as well as in other institutional systems in a well-ordered society require both kinds of action—equity and excellence occurring simultaneously. This is why it is fine and beautiful when white people and people of color attend schools together; one group has the possibility of being redeemed from a false sense of inferiority while the other group has the possibility of being redeemed from a false sense of superiority. Also, individuals may discover in the integrated common school that one can do for another what the other cannot do for oneself.

For these reasons, the fiftieth anniversary of the presence of the spirit of *Brown* among us is celebrated all over this nation and elsewhere in the world because *Brown* saved the United States from the false choice of attempting to achieve excellence without equity. The purpose of *Brown* was to restore equity to public education. And as stated earlier, equity and excellence are complementary and always ought to be kept together. *Brown* clearly stated that segregation "has no place" in public education because segregation often leads to discrimination. And discrimination has no place in a free, open and democratic society. It is contrary to the social contract among citizens in a well-ordered society.

Slowly, some universities are beginning to realize that they have a better chance of surviving when their faculty and student body are diversified. For example, Harvard University, which was founded as a school for white, Anglo-Saxon, New England gentlemen, has learned a lesson about diversity and learned it well. For the school year 2004–2005, a majority of students admitted to the first-year class were women and 40 percent of all students were people of color. Moreover, the proportion of admitted students in the first-year class from the middle Atlantic States was greater than the proportion accepted from New England. Things do change. The population geneticists tell us that a diversified collectivity has a better chance of adapting to a changing environment than one that is homogeneous.

My study a few years ago of the Charleston County public school system in South Carolina (Willie, Edwards and Alves 2002, 99–115) revealed why white people and people of color have different feelings about segregation and diversity in public schools. White people, many of whom have a strong belief in excellence, see nothing wrong with segregated education because white segregated schools in Charleston County and elsewhere in the nation tend to be schools also with a heavy concentration of students connected with affluent families. In Charleston County, these white racially segregated, affluent concentrated schools tended to have the highest achievement test scores in the district. Black people, many of whom have a strong belief in equity, see segregation in public education as something that is wrong, because black segregated schools with a heavy concentration of low-income families in Charleston County tended to have the lowest achievement test scores in the district.

In Charleston, South Carolina, 91 percent of the white students enrolled in white racially segregated, affluent concentrated schools had achievement test scores above the national norm. I should add, however, that these elite schools accommodated only 10 percent of all white students in Charleston County. And in the same school district, only 22 percent of the black students enrolled in black racially segregated, poverty concentrated schools had achievement test scores above the national norm. However, these schools enrolled 52 percent of the black students in this school district. Thus, the schools that were both racially and socioeconomically segregated helped only 10 percent of the white students but harmed a majority of black students in Charleston County, South Carolina.

In these two different kinds of segregated schools, the proportion of high-scoring black students was 69 percentage points less than the proportion of high-scoring whites. My conclusion is that the composition of a school's student body is an important contextual factor significantly related to achievement test scores of students. For example, in racially and socioeconomically mixed schools, black children have better achievement test scores than blacks in racially segregated, low-income concentrated schools. But white children perform less well on achievement tests in racially and socioeconomically mixed schools than whites in racially segregated, affluent concentrated schools. When children who score above the national norm in racially and socioeconomically mixed schools are compared by race, 64 percent of whites and 31 percent of blacks have such scores. Only 33 percentage points separate white students from black students in these fully integrated schools, while 69 percentage points separate black students from white students in fully segregated schools in Charleston County. The message derived from this analysis is simple and clear: If we want to narrow the achievement gap between white children and children of color, one effective method is to create more racially and socioeconomically diverse schools, which is a requirement of *Brown*.

If blacks are to be lifted up and redeemed from a false sense of inferiority because of low achievement test scores in black segregated, poverty concentrated schools, whites must be willing to sacrifice their highest performance in white segregated, affluent concentrated schools by making all schools racially and socioeconomically mixed schools. Sacrifice, of course, is an important component in the building of community and in redeeming those who have missed opportunities in the past. John Rawls has concluded that since none of us deserves our starting place in life, we are obligated to give compensating advantages to those who missed out. This, we will be inclined to do, in a fair and just society. The sacrifice is not great for whites, as a population, since 86 percent in Charleston County now attend schools that are socioeconomically or racially mixed because of court-ordered desegregation. Blacks must be willing to suffer the redemption of whites from a false sense of superiority by trusting that their new participation in racially and socioeconomically mixed schools is real, and not for the purpose of ridicule and betrayal. Such a change would enhance the education of blacks substantially, since only 46 percent attended schools that are socioeconomically or racially integrated when this study was conducted.

Knowledge of the necessity of sacrifice and suffering in schools and elsewhere should be shared with children, parents, and educators as they face the crisis of desegregation, integration, and school reform. Beyond helping others educationally, diverse schools help individuals and their groups make a better adaptation to the world in which they live. All students in schools with diversified student bodies are more inclined to cease their self-centered ways and to develop empathetic relationships with new friends whose way of life may differ from their own. Empathy is an essential concept in community building.

The big questions the *Brown* decision has created for us are these. Should we strive for equity and justice or should we strive for excellence and perfection? There is nothing wrong with perfection and there is something right about justice. So there is no benefit derived from choosing excellence over equity or choosing equity over excellence. My answer, which I hope will become your answer, is that we must strive for both. Excellence without equity could result in arrogant, self-centered, and egocentric attitudes and behavior. And equity without excellence could result in group-centered and ethnocentric attitudes and behavior. Either one or the other alone is harmful; both together are helpful because they jointly enhance reciprocal and complementary relationships between individuals, between groups, and between individuals and groups.

It is the assessment of some analysts of public affairs that *Brown* has failed. I disagree with this assessment because of the empathetic relationships to which implementation of this court order has contributed and because of increased educational attainment for all since announcement of this court order.

1. Before *Brown* (in 1950), the median school year of educational attainment for whites was 40 percent greater than that for people of color; in the year 2000, after *Brown,* the median for whites was less than 1 percent greater than the median for people of color.
2. Before *Brown* (in 1950), about one-third of the adult population twenty-five years of age and older had received a high school education or more; the year 2000, after *Brown,* this proportion had soared to 84 percent.
3. Before *Brown* (in 1950), only 6 percent of the adult population twenty-five years of age and older had completed four or more years of college. In the year 2000, after *Brown,* this proportion had increased to 26 percent.

These facts clearly indicate that *Brown* has not harmed us. Actually, one may hypothesize that based on these findings *Brown* has helped all of us.

It is interesting to analyze variations in the proportion of educational attainment by race and the rate of improvements for white people compared with black people before and after *Brown.*

1. Between 1950 and 2000, the proportion of white adults completing high school represented more than a twofold increase during this fifty-year period.
2. Between 1950 and 2000, the proportion of black adults completing high school represented nearly a sixfold increase during this fifty-year period.
3. Between 1950 and 2000, the proportion of white adults with four or more years of college represented a fourfold increase during this fifty-year period.
4. Between 1950 and today (2000), the proportion of black adults with four or more years of college represented an eight-fold increase during this fifty-year period (U.S. Census Bureau 2001: 131–78).

Blacks continued to lag behind the educational attainment of whites from 1950 to the present time, but their rate of improvement during the years since *Brown* has been greater than the rate of improvement in educational attainment by whites. While the educational attainment gap between all racial groups has not been eliminated, that between black people and white people is narrower today than it was a half century ago. Students in both racial groups have made remarkable progress over the years.

Thus, it is appropriate to declare that the *Brown* court decision restored equity to our national system of public education that tended to focus on excellence and perfection only. And this is good. For those among us who are cynical about the emerging diversity of student bodies, faculty, and staff in learning environments or who are impatient with the rate of change over the years, may I refer you to the wisdom of Harold Kushner. He said that "love is not the admiration of perfection, but the acceptance of an imperfect person with all of his [or her] imperfections . . ." (Kushner 1981, 146–47). In other words, we must develop the capacity "of forgiving and accepting in love a world which has disappointed [us] by not being perfect . . . because it is the only world we have . . ." (Kushner 1981, 147–48). If we do this, we will be "better and stronger" and "live fully, bravely and meaningfully," according to Kushner (Kushner 1981, 147–48). So while we review the weaknesses of *Brown*, let us also be cognizant of the benefits it has conveyed upon all of us, and learn how to transform rather than curse this imperfect world in which we live.

Thus, *Brown*, as an innovation in public education, was not a failure. *Brown* has not failed us; but the law enforcement process in our democratic nation failed *Brown*. Mayors of cities and governors of states who pledge to obey the Constitution of the United States failed to implement *Brown* as the law of the land. They ignored the law, closed public schools, and even ordered the National Guard to prevent desegregation. For these illegal acts, no sanctions were levied against those local and state authorities. When leaders of the civil rights movement broke public laws prohibiting boycotts and conducted mass marches without a permit, they accepted imprisonment. But the leaders of our states and cities in major civil divisions in the United States did not experience punishment for failing to obey public laws. For this reason, I declare that *Brown* did not fail. But some public authorities in this nation failed *Brown*. It is not the privilege of elected executive officers to selectively enforce public laws.

I conclude that the spirit of *Brown* is alive and has spread beyond the boundaries of the United States. In 2004, I was invited by the Faculty of Education of the University of Pretoria to come to South Africa to give a keynote address in an international conference celebrating the tenth anniversary of South Africa as a democracy and the fiftieth anniversary of the *Brown* U.S. Supreme Court decision. Such a conference is testimony that in word and spirit *Brown* continues to live at home and abroad. It is meet and right to honor the wisdom of this court order that has enhanced education for all, although some may not realize it. *Brown,* truly, was an equity case and should be remembered as such because excellence and equity ought always to be kept together. We need both because equity is a correction for the excesses of individualism and excellence is a correction for the excesses of collectivism in a society.

May I conclude with a quotation from my favorite philosopher, Martin Buber. He states that "The fundamental fact of human existence is neither the individual nor the aggregate. . . . Each considered by itself is a mighty abstraction. The individual is a fact of existence in so far as [one] steps into a living relation with the other individuals. The aggregate is a fact of existence in so far as it is built up of living units of relations" (Buber 1947/1955, 203).

Thanks be to the *Brown* court decision that recognized the need to simultaneously advance the interests of individuals as well as the interests of communities. To attempt to advance one without the other as we did in our disproportionate emphasis on excellence and perfection in the past is a way of harming both the community and the individual. This, we need not do; this we dare not do in the name of education.

References

Bates, D. 1962. *The Long Shadow of Little Rock.* Fayetteville: University of Arkansas Press.

Buber, M. 1955. *Between Man and Man.* Boston: Beacon Press (originally published in 1947).

Franklin, J. H. 1974. *From Slavery to Freedom.* 4th ed. New York: Alfred A. Knopf.

Harvard Classics, The. 1938. *American Historical Documents.* New York: P. F. Collier and Son.

Kluger, R. 1975. *Simple Justice.* New York: Vintage.

Kushner, H. S. 1981. *When Bad Things Happen to Good People.* New York: Schocken Books.

Patterson, J. T. 2001. *Brown v. Board of Education.* New York: Oxford University Press.

Rawls, J. 2001. *Justice as Fairness.* Cambridge, MA: Harvard University Press.

Willie, C. V. 1978. *The Sociology of Urban Education.* Lexington, MA: Lexington Books.

Willie, C. V., R. Edwards, and M. J. Alves. 2002. *Student Diversity, Choice and School Improvement,* Westport, CT: Bergin and Garvey.

U.S. Census Bureau. 2001. *Statistical Abstract of the United States.* Washington, D.C.: U.S. Government Printing Office.

CHAPTER 4

Observing the Fiftieth Anniversary of the 1954 United States Supreme Court School Desegregation Decision in *Brown v. The Board of Education of Topeka, Kansas*

CHARLES U. SMITH

As we commemorate the fiftieth anniversary of the *Brown v. the Board of Education of Topeka, Kansas* U.S. Supreme Court public school desegregation decision (hereafter the *Brown* decision), I was tempted to refer to it as a "celebration of the Golden Anniversary of the legal end to racial segregation in the public schools of the United States." When the decision was rendered, on May 17, 1954, I was so elated that I was confident that fifty years later public school racial desegregation would be a thing of the past and a truly "golden celebration" would be highly appropriate. And while I still am convinced that the *Brown* decision was a necessary and fundamental prerequisite for human dignity, race relations, personal/social adjustment, equal educational access, and progress toward the American Ideal, events that have emerged and continuing efforts to obscure, evade, emasculate, and override the decision, demand that we have an "observance" rather than a "celebration" in its "golden" year.

I

There can be no doubt that the *Brown* decision was one of the Court's most important, judicially groundbreaking, precedent-setting ones, with far-reaching impacts on the U.S. Congress, lower federal and state courts, state legislatures, the presidency, federal agencies, private corporations and businesses, and of course, all levels of public and federally assisted educational institutions. To put all of this into proper perspective, I think that it is imperative that we examine, at least briefly, philosophies, societal patterns and court rulings that established, regulated, and limited the roles, status, and behavior of Negroes (blacks) in the United States, prior to the *Brown* ruling.

It is generally accepted that Negro slavery was introduced into the United States colonies at Jamestown, Virginia in 1619. This slavery, though, was not confined to the southern and border states but reached visible and significant numerical levels as far north as New York City (Singer 2003). There is also documented evidence that some Negroes (blacks) served as indentured servants, but it has been clearly shown that the overwhelming majority of Negroes brought from Africa to the colonies from the early 1600s to the 1800s were held as property, and existed in total involuntary servitude—for approximately two and a half centuries.

II

The most notable efforts to modify the slave system and upgrade the status of Negroes were the Dred Scott lawsuits, brought to establish himself and his family as free (nonslave) persons. Dred Scott was born a slave and was owned by Peter Blow in St. Louis, Missouri. Scott subsequently had several owners/masters. From 1830 to 1842 Scott, who married Harriet Robinson, also a slave, spent time in Illinois and Wisconsin, both non-slave states, in service to his then owner, Dr. John Emerson, a military surgeon. In 1842 the Scott family returned to St. Louis with Dr. Emerson and his wife, and Emerson died in 1843.

In 1846, the Scotts sued Mrs. Emerson for their freedom in the St. Louis Circuit and although the Court ruled against them, in 1847 it did permit them to refile their lawsuit. In 1850, the jury in the second trial decided that the Scotts should be free because of their years of residence in the nonslave territories of Wisconsin and Illinois. Mrs. Emerson then appealed to the Missouri Supreme Court in 1852 which overturned the Circuit decision and returned the Scotts to slavery.

In 1853–54, lawyers on Scott's behalf filed suit in the U.S. Federal Court in St. Louis that also ruled against Scott. In 1856–57 the Scott case was appealed to the U.S. Supreme Court (case now named *Scott v. Sanford*). It was the decision of the Court that Scott must remain a slave, not a citizen, and therefore as personal property was not eligible to bring suit in federal court, and that he had never been free. (See the Washington University Libraries and the Missouri State Archives.)

In March of 1857, U.S. Supreme Court Chief Justice Roger Taney stated the ruling for the Court majority that because Scott was black, he was not a citizen and had no right to sue. Further, he said that those who constructed the U.S. Constitution were convinced that "blacks had no rights which the white man was bound to respect, and that the negro might be lawfully and justly reduced to slavery for his own benefit. He was bought and sold and treated as an ordinary article of merchandise and traffic, whenever a profit could be made by it" (Washington University Libraries and Missouri State Archives). Commenting on the case on March 19, 1857, the Albany, New York, *Evening Journal* editorialized: "Five of the nine silk gowns are worn by Slaveholders. More than half its long Bench, is filled with Slaveholders. The Free States with double the population of the Slave States, do not have half the judges. The majority represents a minority of 350,000. The minority represent . . . twenty million."

It is worth noting that a statue and monument to Justice Roger Taney still stands today in downtown Baltimore, Maryland.

The 1857 Dred Scott Supreme Court decision not only established the official legal status of blacks/Negroes in the United States but also provided a rationalization for the notorious "Black Codes" enacted by southern state legislatures after the Civil War to insure total control of virtually all aspects of blacks' existence. The Ku Klux Klan, originally founded in 1865 as a young white gentlemen's "social club," also became, under the leadership of ex-confederate General Nathan Bedford Forrest, an overwhelming extralegal "army" to control southern blacks with their night-riding, burnings, beatings, mutilations, and lynchings.

These patterns of control persisted, successfully keeping blacks in fear and in almost subhuman conditions of life even after President Abraham Lincoln issued the Emancipation Proclamation in 1863. They continued despite Congressional passage of the Thirteeth (1865), Fourteenth (1868), and Fifteenth (1870) Amendments to the U.S. Constitution. (See appendix for these amendments.)

III

The next most famous and precedent-setting legal case that would have broad and longstanding impact on the rights, prerogatives, and way of life of blacks versus whites in the United States was the Louisiana *Plessy v. Ferguson* lawsuit that was concluded by another race-defining ruling by the U.S. Supreme Court in 1896, thirty-nine years after the Dred Scott decision.

Homer Plessy, a light-skinned Negro who could pass for "white," agreed to be a test case and brought suit in 1890, supported by the Citizens Committee to Test the Constitutionality of the Louisiana Separate Car Law. The Louisiana district court ruled that the State had the power to regulate railroad companies operating solely within its borders and concluded that the Louisiana Separate Car Act was constitutional. The decision was appealed to the state supreme court in 1893 and was appealed again to the U.S. Supreme Court in 1896 (Zimmerman 1997).

When the case, now *Plessy v. Ferguson,* got to the U.S. Supreme Court, counsel for Plessy argued for relief under the "equal protection" clause of the Fourteeth Amendment and the freedom from slavery guarantee of the Thirteenth Amendment, both to no avail. The majority of the justices agreed that separation of the races does not "stamp" blacks as inferior because both blacks and whites had "equal" facilities, though separate. "One justice, John Marshall Harlan, disagreed strongly from the majority and stated every one knows that the statute in question had as its origin the purpose, not so much to exclude white persons from railroad cars occupied by blacks, as to exclude colored people from coaches occupied by or assigned to white persons" (Zimmerman 1997). This decision was the basis and legal justification for segregation of blacks and whites in virtually all aspects of public and private life for the next half century, especially, but not exclusively, in the South. "Separate but equal" racial segregation of blacks and whites was established, practiced, and overseen by law enforcement officers, judges, courts, schools, buses, eating places, toilets, drinking fountains, parks, playgrounds, hospitals and medical facilities, railroads, churches, night clubs, parks and recreational facilities, public housing, doctors' offices, athletic sports and games, financial institutions, dating, courtship, marriage and family life, on developing interstate highways and in emerging television productions. While pervasive in the South, racial segregation, now fully sanctioned by federal law, was frequently practiced in northern cities and states, including New York City where de facto segregation resulted in many celebrated cases of black exclusion.

IV

In 1910, shortly after the turn of the twentieth century, the National Association for the Advancement of Colored People (NAACP) was founded, with Dr. W. E. B. DuBois among its interracial group of organizers. It is hardly an accident that the NAACP continues to retain its interracial composition in its leadership and its program thrusts. By the 1930s, it was determined that the most feasible and effective strategy and tactic, for blacks generally and the NAACP, to impact and improve the status and life for blacks was to use the very institutions that established the "separate but equal" mandate, namely the judiciary, especially the federal courts.

Finch (1981) reports that as early as 1910, the year of its founding, the NAACP intervened in three legal cases involving justice for blacks and achieved varying degrees of success. By the time of its incorporation in 1912 the formally stated objectives of the NAACP were:

> To promote equality of rights and eradicate caste or race prejudice among the citizens of the United States: to advance the interests of colored citizens: to secure for them impartial suffrage: and to increase their opportunities for securing justice in the courts, education for their children, employment according to their ability, and complete equality before the law. (Finch 1981, quoted by Smith 1984)

> With litigation in the courts, especially federal courts, as its main strategy and racial discrimination in education as a high priority, the NAACP began systematically to attack problems [of] equity, access, and compensation in public education, including colleges, universities. and professional schools. . . . (Smith 1984)

Charles Houston, former vice dean of the Howard University Law School, became the full-time legal counsel for the NAACP in 1935 and soon recruited Thurgood Marshall of Baltimore, Maryland as his chief assistant. These two lawyers, supported by the NAACP Legal Defense and Educational Fund (established in 1939), assisted other lawyers and won some important legal victories in education from the 1930s to the 1950s in the southern and border states.

Some noteworthy cases argued successfully in this period were:

Murray v. University of Maryland Law School (admission), 1935
Missouri ex rel Gaines v. Canada (admission), 1938
Alston v. Virginia (salary equality), 1940
Sipuel v. Board of Regents (admission)–Oklahoma, 1948
Hawkins v. Florida Bd. of Control (admission), 1949–1956
McLaurin v. Oklahoma Bd. of Regents (admission), 1950
Sweatt v. Painter (admission)–Texas, 1950.

In most of the above cases, " . . . the plaintiffs won permission to enter previously all-white institutions. But admission was in the context of 'separate but equal': the Court did not consider the legality of racial segregation in public education. The Court's general stipulation was that the states involved must provide equal schooling for the black plaintiffs, or admit them to the institutions reserved for whites . . ." (Smith 1975). The states of Oklahoma and Texas, respectively, immediately set up and built law schools for one person. Neither Sipuel nor Sweatt attended these hastily devised law schools "on the grounds that they were not equal to the long-established schools for whites . . ." (Smith, 1975). The U.S. Supreme Court concurred with their claim and ruled that they were legally eligible to attend the white institutions. Thus, the Court began to broach the question of whether separate facilities could indeed be equal—a key element in the later *Brown* decision.

Herman Sweatt attempted to enroll in the law college of the University of Texas for the February 1946 term and was denied by the school solely because he was a Negro (black). Sweatt immediately filed suit against The University of Texas officials to compel his admission. Because there was no state law school for Negroes (blacks) at the time and Texas state officials recognized that refusing to admit Sweatt denied him equal protection of the laws guaranteed by the Fourteenth Amendment, they immediately began setting up a law school for him at the all-black Texas Southern University in Houston. Sweatt refused to attend this *new* school. Sweatt did not get the relief that he sought in the State trial court of Civil Appeals or the Texas Supreme Court.

The U.S. Supreme Court agreed to hear the case, now known as *Sweatt v. Painter,* in April 1950. In June 1950, the Court ruled that the law school provided for Sweatt could not be compared to the University of Texas Law School because it did not have the longstanding traditions, prestige, reputation for excellence, successful alumni, or financial support resources. Such differences therefore would not give

Sweatt the equal protection of the laws guaranteed by the Fourteenth Amendment. The U.S. Supreme Court said: "We hold that the Equal Protection Amendment requires that the Petitioner be admitted to the University of Texas Law School. The (Texas Supreme Court) judgment is reversed . . . " (Text—Supreme Court of the United States. *Sweatt v. Painter,* June 5, 1950). This opinion, delivered by Chief Justice Vinson, stated unequivocally that equality of educational programs, to comply with the requirements of the Fourteenth Amendment, must include intangible qualities and elements that are essential in the study of the law. Comparing the new law school set up for Sweatt (and other blacks/ Negroes), Vinson stated:

> Whether the University of Texas Law School is compared with the original or the new law school, we cannot find substantial equality in the educational opportunities offered white and Negro law students by the State. In terms of number of faculty, variety of courses and opportunity for specialization, size of the student body, scope of the library . . . and similar activities, the University of Texas Law School is superior. What is more important, the University of Texas Law School possesses to a far greater degree those qualities which are incapable of objective measurement which make for greatness in a law school. Such qualities include reputation of the faculty, experience of the administration, position and influence of the alumni, standing in the community, traditions and prestige. It is difficult to believe that one who had a free choice between these two law schools would consider the question closed.
>
> Moreover, although the law is a highly learned profession, we are well aware that it is an intensely practical one. The law school, the proving ground for legal learning and practice, cannot be effective in isolation from the individuals and institutions with which the law interacts. Few students and no one who has practiced law would choose to study in an academic vacuum, removed from the interplay of ideas and the exchange with which the law is concerned. The law school to which Texas is willing to admit petitioner excludes from its student body members of the racial groups [that make up] 85% of the population of the State and include most of the lawyers, witnesses, jurors, judges, and other officials with whom petitioner will inevitably be dealing when he becomes a member of the Texas Bar. With such a substantial and significant segment of society excluded, we cannot conclude that the education offered petitioner is

substantially equal to that he would receive if admitted to the University of Texas Law School. (*Sweatt v. Painter,* June 5, 1950)

These portions of the *Sweatt* ruling are quoted extensively because the Court's conclusion in this case regarding the essentiality of "intangibles" in racial equality is highly relevant to the *Brown* decision that followed four years later.

In the four preceding sections, I have gone into some detail about war and conflicts; defeats and humiliations suffered by blacks; court rulings favoring whites; the extralegal domination of blacks by whites; and amount of time required to change/improve the role, status, humanity, and political and economic access of blacks in the hundred years that elapsed after *Dred Scott* and before the *Brown* decision. An uneven continuum may be observed/constructed about the existence of Negroes/blacks in the U.S. colonies and then the states:

1619–1856—Most blacks, especially in the South, held as subhuman slaves.

1857—*Dred Scott* Decision–Supreme Court affirmed that blacks were property and therefore did not have human rights.

1863—President Lincoln issued the Emancipation Proclamation that construed blacks as humans and gave many freedom in theory.

1865, 1868, 1870—13th, 14th, and 15th Constitutional amendments passed, legally freeing all blacks from slavery, granting them equal protection of the laws and due legal process, respectively.

1896–1946—Over half a century dominated by Supreme Court ruling in *Plessy* that blacks were citizens entitled to political equity so long as virtually all activities, accesses, facilities, opportunities, educational programs, and residence areas were "equal," but kept racially separate.

1910–1949—NAACP lawsuits chipped away at the sham of "separate but equal" in the treatment of blacks; a number of significant victories were harbingers of major improvements in the lives and existence of blacks.

1950—Supreme Court ruled in *Sweatt v. Painter* that "intangibles" must be considered in determining whether separate facilities are indeed equal.

1954—The *Brown* decision by the U.S. Supreme Court.

The monumental decision regarding racial segregation in the public educational institutions of the United States rendered by the U.S. Supreme Court (the Court) on May 17, 1954, came after its consideration of appeals from lower court decisions in Virginia, South Carolina, Delaware, and Kansas. The case became known as the "Brown decision" because appellants are usually listed in alphabetical order by surnames and Linda Brown was first among these litigants. In this case the Court dealt specifically and exclusively with racial segregation and did not consider other *tangible* factors that might otherwise affect equality for blacks.

The Court said:

> In the instant case . . . Here, unlike *Sweatt v. Painter,* there are findings . . . that the Negro and white schools involved have been equalized, or are being equalized, with respect to buildings, curricula, qualifications and salaries of teachers, and other "tangible" factors. Our decision, therefore, cannot turn on merely a comparison of these tangible factors in the Negro and white schools involved in each of the cases. *We must look instead to the effect of desegregation itself on public education.* (Court text; emphasis added)

The Court also indicated that it could not go back to the time of *Plessy,* but must consider public education, its role, impact, and importance in the United States at the present time (1954). Additionally, it noted the tremendous importance of education for a democratic society and "awakening the child to cultural values and helping children to adjust normally to their environment."

Quoting the Court:

> We come then to the question presented: Does segregation of children in public schools solely on the basis of race, even though the physical facilities and other "tangible" factors may be equal, deprive the children of the minority group of equal educational opportunities? *We believe it does.*

The basis for this determination and ruling is shown in other statements by the Court:

To separate them from others of similar age and qualifications solely because of their race generates a feeling of inferiority as to their status in the community that may affect their hearts and minds in a way unlikely ever to be undone.

Segregation of white and colored children in public schools has a determined effect upon the colored children. The impact is greater when it has the sanction of the law; for the policy of separating the races is usually interpreted as denoting the inferiority of the Negro groups. A sense of inferiority affects the motivation of children to learn. Segregation with the sanction of law, therefore, has a tendency to retard the educational and mental development of Negro children.

We conclude that in the field of public education the doctrine of "separate but equal" has no place. Separate educational facilities are inherently unequal. Therefore, we hold that the plaintiffs and others similarly situated for whom the actions have been brought by reason of the segregation complained of, deprived of the equal protection of the laws guaranteed by the Fourteenth Amendment. We have now announced that such segregation is denial of the equal protection of the laws. (Smith 1975; reprinted 1996; emphasis added)

V

With all nine justices concurring, Chief Justice Earl Warren delivered the *Brown* ruling. I think that the Court's unanimity in this decision is important for two significant reasons. First, neither the *Dred Scott* nor the *Plessy* rulings were rendered by totally concurring Courts. Second, the members of the *Brown* Court were well aware of the public responses that such a precedent-shattering and precedent-making declaration would provoke, and they wanted to have the weight and prestige of the full Court undergirding this epochal decision. With this decision, the Warren Court ignored *stare decisis* with regard to the *de jure* racial segregation of public schools in the South, as well as the *de facto* racial segregation in northern public schools.

The sentence in the *Brown* decision stating that "Separate educational facilities are inherently unequal" makes it unequivocally clear that no matter how good educational facilities and resources are, if they support racial segregation, they are forever unequal—and cannot ever be made equal because they are separate. (Note that in the year 2004, fifty years after the *Brown* decision, many whites and blacks were advocating and working for the reestablishment of separate schools for blacks and whites without realizing or caring that to do so would violate the federal law of the land.)

It is essential that everyone understands the rationale of the *Brown* decision, namely that it was not about pedagogy—improving "reading, writing, and (a)rithmetic," or elevating test scores or the quality of teaching and learning—but rather about *what racial segregation does to the hearts and minds and personalities of those who are segregated because of race.* Some, especially lawyers, criticized the Court for using psychological and sociological research findings in reaching its conclusion, with the claim that such data had no place in such an important ruling.

Much of the immediate reaction to the *Brown* decision, especially by elected and appointed public officials in the South, was blatantly negative. In the North, many public officials blithely ignored the decision, no doubt feeling that they did not have a problem because there were no legal requirements for racial segregation in their public schools. Southern legislators and education officials responded to the decision with interposition declarations, pupil assignment laws, "health and safety" regulations, use of testing (perhaps to prove that blacks were too ignorant to go to school), all-white "Christian" academies, white flight to the suburbs, unaccredited charter schools, school vouchers, and "homeschooling." The ultimate defiant step was taken by Prince Edward County in Virginia by closing its public school system entirely for three years to avoid compliance with the *Brown* ruling. The greatest show of force to enable desegregation came when President Eisenhower reluctantly sent federal troops to Little Rock, Arkansas to insure that nine black students safely desegregated Central High School. Anti-desegregation activities are continuing today, with growing evidence of their intensification.

However, the *Brown* decision was destined to produce broad activity for change and the improvement in many facets of life for blacks, just as the *Plessy* doctrine of separate but equal dominated the lives of blacks for the previous half-century. Although the *Brown* decision was specifically directed at racial segregation in public education (as *Plessy* was rendered about public transportation), black and white people came to use the ruling to fight racial segregation and discrimination in many different facets of life. For the first time in U.S. history, the highest Court in the land had declared that racial segregation was illegal—notwithstanding the fact that public education was the focus.

In 1955, one year after the *Brown* decision, Rosa Parks decided that she was tired of being segregated on city buses and refused to move to the back of the bus in Montgomery, Alabama. This event is widely accepted as the precipitating event for the massive civil rights movement of the 1950s and 1960s. Only a few months later, in May of 1956, Florida A&M University students Wilhelmina Jakes and Carrie Patterson refused to move to the back of a city bus, thereby igniting the Tallahassee,

Florida bus boycott and protest that lasted for over two years. In January 1960, four freshman male students at North Carolina A&T University "sat in" at the white-only lunch counter at the Woolworth department store in Greensboro, North Carolina, an incident that gained nationwide attention. Black students at other historically black colleges and universities in the South organized and participated in "sit-ins," mass marches, "swim-ins," strikes, lunch counter demonstrations, and mass meetings, to overcome racial segregation and discrimination. In many such instances and activities, nonstudent, adult blacks, mainly in the southern and border states, joined with the students, supported them with funds and legal counsel, and organized and carried out civil rights activities of their own.

Dr. Martin Luther King Jr. became the symbolic leader of the civil rights movement and the actual, in person, leader of many protest and public awareness campaigns. This civil rights era, traceable almost directly to the 1954 *Brown* decision, was unprecedented, and included activities by whites and other groups of nonwhites. The NAACP, also perhaps encouraged and stimulated by the *Brown* decision, if anything, became more active with civil rights lawsuits after the 1954 ruling. With permission from *The Negro Educational Review* and the NAACP Legal Defense and Education Fund, a list of some of the mostly successful cases is presented below. Several significant cases completed before the *Brown* decision are included because they are part of the NAACP's continuum of important court rulings on civil rights and race relations.

1948 Higher Education (*Sipuel v. University of Oklahoma,*
–1950 *Sweatt v. Painter, McLauren v. Oklahoma State Regents*)
      Supreme Court outlaws exclusion of blacks from the state law schools and segregation of a black within a state university.

1954 Education (*Brown v. Board of Education*)
      Supreme Court rules racial segregation in public schools violates the Fourteenth Amendment and overrules "separate but equal" doctrine.

1954 Education (*Boiling v. Sharpe*)
      In this companion case to *Brown v. Board of Education,* the U.S. Supreme Court unanimously ruled " . . . that racial segregation in public schools of the District of Columbia is denial of the due process of law."

1955   Education (*Brown v. Board of Education II*)
Supreme Court holds that segregation in school must end "with all deliberate speed."

1961   Higher Education (*Holmes v. Danner*)
Charlayne Hunter and Hamilton Holmes admitted to the University of Georgia after a series of court battles.

1961   Higher Education (*Meredith v. Fair*)
Legal Defense Fund conducts a long and tenacious legal campaign which results in the admission of James Meredith to the University of Mississippi.

1963   Higher Education (*Lucy v. Adams*)
Federal district court orders University of Alabama to admit two black students. Governor Wallace "stands in the schoolhouse door" to prevent integration. President Kennedy mobilizes National Guard. Vivian Malone and James Hood admitted.

1963   Higher education (*Gant v. Clemson College*)
Court of Appeals orders first black student admitted to Clemson College in South Carolina.

1964   Education (*Griffin v. School Board of Prince Edward County, Virginia*)
The Supreme Court ruled that the County's plans providing financial assistance for the support of a private educational system was a denial of equal protection of the law. Prince Edward County had closed its public school system in 1959, rather than comply with the 1954 *Brown* decision.

1965   Education (*Bradley v. School Board, Gilliam v. School Board, Rodgers v. Paul*)
Supreme Court declares faculty desegregation is a necessary part of all school desegregation plans.

1967   Education (*Lee v. Macon County Board of Education*)
Supreme Court affirms U.S. district court decision ordering desegregation of all Alabama school districts in first statewide

suit; and holds state tuition grants to whites attending private segregation schools unconstitutional.

1969   Education (*Alexander v. Holmes County Board of Education*)
HEW asks additional extension of time for 33 Mississippi school districts to desegregate. Legal Defense Fund appeals to Supreme Court. Court responds by directing all school districts to terminate dual school systems at once and ends "all deliberate speed" doctrine.

1971   (*Swann v. Charlotte-Mecklenburg Board of Education*)
Supreme Court upholds use of all conventional means to dismantle dual school systems and create unitary systems. Chief Justice Burger, writing for unanimous Court, states " . . . bus transportation has long been a part of all public educational systems and it is not likely that a truly effective remedy could be devised without continued reliance upon it." Court also strikes down North Carolina and New York anti-busing statutes.

1972   Education (*Wright v. City of Emporia, Virginia, Cotton v. Scotland Neck Board of Education*)
Supreme Court rules that ten states with heavy concentrations of white students cannot secede from largely black county school systems because this would impede efforts to dismantle the segregated school systems that had operated by law in those counties.

1973   Higher Education (*Adams v. Richardson*)
The United District of Columbia rules that ten states (including Florida) were maintaining racially segregated systems of higher education with financial assistance from the Department of Health, Education, and Welfare. The Court ordered these states to act immediately to desegregate their institutions of higher education.

1974   Education (*Bradley v. Milliken*)
The Supreme Court, in a five to four decision, reversed the Court of Appeals order requiring inter-district desegregation and merger between Detroit and its suburbs.

The 1971 case of *Swann v. Charlotte-Mecklenburg* and the 1973 case of *Adams v. Richardson,* both decided after the passage of the 1964 Civil Rights Act enacted by Congress (to be discussed later in this chapter), are of special interest among the cases listed above. The *Swann* decision represented only the second time that the U.S. Supreme Court rendered a unanimous decision favorable to blacks in civil rights cases. Even more importantly, the decision delivered by Chief Justice Warren Burger ordered busing as necessary to implement racial desegregation in North Carolina, and voided antibusing statutes in both North Carolina and New York. Ironically, Justice Burger had been appointed to the Supreme Court by President Richard Nixon who vociferously opposed busing to desegregate.

For the most part, state systems of higher education had ignored the *Brown* decision, probably assuming or hoping that the 1954 ruling applied only to K–12 school systems. The *Adams v. Richardson* ruling (1973) by the United States District Court for the District of Columbia removed all doubt that in *Brown* "desegregation of public education" in the United States also included undergraduate and graduate programs at public universities, four-year colleges, and technical and community colleges. The Adams lawsuit was filed by the NAACP in 1970 because between January 1969 and February 1970, the U.S. Department of Health, Education, and Welfare (HEW) determined that ten states, Louisiana, Mississippi, Oklahoma, North Carolina, Florida, Arkansas, Pennsylvania, Georgia, and Virginia, were still operating racially segregated systems of higher education. HEW requested each of these states to submit a plan for desegregation within 120 days or less. Arkansas, Pennsylvania, Maryland, Georgia, and Virginia submitted plans that were unacceptable to HEW. As late as February 1973—a time lapse of three years—Louisiana, Mississippi, Oklahoma, North Carolina, and Florida had submitted no plans at all (Smith, 1975). The State of Louisiana has never filed a plan, even to this day.

In 1970, the NAACP filed a class action suit on behalf of John Quincy Adams, thirty-one other students and "two other citizens and taxpayers" in the Federal District Court of the District of Columbia, Judge John Pratt presiding. The NAACP argued that HEW was violating the Civil Rights Act of 1964 by giving federal financial support to these segregated higher education systems. In 1972, Judge Pratt ruled in favor of the plaintiffs. His subsequent order to HEW was appealed to the DC Court of Appeals in 1973, which upheld his order. This lawsuit, pursuant to the *Brown* decision and based upon the Civil Rights Act of 1964, was highly unusual because it revealed a federal agency (HEW) violating provisions of a federal law, namely, the 1964 Civil Rights Act, that it was bound to enforce.

Because the *Brown* decision clearly focused on racial inequity, racial segregation, and discrimination, it probably influenced the U.S. Congress to pass a little-known civil rights act in 1957. The main accomplishment of the Civil Rights Act of 1957 was the creation of the federal Commission on Civil Rights. Its duties were/are to investigate written allegations by citizens who claim that they have been denied the right to vote; to collect data concerning the denial of equal protection of the laws under the Constitution; and to appraise the laws and policies of the federal government with respect to equal protection of the laws of the Constitution. This Commission became an important component of the later 1964 Civil Rights Act passed by Congress.

Six years after the *Brown* decision President John F. Kennedy issued Executive Order 10925 that called for "affirmative action" in employment, compensation, and promotion of all persons without regard to race. This order also created the Committee on Equal Employment to monitor and report on affirmative steps by government contractors to promote compliance with the order. This was (as far as I can determine) the first time that a U.S. Chief Executive used the expression "affirmative action" and I have no doubt that President Kennedy took the *Brown* decision into consideration in issuing his order. In 1965, President Lyndon Johnson issued Executive Order 11246 that further supported President Kennedy's concern and required government contractors to "take affirmative action" in the hiring of minorities.

The most comprehensive civil rights legislation ever passed by the United States Congress was the Civil Rights Act of 1964 (the Act). This Act, previously referred to, was passed by Congress on July 2, 1964, ten years and two months after the *Brown* decision on May 17, 1954. It was also passed after the longest filibuster in the history of the United States Congress, eighty-one days, led by Florida's senior Senator Spessard Holland.

Of the Act's ten titles, five are most relevant to this paper and the 1954 *Brown* decision: namely Titles II, III, IV, VI and VII.

- Title II prohibited discrimination in places of public accommodation such as hotels and motels, unless such places were owner-occupied and had only five rooms or fewer.
- Title III mandated the desegregation of public facilities, such as buses, trains, parks, hospitals, beaches and playgrounds, and autho-

rized the U.S. Attorney General to bring lawsuits as needed to enforce desegregation.

- Title IV Desegregation of Public Education provided for the enforcement of racial desegregation by authorizing technical and financial assistance to assist with compliance and the withholding of such assistance from noncomplying school systems. It also authorized the U.S. Attorney General to bring lawsuits in the name of the government on behalf of students and parents seeking desegregation but without the means to sue on their own.
- Title VI Nondiscrimination in Federally Assisted Programs prohibited discrimination in any programs or activities receiving federal financial assistance. This included such operations and entities as private schools receiving tax exemptions, private hospitals, state road and highway maintenance and construction, banks, credit unions, and state military units. Appropriate federal departments were also authorized to take actions necessary to carry out this policy.
- Title VII established the Equal Employment Opportunity Commission to insure equal access to jobs and to eliminate unlawful employment practices.

The entire 1964 Civil Rights Act was probably related to the *Brown* decision, but the titles listed above are clearly the domains of racial desegregation and equal protection of the laws so forcefully enunciated in *Brown.*

In 1965, Congress passed the Voting Rights Act that removed barriers in many local areas that prevented blacks from exercising the franchise. Also, in 1965, Congress passed the Higher Education Act, with Title I, Strengthening Developing Institutions, which was largely to aid historically black colleges and universities but quickly had to include growing numbers of predominantly white colleges. Title IX of this act is probably a part of the *Brown* legacy, because it mandates equality for women student athletes, by providing for them equity in athletic programs and funding for them on a par with the finding for male student athletes.

VII

At the beginning of this essay, I expressed reservations about *celebrating* the fiftieth anniversary of the *Brown* decision of 1954. Yet, recollecting how things were one hundred years before *Brown,* and then fifty years before *Brown,* there may very well be grounds for a truly *golden* anniversary now fifty years after *Brown.* We have moved from the debilitating and discouraging denial of humanity for blacks by the unforgettable rhetoric of Justice Roger Taney in *Dred Scott,* and the marginal and still restrictive "separate but equal" murky status for blacks as limited humans by the *Plessy* ruling, to the brightness and clarity of full humanity and equal rights for blacks by the unprecedented and illuminating Supreme Court unanimity fifty years later with the *Brown* decision. I therefore conclude that there is just cause for the Nation to celebrate in the year 2004!

As outlined in some detail above, many changes and improvements beyond public school desegregation have taken place in the lives of both blacks and whites, as well as other minorities and are traceable to the far-reaching influence of the *Brown* decision. However, as one looks at the present scene regarding public school desegregation and other facets of black-white life in the United States, it is clear that the promise of *Brown* and the hopes that accompanied it are faced with strong efforts to negate it and circumvent a unanimous Supreme Court ruling that will stand forever as the law of the land by which all citizens should be governed.

In 1973, the Federal District Court for the District of Columbia ruled that public institutions of higher education must desegregate. In 1978, the United States Supreme Court ruled in the *Bakke* case that race could be legitimately used as a factor in admission to higher education programs. Yet, despite these rulings, especially the Supreme Court decision in *Bakke,* in 1996 an inferior court, the United States Court of Appeal for the Fifth Circuit in the State of Texas, denied the admission of Cheryl Hopwood and other black applicants to the University of Texas Law School. Directly in opposition to the *Bakke* ruling by the highest court in the land, the Texas Federal Appeals Court concluded " . . . the law school may not use race as a factor in law school admissions . . ." (text of the ruling March 8, 1996). It should be worth noting that the governor of the State of Texas at this time was George W. Bush, now President of the United States.

Three years later, on November 9, 1999, J. E. B. (Jeb) Bush, governor of Florida and brother of President George W. Bush, issued an executive order titled "One Florida Initiative." He said, "With my One Florida Initiative, we can increase opportunity and diversity in the state's universities . . . without using policies that discriminate or pit one racial group against another. . . . The education component of the One Florida Initiative states 'Eliminate race and ethnicity as a factor in university admissions.'"

There is no law that requires "ethnic diversity" in public university admissions. There is ample federal law that mandates racial desegregation, namely, the *Brown* decision, Title IV of the 1964 Civil Rights Act, the 1973 *Adams v. Richardson* ruling (that specifically listed Florida among the states being ordered to desegregate), and the 1978 *Bakke* Supreme Court Decision that said that race could be a factor in university admissions.

It is incredible that the appeals court ruling in Texas and the executive order of the Florida governor have been operating without challenge from the United States Attorney General (or other federal agency). However, both of these instances document the barriers that still exist or are being erected to oppose the *Brown* decision. In addition, in 1994 and still continuing, Ward Connerly has been going about the country trying to get states to pass constitutional amendments banning affirmative action.

Christian academies, charter schools, home schooling, private school vouchers (using public funds), "white flight," all-black schools and all-white schools still abound and seem to be growing in number and influence. Add to this the study by the Southern Education Foundation, The Civil Rights Project, and the Harvard Project on School Desegregation that found "that the 1991–1996 period has seen the largest backward movement toward segregation for blacks since the landmark 1954 *Brown* decision" (Harvard University *Gazette,* 1997).

With so much resistance to and evasion of the *Brown* decision, fifty years later, aided by a deliberate opposing ruling of a lower court, plus the negating machinations of at least one elected state chief executive, one might easily become discouraged about the future of racial desegregation mandated by the *Brown* decision, other federal court decisions and United States law enacted by Congress.

However, the hope and promise of the *Brown* decision were strongly endorsed and affirmed on June 23, 2003, when the United States Supreme Court ruled in *Grutter v. Bollinger* that the University of Michigan could use race in its admission procedures. Writing for the Court majority, Justice Sandra Day O'Connor said, "The Equal Protection Clause does not prohibit the Law School's narrowly tailored use of race in its admissions decisions to further a compelling interest in obtaining the educational benefits that flow from a diverse student body" (Court text, 2003).

University of Michigan President Mary Sue Coleman said of the Court's endorsement of their affirmative action program: "This is a tremendous victory for the University of Michigan, for all of higher education. . . . A majority of the Court has firmly endorsed the principle of diversity articulated by Justice Powell in the *Bakke* decision. . . . This is a resounding affirmation that will be heard across the land—from our college classrooms to our corporate boardrooms" (University of Michigan News Service, 2003). There can be no doubt that the Supreme Court ruling in the University of Michigan affirmative action case aroused the interest of many regarding affirmative action programs, reenergized civil rights activists jaded by opposition and denial, and stimulated scholar/activists, such as myself, to continue to do the research, publish the reports, and continue to participate in the process of building a *democracy* in the United States, far beyond the imagination and dreams of the Founding Fathers.

Appendix

Cited Constitutional Amendments:

- Article XIII Eliminated slavery and involuntary servitude except as punishment for a crime
- Article XIV Established citizenship rights, established due legal process and equal protection of the laws
- Article XV Established the right of citizens to vote regardless of race, color or previous condition of servitude

Members of the United States Supreme Court Who Rendered the 1954 *Brown* decision

- Chief Justice Earl Warren
- Associate Justices Hugo Black, Stanley Reed, Felix Frankfurter, William O. Douglas, Robert Jackson, Harold Burton, Tom Clark, and Sherman Minton

References

Adams v. Richardson 1974. Federal District Court of the District of Columbia. Washington, D.C.
Albany Evening Journal. 1857. March 29. Albany, New York.
Brown, et. al. v. Board of Education of Topeka, Kansas. 1954. 347 U.S. 483, 490.
Civil Rights Act of 1957. 1957. U.S.C.

Civil Rights Act of 1964. 1964. U.S.C.

Cheryl J. Hopwood, et. al. v. State of Texas. No. 84–50569. 1996. U.S. Court of Appeals for the Fifth Circuit.

Executive Order No. 3 C.E.R. 1961. Establishing the President's Committee on Equal Employment Opportunity. The White House.

Finch, M. 1981. *The NAACP: Its Fight for Justice.* Metuchen, NJ and London: Scarecrow Press.

Higher Education Act of 1965. 1965. U.S.C.

National Study Finds School Segregation increasing. 1997. Harvard University *Gazette.* Cambridge, MA.

One Florida. Executive Order of the Governor of Florida. (1999). The Florida Capitol, Office of the Governor.

Plessy v. Ferguson. 1896. 263 U.S. 8. 537.

Regents of the University of California at Davis v. Alan Bakke. 1978. U.S. Encyclopedia. com. (2004). Infoplease. (2004).

Singer, A. 2003. "19th Century New York City's Complicity with Slavery: Documenting the Case for Reparations." *The Negro Educational Review* 54: 17–29

Smith, C. 1975. "Public School Desegregation and the Law." *Social Forces* 54: 317–27.

Smith, C. 1984. "The Role of the NAACP in Public Education." *The Negro Educational Review* 34: 92–101.

Smith, C. (1996). *Migration, Education and Race Relations.* Silver Spring, MD: Beckham House.

Sweatt v. Painter. 1950. 339 U.S. 629, 70 S. Ct. 848, 941, 94 L. Ed.114.

"U.S. Supreme Court Rules on the University of Michigan cases." 2003. University of Michigan News Service. Ann Arbor.

Voting Rights Act of 1965. 1965. U.S.C.

Zimmerman, T. 1997. *Plessy v. Ferguson.* Essay published on the Internet.

CHAPTER 5

Remembering Little Rock, 1957

LESTER P. MONTS

Recounting history is a selective process.
What we choose to remember and acknowledge
is based largely on how it affects our present-day lives.

The year 2004 marked the *fiftieth* anniversary of a landmark case about diversity in education. The 1954 *Brown v. Board of Education of Topeka, Kansas* case and subsequent Supreme Court ruling had major national significance in the field of public education, especially for the southern states where the doctrine of "separate but equal" was mandated by law. This essay is a reflection on the period before and after the *Brown* decision and how it affected my personal life and my educational experience in Little Rock, Arkansas.

Prior to the *Brown* decision, all levels of public education in the South operated under the "separate but equal" doctrine, which was based on the 1896 Supreme Court ruling in the case *Plessy v. Ferguson.* That ruling was overturned in the *Brown* case, bringing about a new era of educational opportunity for African Americans in all regions of the nation; it brought hope that access to quality education and its accompanying benefits were now within their reach. Yet for people in the South who were still living with the legacy of slavery, there would be no rapid transformation of social and political systems based on segregation of the races.

Attending public schools in Little Rock, Arkansas, in the 1950s–60s, I experienced firsthand the meaning of "separate but equal." Black schools routinely were given the hand-me-downs from the white schools—books, sports equipment, musical instruments, even auditorium seats. Black families often complained about having their students take public transportation far distances across town to attend the one black high school in the city, while white students not only had the convenience of a high school in their part of town, but if they lived too far, school buses were made available to them.

Outside of school, segregation affected all aspects of employment and access to social and government services. Segregation was the law of the land, severely limiting black people's opportunities for gainful employment. Blacks performed menial jobs as maids, janitors, and day laborers. Although there were a few black lawyers, doctors, and small business owners, the two main professions available to educated blacks were in education and the ministry. Little Rock's one black officer walked a beat only in the small black commercial district. He did not have the authority to issue tickets or arrest a white person. Public recreation facilities were closed to black youth. The downtown Boys Club, YMCA, YWCA and the facilities of most civic organizations operated on a "whites only" policy. Blacks were forced to sit in the back of the bus and use restrooms and water fountains separate from whites. Upscale restaurants, soda fountains, cafeterias, even McDonalds did not serve black patrons. Blacks could not use the downtown public library. Feelings of neglect and despair were rampant in black communities. However, people believed in the American dream that through education, equal opportunity, freedom, and justice were attainable.

Attending black schools in Little Rock offered some benefits not available to students in rural schools. After all, we did attend accredited schools and had serviceable school buildings and opportunities to attend college. At the time only four colleges—Arkansas AM&N College, Philander Smith College, Arkansas Baptist College, and Shorter College—were open to black enrollment among the twenty-plus colleges in the state. We had outstanding teachers. Many received bachelor's degrees from Fisk University, Morehouse College, Tuskegee Institute, Philander Smith College, Arkansas AM&N College, and other prestigious black colleges. A few had completed master's and doctoral degrees from major universities outside of Arkansas. Although black teachers were forced to teach under less than desirable conditions, with inadequate educational resources, they were dedicated and nurturing people who were committed to sound educational principles.

The children of sharecroppers who lived in rural, agricultural areas of the state had less chance to receive a quality education. They experienced what was called a "split session." Under this policy adopted by rural school districts, black schools were closed during the cotton harvest in the fall because the students were needed to pick and process the cotton crop. Moreover, it was commonplace for teachers in the rural schools to hold only a high school diploma. Students attending these schools had little in the way of books and other learning materials, and the school buildings, often just one-room shacks, were deplorable. My grandfather moved his family from the rural delta region of southeastern Arkansas where these conditions existed, to Little Rock to provide my mother and her siblings a chance to attend the only accredited black high school in the state.

The Court's ruling in the *Brown* case, however, did not result in the immediate integration of public schools in the south. Pockets of resistance to the order began to emerge, which slowed progress in certain regions. Granted, numerous school districts followed the Court's ruling without incident and made the necessary changes to integrate; Arkansas was one of two southern states to announce within a week of the *Brown* decision its plans to desegregate its schools. The Board of Education in Little Rock was among the first to move in that direction. Little Rock had established a reputation for being a progressive southern city with good race relations. Many observers believed the schools could break down the barriers of segregation with a carefully developed program. Yet there were others in the city and state who called for resistance to the Court's ruling and set out to sustain a campaign of resistance often accompanied by violence.

The first major nationwide challenge to the *Brown* decision occurred in Little Rock in 1957. The action was the result of a suit filed in federal district court against the local school board by Daisy Bates, president of the local branch of the NAACP and author of the award-winning book, *The Long Shadow of Little Rock*. Ms. Bates and other black leaders believed that the desegregation process proposed by the Little Rock school board was progressing too slowly. The Court's action sped the process along and by the summer of 1957, nine black students were scheduled to enroll at Central High School in the fall.

By the beginning of the 1957 school year, media reports and school board bulletins had provided the public with ample coverage of the desegregation plan. During the first week of classes, Governor Orval E. Faubus called out the state's National Guard to surround Little Rock Central High School and prevent any black students from entering. He claimed that such action was necessary to prevent rioting and to ward off caravans of protesters headed to Little Rock to commit violence against citizens and property. He later espoused the view that his actions were based on the southern doctrine of "states' rights." Meetings and telegrams between President Eisenhower and Governor Faubus, along with court injunctions, kept the nine students away from school for nearly three weeks.

When the students returned to school in late September, Little Rock policemen surrounded Central High. Hundreds of curiosity seekers and protesters congregated in front of the school. Little Rock's mayor ordered the local police to quietly accompany the nine black students into the school through a side door after classes had begun. When it was announced that the students were in the school, a mob of violent segregationists broke through the police barricades and rushed toward the entrance. Many white parents entered the school to remove their sons and daughters. Fearful that the police did not have the capacity to restrain the mob, the school administration moved the black students out a side door. The local police could not control the riot being perpetrated by mobs of protesters. Black students, national news reporters, sympathetic bystanders, and anyone else who showed a tolerance for law and order was attacked and a melee ensued.

The national media had a field day reporting on the violence being perpetrated by ardent segregationists. Amid the chaos, Relman Morin of Associated Press wrote,

> Crowds clustered at both ends of the school set up a storm of fierce howling and surged towards the lines of police and state troopers. The explosive climax came, after the school had been under siege since 8:45 A.M., when the Negroes walked quietly through the doors. Police, armed with riot guns and tear gas, had kept the crowd under control. Inside, meanwhile, students reported seeing Negroes with blood on their clothes. The crowd beat three newspapermen. All three were employed by *Life* magazine. James L. Hicks, a reporter for the *New York Amsterdam News,* wrote about the beatings received by four black newsmen: "At Park Street we came face to face with a mob of about 100 whites standing on the corner. When they saw us, they rushed toward us yelling 'Here come the niggers.' A man threw a punch at Wilson [editor of the *Tri-State Journal*], another kicked Newson [reporter, *Afro-American Newspaper*], and a one-armed man slugged me beside my right ear. We turned to run and found ourselves trapped by the crowds whom we had passed as we walked up the street to the school. As we met, a group of five men, the mob

yelled 'stop them,' 'kill them . . . ' Many of these beatings occurred as local police and state troopers stood watching."

In 1957, I was a spry ten-year-old fourth grader. The segregation that existed during that time mattered little to me because it was simply the life I knew. My parents were aware of the emerging calamity and made efforts to shelter us from the harsh aspects of these events. At the time, such things were not discussed with children my age. When the crisis at Central High School erupted, it was a surprise, it was a frightening end to my assumption about what I had deemed a safe and secure school and home life.

My sense of well-being all changed on a September day during recess when two hundred children at Stephens Elementary School ceased playing and stared at a rumble emanating from the sky. The sound of large transport airplanes overhead was frightening, especially since we had been conditioned during this Cold War period to believe that an attack by the Russian army was imminent. We stood bewildered and learned later that the planes carried troops from the U.S. Army 101st Airborne Division headed to Little Rock Air Force Base with orders to dispatch immediately to Central High School to force compliance with the federal court school desegregation order.

President Eisenhower sent the federal troops to Little Rock in response to calls from Mayor Woodrow Mann and Congressman Brooks Hayes to bring about law and order and force compliance with the federal court order to desegregate Central High School. In a message to the nation, Eisenhower stated: "Under the leadership of demagogic extremists, disorderly mobs have deliberately prevented the carrying out of proper orders from a federal court. Mob rule cannot be allowed to override the decisions of our courts."

The terrorism that accompanied these events is not easily forgotten. The anti-integration forces (mainly the White Citizens Council and the KKK) began to conduct a campaign of terror on the black community and on anyone who had even moderate leanings toward school integration. The superintendent of schools and the city mayor received daily death threats and had their homes and cars riveted with bullets. Bombings occurred at the homes of NAACP President Daisy Bates and Carlotta Walls, one of the nine black students attending Central High School. In further acts of violence, the offices of the Little Rock Public Schools were bombed. In many instances, some of the parents of the Little Rock Nine lost their jobs at white-owned businesses. Night riders, gangs of white thugs, drove through black neighborhoods break-ing windows and attacking people on the street. At my elementary school, we experienced weekly bomb threats, creating an environment of fear and disillusionment.

Hatred and bigotry came from some of the most unlikely people. Wesley Pruden, a white minister and ardent segregationist, ran newspa-per advertisements opposing integration. He asked such questions as: At social functions would black males and white females dance together? Would black students join clubs and travel with whites? Would black and white students use the same restrooms? Would black males and white females enact "tender love scenes" in school dramas?

The national and international media extensively publicized the hate and anger directed toward the nine black students attending Central High School. Books written about Daisy Bates and several of the nine students themselves also tell the story. Let me ask: How many of us had federal troops provide transportation to and from school and accompany us to each of our classes? How many of us could have stood up to these acts of violence? These were high school students whose ages ranged from fifteen to seventeen. Because their families wanted them to receive the best education available, people wanted to kill them. It is a sad com-mentary on our "civilized" society and it is an episode in American his-tory that we should not forget.

Ironically, had the process of integration been left to the students, black and white, today, we might be looking back on a very different scenario. The acts of violence against the nine students were commit-ted by outside agitators and a small gang of student thugs. Several white students befriended the nine black students, deploring what they were being subjected to both in and outside the halls of Central High School. The student newspaper ran editorials condemning the violence going on outside the school during the height of the crisis. A white student was quoted in the *San Francisco Chronicle* saying, "If parents would just go home and let us alone, we'll be all right. . . . We just want them to leave us be. We can do it."

In 1962, Ernest Green, the first black student to graduate from Cen-tral High School, spoke about his experience with the white students:

> In looking through my clippings, I think of all the things that have happened at Central, the most significant thing was the friendly atti-tude that students showed toward me the day of the rioting. The type of thing that was going on outside, people beaten, cursed, the mob

hysterics and all of this going on outside . . . we inside the school didn't realize the problems that were occurring and continually students were befriending us. I remember one case in particular in my physics class. I was three weeks behind in my assignments, and a couple of fellows offered to give me notes and to help me catch up on the work that I had missed. I was amazed at this kind of attitude being shown toward the Negroes.

The Little Rock Nine—Ernest Green, Carlotta Walls, Elizabeth Ekford, Jefferson Thomas, Terrance Roberts, Minnijean Brown, Gloria Ray, Thelma Mothershead, Melba Pattilo—are nine of the bravest people I have ever known. They and their families are the true heroes of the Central High School crisis. Their courage and resilience galvanized black and white resistance to racial oppression in Arkansas and the nation.

Today, Little Rock Central High School stands as a proud reminder of when in 1957 it served as a symbol of southern resistance to school desegregation. A magnificent edifice, Central High School was lauded for its architectural beauty and the quality of education it offered in a state that was near the bottom nationally in public education rankings. When the school opened its doors to students in 1927, the *New York Times* noted that at a cost of $1,500,000 it was the most expensive ever constructed in the United States. Now fifty years beyond the 1957 crisis, Central High School is a much different place. Today, the once all white neighborhood surrounding the school is predominately black and the majority of students at Central High are African American.

Several ceremonies have occurred over the years to commemorate the tumultuous events of the previous era. In 1997, President Clinton, former school administrators, city officials, and students gathered on the steps of the school for the fortieth anniversary of the historic events surrounding the 1957 crisis. Each of the nine students returned to the high school to which they were once denied enrollment to accept commendations from the President of the United States.

For me, it was overwhelming to watch and read the national media coverage of the celebratory atmosphere of these events and the "former-foes-now-friends" ambiance of the occasion; it was quite a contrast to one of the most violent periods in civil rights history. As part of the fortieth anniversary, the Mobil Oil station across the street from Central High School that was so prominently seen in the media coverage, had after years of neglect been restored to its original appearance and turned into the Central High School Visitors Center and Museum. Directly across the street from the Museum, a well-manicured park has been created with engraved plaques and monuments erected as a lasting remembrance for the struggle for school integration. (To provide longevity, the Museum and monument garden are funded and maintained by the State Parks Department.) The contrast between the present-day environment and the events of September 1957 is testimony to the enormous sacrifices made by people of both races and all levels of authority to remedy the inequities and injustices resulting from state-mandated segregation and Jim Crow laws of the South.

The integration of Little Rock Central High School was one of many episodes in the struggle for equality in our society. It occurred at the time that Dr. Martin Luther King Jr. began to emerge as the quintessential leader of the civil rights movement after being arrested during the Montgomery Bus Boycott of 1955. Education was important to King and those involved in the civil rights movement because they understood that it was the stepping stone to political and economic prosperity for African Americans. In his book, *Strive toward Freedom: The Montgomery Story* (1958), Dr. King wrote: "It is one thing to agree that the goal of integration is morally and legally right; it is another thing to commit oneself positively and actively to the ideal of integration—the former is intellectual assent, the latter is actual belief. These are days that demand practices to match profession. This is no day to pay lip service to integration; we must pay life service to it."

The Supreme Court decision of 1954 and the crisis at Central High School served as catalysts for efforts that changed a nation. Dr. King firmly believed providing quality education to all would lead the nation toward the ideal of equality and justice. It is a belief we are still trying to make a reality.

CHAPTER 6

Frasier v. UNC—A Personal Account

RALPH K. FRASIER

No state shall make or enforce any law which shall abridge the privileges or
immunities of citizens of the United States, nor shall any state deprive
any person of life, liberty . . . without due process of law
nor deny to any person within its jurisdiction
the equal protection of the law.

—Fourteenth Amendment to the Constitution of the United States

PORTER, WRIGHT, MORRIS & ARTHUR, LLP
LEROY BENJAMIN FRASIER, JR.
RALPH KENNEDY FRASIER
AND
JOHN LEWIS BRANDON, PLAINTIFFS
V.
THE BOARD OF TRUSTEES OF THE UNIVERSITY OF NORTH CAROLINA
(UNIVERSITY OF NORTH CAROLINA)
GORDON GRAY, PRESIDENT UNIVERSITY OF NORTH CAROLINA
(JAMES HARRIS PURKS, ACTING PRESIDENT)
CORYDON P. SPRUILL, DEAN OF THE GENERAL COLLEGE OF THE
UNIVERSITY OF NORTH CAROLINA
(CECIL JOHNSON, SUCCESSOR)
CLIFFORD LYONS, DEAN OF THE UNDERGRADUATE SCHOOL OF ARTS AND
SCIENCES
(J. CARLYLE STITTERSON, SUCCESSOR)
AND
LEE ROY WELLS ARMSTRONG, DIRECTOR OF ADMISSIONS
UNIVERSITY OF NORTH CAROLINA, DEFENDANTS

Every newspaper, most magazines and especially, the bar journals, have paused this year [2004] to recognize the most important U.S. Court ruling of the past century and perhaps of all time. Certainly, for African Americans, the decision has caused greater changes in our lifetime than any other. Prior to 1954, seventeen states had laws requiring segregation of some aspect of society—law enforcement, housing, marriage, adoption, education, healthcare, burial, transportation, employment, entertainment, food service, hotels. Most of the seventeen required segregation in all of those categories.

Brown v. Board of Education of Topeka, Kansas began the change of the mindset of the entire country which had accepted or, at least tolerated, the rationale of the 1896 decision in *Plessy v. Ferguson* that "separate facilities for the races are permissible . . . so long as the facilities were equal." *Plessy* recognized, as fact, that segregation was required because of fears, prides, and prejudices which were rampart in the South and latent in the North. Segregation sought to prevent dilution of blood or dissipation of faith—the instinct for self-preservation. "Negroes do not have the capacity to absorb white education. Desegregation will result in lowering the intelligence of whites. . . ." *Brown* reversed *Plessy* and turned the underlying rationale upside down.

Much of the 2004 writing focuses on the trend toward resegregating the races in public education. Janine Hancock Jones, a young African American lawyer from Columbus, Ohio, writing in the Spring issue of *Columbus Bar Briefs,* analyzes trends in Columbus schools and concludes that we are back *to* the fifties. Unfortunately, the court did not set a timetable for enforcement and directed desegregation with "all deliberate speed"—interpreted as a euphemism for delay.

In 1954, one hundred members of Congress issued the Southern Manifesto encouraging massive resistance and pledging the "use of all lawful means to bring about a reversal." The U.S. Attorney General, Herbert Brownell, called together the southern state attorneys general seeking their professional help in eliminating segregation. Many informed Brownell that they were potential gubernatorial candidates and that it would be political suicide to support desegregation.

No, Janine, we ain't back to the fifties.

Like the *Brown* decision, *Frasier* was not simply an action challenging the right of three plaintiffs to attend one of the institutions of higher education within the State of North Carolina which historically had limited access to its undergraduate schools to white citizens. Rather, the suit was one of a series seeking to dismantle a system of deeply entrenched racial segregation and subjugation of black citizens by white masters.

The rigid segregation patterns were vestiges of slavery which later gave way to one of the greatest legal fictions ever visited upon citizens of the United States. Separation of the races had been a policy adopted and adhered to by many states since the Civil War. Courts had consistently held that separation did not per se create inequality. So long as there was no discrimination and facilities and opportunities offered were equal, the courts uniformly held that states were within their rights and that no right guaranteed by the Constitution of the United States had been violated.

In *Plessy v. Ferguson* [16 Sup. Ct., 1138, 163 U.S. 537 (1896)], the United States sanctioned segregated facilities so long as separate facilities were equal in their character and quality. In the southern states, in health care, transportation, education, law enforcement, public accommodations, employment, housing or government services, equality never existed nor was equality contemplated.

Beginning in 1951, the University of North Carolina conceded that the state failed to provide separate but equal graduate and professional facilities. In fact, in most instances no facilities for graduate and professional education of black citizens were available in the state; and hence, begrudgingly, UNC accepted blacks in graduate and professional schools. From June 1951 to September 1955, four black students had earned LLB degrees and one had been awarded a medical degree. As of September 1955, four blacks were enrolled in law school, two in the graduate school, and one in the school of medicine.

Since many who will read this were born after 1954, I want to identify some bodies and agencies just to give a flavor of leadership of the day and I also want to point to a few bodies and individuals who had a profound effect on me. With rare exceptions, the government's leadership structure was composed of white males. In a few agencies (primarily dealing with education) a handful of white women held positions.

President Dwight Eisenhower interviewed approximately 520 white males and females for executive posts within his administration. In the Judiciary, all members of the U.S. Supreme Court, the U.S. Fourth Circuit Court of Appeals, the U.S. District Courts sitting in North Carolina and at the state level, the State Supreme Court, Superior Courts, and North Carolina Special Courts were presided over by only white males. Not only were those courts and their clerks and administrators all white, but so, too, were all employees above the rank of janitor.

One of the ugliest electoral campaigns in the history of the United States was the 1950 senatorial race in North Carolina, between Willis Smith and Frank Porter Graham. Graham, a liberal, was appointed to fill the vacancy created by the death of Senator J. Melvin Broughton. That campaign was more racist than any campaign South Carolina, Georgia, Mississippi, Alabama, or other Deep South states imagined. Senator Smith's campaign was guided substantially by Jesse Helms. The Smith-Helms platform promoting bigotry defeated Graham. Smith was succeeded in the Senate by W. Kerr Scott. Serving also during the mid-fifties was Senator Samuel J. Ervin, widely known as the constitutional scholar who presided over the Watergate hearings and the ouster of President Richard Nixon. However, Senator Ervin was known by blacks in North Carolina as a bigot of the first order. His record in the Senate and, before that, as a member of the North Carolina judiciary, took advantage of every opportunity to curtail the rights of black citizens.

During the mid-fifties, Jesse Helms was not an elected official; rather, he was a vice president of the NBC affiliate in Raleigh, WRAL, where he delivered a twice daily editorial commentary on issues of the day. It so happened that the issues most days centered on civil rights and Helms continued the bigotry and racism for which he was well known. James K. Dorsett Jr. was his son-in-law and a member of Senator Smith's Raleigh law firm. Dorsett also later served in an official capacity in Helms's campaigns.

The trustees of North Carolina's universities were appointed by the all-white North Carolina Legislature and hence, the hundred members of the University of North Carolina's Board of Trustees, not surprisingly, were all white. All county sheriffs were white; all members of the State Highway Patrol were white; all county commissioners were white; most restaurants were white; all hotels were white. The restaurants and theaters which admitted blacks admitted them only in theater balconies or take-out windows at restaurants. I was grown and married with children before I ever stayed in a hotel or motel. When blacks traveled, they were going to see someone. The black extended family was extended, in part, because of the necessity of visiting with friends and families whenever one traveled. If you did not have a "somebody" you didn't go.

Now back to 1954. On May 17, 1954, I was an eleventh grade student at Hillside High School in Durham, North Carolina. I remember that afternoon during Mae Bass Spaulding's Latin class, when an announcement was made over the public address system informing the school of the U.S. Supreme Court's *Brown* decision. For the balance of the class period, our discussion focused exclusively on the anticipated consequences of the decision and, based upon what little we had heard over the public address system, it was everybody's belief that at the beginning of the fall 1954 term, probably half of our student body would enroll at Durham High School since approximately that percentage lived closer to Durham High than to Hillside. It was our view that the Court's mandate would be implemented "with all deliberate speed" with the emphasis on *speed*. We were not prepared for the deceit, hypocrisy, and chicanery that would follow. The Court ruled, in part, "we conclude that in the field of public education, the doctrine of 'separate but equal' has no place. Separate educational facilities are inherently unequal."

Reaction to the *Brown* decision was varied in North Carolina. Governor William B. Umstead said that he was "terribly disappointed" with the Court's ruling. Frank Porter Graham, then United Nations mediator and former president of the University of North Carolina, told a group in Washington that the Court's decision must be "accepted in good faith and wisdom" by everyone. He saw such an attitude as a "moral imperative." This view, however, was not the view of the 1954 UNC administration or trustees. Even before the *Brown* decision was announced, the Board of Trustees of the University of North Carolina had gone on record with respect to undergraduate admissions, adopting a policy to exclude Negroes from the undergraduate schools.

Following the *Brown* decision, interested students from the UNC YM/YWCA determined that the time was right for them to make a difference. A delegation from the Y led by William O. Loftquist visited with H. M. Holmes, principal of Hillside High School in Durham. The Y delegation expressed the need to have black undergraduate students on campus and pledged the full support of their organization as well as the support of the individual members. Included among the leadership supporting the desegregation of the university was Charles Kuralt, editor of the UNC *Daily Tar Heel* newspaper, later to become the renowned CBS correspondent.

Mr. Holmes understood that persons undertaking a challenge to state and university policy would do so at great risk. He knew the social, political, and economic structure at the time and it was quite certain that political, social, and economic pressure would be applied to applicants and their families. Mr. Holmes informed the Durham Committee on Negro Affairs ("Durham Committee") which concluded that the effort was worthy and timely and sought to identify students whose families could be somewhat insulated from the pressures likely to be exerted. Both of my parents were employees of North Carolina Mutual Life Insurance Company, at the time the largest black-controlled enterprise in the world. My mother's brother was president. Their employment was quite secure. John Lewis Brandon, another member of our Hillside class, was the son of custodial employees at Duke University whose wages were so low that the Durham committee could afford to counter any economic retaliation.

My father was a former president of the Durham Committee, former president of the Hillside Parent Teacher's Association, and very much a community activist. He, more than we, decided that my brother LeRoy and I should submit applications for admission to the University of North Carolina. On May 18, 1955, LeRoy, John Brandon, and I received letters from Roy Armstrong, Director of Admissions, which stated in part: "The Trustees of the University have not yet changed the policy of admission of Negro students to the University. Negroes are eligible to make application to come to the University for graduate and professional study not offered at a Negro college in North Carolina. Negroes are not eligible to apply for admission to the undergraduate division of the University."

There followed a torrent of publicity and a call for a meeting of the board of trustees. The one hundred members of the Board were all elected by the General Assembly and represented the ultimate political payoff for "supporters of good government." By statute, the governor was *ex officio* the presiding officer. In the intervening year Governor Umstead died and was succeeded by Luther H. Hodges.

At a meeting on May 23, 1955, 89 members were present and voted unanimously to adopt the following resolution:

> The State of North Carolina, having spent millions of dollars in providing adequate and equal educational facilities in the undergraduate departments of its institutions of higher learning for all races, it is hereby declared to be the policy of the Board of Trustees of the consolidated University of North Carolina, that applications of Negroes to the undergraduate schools of the three branches of the consolidated university, be not accepted.

The 89 affirmative votes included the votes of 22 lawyer-members later to be interpreted as 22 views on the legality of the trustees' resolution and the rejection of a contrary construction of the *Brown* decision. Judge John J. Parker of the U.S. Fourth Circuit Court of Appeals was a member of the Board of Trustees but was not present at the May 23 meeting. On June 1, Judge Parker wrote Governor Hodges suggesting that the Board probably thought that the *Brown* decision was not final in light of a motion for rehearing pending before the Supreme Court. Judge Parker stated that on May 31 the Court reaffirmed *Brown* (*Brown II*) and, based upon that development, Judge Parker suggested that a meeting of the Board be called to reconsider its action. Parker concluded that the Board of Trustees of a state university could not afford to put itself in the position of defying the law or of directing officials of the University to disregard it: "On the contrary, I think it is the duty of the Board not only to obey the law as declared by the Supreme Court, but also to take the lead in providing for its peaceful observance by our people. If the problem is approached in this spirit, many difficulties which now appear troublesome will be solved without friction."

Another view was expressed by Donald O. Fowler, president of the Student Government at the University. He wrote:

It is my considered judgment that the majority of students at Chapel Hill would support the recent action of the Board of Trustees to refrain from integration at this time. I can reach no other conclusion as a result of the countless number of comments which have been directed to me during the past several weeks. I feel confident that the students at Chapel Hill have the utmost confidence in the wisdom of our state and university officials and at this crucial period, pledge our cooperation and full support of their action.

Those who are interested can read *Frasier v. the Board of Trustees of the University of North Carolina,* [134 Fed supp. 589, decided September 16, 1955(2)] as well as *Board of Trustees of the University of North Carolina, et al. v. Frasier, et al.,* [350 U.S. 979, 76 S Ct 467, decided March 5, 1956(7)]. I won't spend much time discussing the case either at the District Court level or the Supreme Court. It's relatively straightforward. Three plaintiffs in a class action against the Board of Trustees of the University of North Carolina sought a declaratory judgment that certain orders of the Board of Trustees which deny admission to undergraduate schools to members of the Negro race are in violation of the equal protection clause of the Fourteenth Amendment of the Constitution. The complaint also sought an injunction restraining the University from denying admission to Negroes solely because of their race and color.

Citing the *Brown* decision previously discussed, Judge Morris A. Soper, writing for the three judge District Court Panel (including Armistead Dobie, from the United States Court of Appeals for the Fourth Circuit and Johnson J. Hayes of the U.S. District Court for the Middle District of North Carolina), adopted the language from the *Brown* decision: "We conclude that in the field of public education, the doctrine of 'separate but equal' has no place. Separate educational facilities are inherently unequal." Next, the Court swiftly dispatched the university's suggestion that the reasoning in the *Brown* decision did not apply with equal force to colleges as to primary schools. The court concluded "indeed it is fair to say that they apply with greater force to students of mature age in the concluding years of their formal education as they are about to engage in the serious business of adult life."

The U.S. Supreme Court affirmed. The legal team for the state included William B. Rodman Jr., Attorney General, and I. Beverly Lake, Assistant Attorney General, and for the plaintiffs able counsel were Conrad O. Pearson, Floyd B. McKissick, John H. Wheeler, William A. Marsh Jr., E. A. Gadsden, Milton E. Johnson and joining at the Supreme Court, Thurgood Marshall and Robert L. Carter.

The District Court opinion was rendered on September 16, 1955, my seventeenth birthday, and we enrolled on that date.

William Friday, who became president of the university in 1956, recently said that UNC was a leader among southern universities. He described desegregation as moving slowly through gradual acceptance of what was the progressive thing to do—an attitude that continues to give UNC the reputation for being one of the most forward-thinking universities in the Nation: "When the *Brown* decision was made, this brought an end to the old traditional attitude about separate but equal. . . . It was the university itself that had to set the pace." Throughout all the conflicts and victories for black equality, Friday said the university played a vital role in bringing people together and changing the views of people all over the state.

I guess that is why the revisionist history will next have Friday, Rodman, and Lake on the U.S. Supreme Court steps joining hands with Billy Marsh and Thurgood Marshall singing "We Shall Overcome." Or should we forget that Governor Luther Hodges as *ex officio* chair of the Board of Trustees and its Executive Committee directed Attorney General Rodman to appeal the three judge Federal District Court decision and appointed Thomas J. Pearsall chair of a committee to confer with the attorney general "to . . . advise and direct with respect to the scope and extent of the appeal to be taken and matters incidental to the appeal and the enforcement of the court's decree. . . ." This is the same "progressive" Thomas Pearsall who developed North Carolina's Pearsall Plan under which the public school system would be abolished if North Carolina were faced with a directive to desegregate the public schools. This is the same progressive university that required that the black students live in a segregated quadrant of a dormitory; that initially denied black students access to the swimming pool, the student section for athletic events, the Carolina Inn, and other university facilities.

It should also be noted that while the University dominated all aspects of the Chapel Hill community, nothing was done to foster access to restaurants, theaters, and other public accommodation facilities.

That sums up the posture of the participants in that litigation except that it should be noted that we recently gained access to work papers of Attorney General Rodman and Assistant Attorney General I. Beverly Lake. It is clear from some of the internal memoranda that they had no real expectation of success either at the District Court or the Supreme Court level. I suppose, in a sense, I would rather have had them deeply committed to the position which they espoused rather than acting hypocritically for political purposes. An August 30, 1955 memorandum from Lake to Rodman asserts:

I do not believe that there is the remotest possibility of our ultimate success. I do believe that we have here an opportunity to demonstrate both to the people of North Carolina and to the NAACP that we intend to fight integration at every step and that we have nothing of which we feel ashamed. Such a presentation by this office will, in my opinion, give to the people of the state some very badly needed encouragement.

On September 1, 1955, Rodman wrote to then Governor Luther H. Hodges (who had succeeded Governor Umstead on his death in November 1954): "nowhere have I found reasonable hope that we can succeed."

Frasier v. UNC extended *Brown* to higher education and was the top North Carolina news story of 1955 and number 8 in North Carolina for the twentieth century.

I'd like to spend a few moments focusing on a few of the events and people who had a profound effect on my career. During the summer of 1964, the Congress was debating the Civil Rights Act of 1964 which, if enacted, would have a profound effect on public accommodations and employment. At the time, Roland Hayes was an assistant manager in the Church Street office of Wachovia Bank & Trust Company in Winston-Salem. That role was very unusual because at the time, most majority businesses did not employ blacks in managerial positions. Wachovia was unique in that in the 1930s it had acquired the black-owned and managed Church Street Bank. The black president of the bank was president by day but at night he was a custodian at Wachovia. In the latter role, he became acquainted with much of the Wachovia senior management. With the black bank on the verge of collapse, its president prevailed on Wachovia management to acquire and save the Church Street Bank. After a period of all-white management, Wachovia operated the Church Street office solely with black employees at all levels well into the 1960s. Generally, those employees were restricted to that location and did not have the mobility to move through the ranks of the largest bank in the Southeast. Nevertheless, and despite those limitations, the Church Street office provided a training ground for a few fortunate blacks to experience banking in a major financial institution. In fact, during the sixties and seventies, if you looked around the country at black-owned banks, you would find that most of the executive management were alumni of the Wachovia Church Street office.

During the summer of 1964, I was slated to join my classmate, Maynard Jackson, in Boston where he had worked prior to coming to law school. He had been a successful sales manager of Colliers Encyclopedias. Maynard had taught me the sales spiel and I had every intention of going to Boston. Roland Hayes, the Church Street Assistant Manager, suggested—in fact dared me to submit an employment inquiry to Wachovia to see how they would respond. I wrote the Director of Human Resources explaining why he needed to hire me. He invited me for an interview, and to our amazement, he offered summer employment *in the main office*. Even more surprising, at the end of the summer, I was offered a full-time position to commence upon completion of my final semester in law school. I accepted.

As all lawyers know, before you gain approval to take any bar examination, you are required to satisfy a character and fitness test established by the State Board of Law Examiners. In North Carolina that included reference checking, and as was the case of black applicants, an inquisition before Edward L. Cannon, secretary of the North Carolina State Bar, the licensing agency. During his tenure, the Cannon inquisition was dreaded almost as much as the bar exam. The character and fitness passage for black applicants was only slightly better than the passage rate on the bar exam. Such things as NAACP membership, participation in civil rights activities, and other "communist inspired activity" subjected blacks to a grueling process and many were rejected as "unfit."

Prior to taking the 1965 bar exam, I sought to arrange my interview with Mr. Cannon. When I made inquiry, I learned that Mr. Cannon's son was taking the bar that year and, as a result, he had recused himself from the interview and examination process. In Cannon's absence, interviews were conducted by the assistant secretary, B. E. James. I talked with Mr. James by phone and he informed me that on the morning prior to my call, he had been in Winston-Salem and had interviewed the entire Wake Forest University third year law class. Under Cannon, the interview for blacks lasted the better part of a day for each applicant. It was amazing that at Wake Forest, the entire class could be interviewed in a morning. Mr. James suggested that rather than coming back to Winston-Salem or have me come to Raleigh, it would be just as well to have a member of the Winston-Salem Bar conduct an interview and that would satisfy the requirement. You can imagine how elated I was by that development.

The next hurdle was to prepare for the exam itself. Two bar review courses were offered—one at Duke University in Durham and one at Wake Forest University in Winston-Salem. Since I was working and living in Winston-Salem, I sought to register for the bar review course at Wake Forest. I was informed that Negroes were not eligible to register for courses conducted at Wake Forest and told that I would have to make other arrangements and to "get over it." The only other arrangement was the course at Duke, ninety miles away. Since I was working full time, I decided not to commute every day, but registered at Duke, obtained the review materials, and conducted my own course.

After passing the bar exam, and being admitted to the North Carolina State Bar, I made an application for membership in the North Carolina Bar Association, Inc., the professional trade association. My application was the subject of great debate at the Association's April 1966 meeting. Moses Burt and Floyd McKissick had applied earlier and their applications had been "held over" to the April meeting. A motion to defer action on those three applications was defeated in favor of a motion to reject the applications of Burt and McKissick and defer action on my application until the Association's July meeting. At the April 1966 meeting, 57 applications were approved. At the July 2, 1966 meeting, heated debate continued. In the end, Romallus O. Murphy and I were rejected and sixteen applicants were approved, having passed a three-prong test— (1) white male, (2) lawyer, and (3) the ability to fog a mirror. Though the Association's sanitized minutes don't mention it, Burt, McKissick, Murphy, and I are black. One of the leaders of maintaining a segregated association was James K. Dorsett Jr., whom I mentioned earlier.

Dorsett, the son-in-law of Willis Smith, former member of the North Carolina Legislature, former president of the North Carolina Bar Association, and a prominent Raleigh lawyer, had argued that blacks should not be admitted since the North Carolina Bar Association, in addition to professional activities, also sponsored social activities for its members and their spouses and that it would be inappropriate to have blacks in this latter setting.

Several years later, Dorsett, who knew very little about banking but was politically connected, was named Executive Vice President, General Counsel, and Secretary of Wachovia and I became one of his direct reports. This was genuine stress. Some months later, Dorsett was approving the payment of annual dues to various professional associations for the staff lawyers. He noted that I had not sought reimbursement for membership dues in the North Carolina Bar Association. I explained that I was not a member because "the bastards had denied my application and that I will not join until they offer me an apology." Dorsett responded that "you shouldn't be that way. You should get over that."

For many years my resentment toward Wake Forest University was quite intense, but not nearly as intense as my resentment of Dorsett. Despite the overall positive experience and success that I enjoyed at Wachovia, I seethed with resentment every time I saw Dorsett. That resentment was partly responsible for my vulnerability to an offer for an opportunity in Ohio. For over twenty-five years, I thought of Dorsett every single day. I didn't "get over it."

About five years ago, I attended a meeting in Reno, Nevada. The travel schedule required that I arrive early in the afternoon of the day prior to my meeting. I decided that with that available time, I would compose a letter to Dorsett in an effort to "get over it." Before sitting down to write, I looked through some of the reading material that I had brought, including the *North Carolina Bar Quarterly,* and saw that James K. Dorsett Jr. had died. I felt cheated out of the opportunity to inform him of the impact he had on my life. It occurred to me, however, that I may have been the loser for harboring resentment all those years to no good end.

Recently, I read an article about long-standing resentment. In 1930, a black Baltimore resident who lived approximately three blocks from the University of Maryland Law School, enrolled in the Law School at Howard University—forty miles away because he was not eligible to enter the University of Maryland due to his race and color. Over sixty years later, after the black lawyer had attained some degree of prominence, the University of Maryland decided to honor a distinguished native son by commissioning a bust and naming the new University of Maryland Law School facility in his honor. The bust was done, the facility was built and Thurgood Marshall declined to participate in the dedication ceremony, stating that "I wasn't good enough in 1930 and I won't be good enough now." He never "got over it."

Reading that story gave me comfort and I then was able to assert with deep conviction that I will "get over it" with respect to Faubus, Thurmond, Talmadge, Wallace, Umstead, Hodges, Ervin, Smith, Helms, Wake Forest, Dorsett, and a thousand other bigots when the resentment is wrested from my cold, dead hand.

CHAPTER 7

Brown v. Board and Columbus

ROBERT M. DUNCAN

I

In May, 1954, I was in the United States Army at Fort Richardson, Alaska. I had been deferred from service to attend law school. My dear friend and barracks roommate, a nonblack from North Carolina, having completed a graduate degree, similarly was fulfilling his military obligation. We were together the afternoon of May 17, 1954, when we heard about the decision in *Brown v. Board of Education*.[1] I remarked that the decision was a critically important fundamental change in the law which will be good for America. He responded that the decision would be unacceptable to most white people, and that it would be hard to make it work. We were both right. Certainly, in 1954, no prescience would have ever allowed me to imagine that I, an African American, would become a United States District Judge and preside over a full-fledged school desegregation case.

In 1948, after graduating from The Ohio State University College of Education, I wanted to live in Columbus and become a public school teacher at the secondary level. However, getting a position at Champion Junior High School, the only secondary school in the District where African American teachers were employed, seemed virtually impossible.

1. 347 U.S. 483 (1954)

There was a long waiting list. Ironically, after examining alternatives, I decided to go to law school.

Fate would have it that after my appointment as a federal judge in July 1974, I inherited a docket of cases which included *Penick, et al. v. Columbus Board of Education.*[2] Fourteen students filed suit against the Columbus Board of Education and various other defendants alleging that the defendants' purposeful conduct caused and was perpetuating racial segregation in the public schools. To the best of my knowledge, the Columbus case was one of the last desegregation cases involving a large urban school district to be litigated. There was a large body of relevant case law available which was instructive. Also before the trial, I had the opportunity to attend a seminar on "Education and the Courts" sponsored by the Danforth Foundation. There I met a number of federal judges who presided over well-known school desegregation cases including some from northern communities. I benefited from hearing comments from school superintendents from urban areas that had been required to implement desegregation remedies. The seminar provoked critical thinking about a broad range of extremely important legal and social issues arising from and related to school desegregation. I will always be grateful to the Danforth Foundation for sponsoring the seminar.

II

The trial to the Court in *Penick, et al. v. Columbus Board of Education* began on April 19, 1976 and concluded June 17, 1976. There were 70 witnesses, over 600 exhibits, and 6,600 pages of transcript. All the lawyers in the case represented their clients in a very professional manner and certainly were among the best ever to appear before me. Accordingly, the issues were sharply and feverishly contested.

In the process of making findings of fact and conclusions of law, I first reviewed the evidence regarding activities and events that took place before *Brown* was decided, and then post-*Brown* evidence.

If the District had been unlawfully segregated by race, after the May 1954 decision, the duty to desegregate arose. The evidence clearly indicated that prior to *Brown,* over the years Columbus officials—using race-based student school attendance assignment, optional attendance zones, zone boundary changes, placement of faculty and staff based on race and

2. 429F. Supp. 229 (1977)

other strategies—intentionally caused an enclave of east side schools to effectively be maintained as one race: African American. Predecessors of the Columbus defendants had caused some black children to be educated in schools that were predominantly white; however, the officials also deliberately caused at least five schools to be overwhelmingly black schools. These schools remained one race[3] until the remedial order was effective in 1979.[4]

Post-*Brown,* not only was there a responsibility to desegregate but also a clear mandate not to intentionally cause more segregation. Nevertheless, the board's school construction site decisions increased racial impaction.

After World War II, Columbus experienced meteoric growth. By the end of the 1960s there were more than 110,000 students in the district. Large increases in school population required that more schools be built. Despite objections from citizens and civic and community groups, the school board[5] majority, adhering to a neighborhood school policy, decided to build a number of new schools in areas where they would be one race: white. Alternative building sites available in other areas would have lessened the district's segregation of students by race.

Drawing reasonable inferences from the facts, there was sufficient proof that the intentional acts and omissions of school officials resulted in furtherance and continuance of segregation. The *Washington v. Davis* "discriminatory purpose" standard proof was met and the Columbus School District was judged to be a "dual" system—one that was intentionally organized and operated by school officials as part white and part black.[6]

The defendants were permanently enjoined from discriminating on the basis of race and from promoting or maintaining unconstitutional racial segregation in the Columbus school facilities.[7] A Board proposed a

3. One race school: one in which 90 percent or more of the students are of a single race.

4. *Penick v. Columbus Board of Education,* 429 F. Supp. 229,236

5. 426 U.S. 229.

6. While the term "dual" is comparatively well understood in school desegregation matters, the use of the word "unitary" is not. In *Board of Education Oklahoma City Schools v. Dowell* [498 U.S. 237, 245 (1991)], Chief Justice Rehnquist noted that the use of the term "unitary" has been used inconsistently by lower courts. Some courts have used it to identify a school district that has completely remedied all vestiges of past discrimination. Other courts have used "unitary" to describe any school district that has currently desegregated student assignments. Under that interpretation a school district could be called "unitary" and, nevertheless, still contain vestiges of past discrimination. The Chief Justice declined to define the term more precisely.

7. See *Penick v. Columbus Board of Education,* 429 F. Supp. 229 (S.D. Ohio 1977), *aff'd,* 583 F. 2d 787 (6th Cir. 1978, *aff'd,* 443 U.S. 449 (1979).

system-wide remedial plan that was approved by October 7, 1977.[8] The remedy order included pupil reassignment to achieve racial balance. A subsequent round of appellate litigation left the same remedies intact.[9] Busing began in September 1979.

It was good fortune that Dr. LaVerne Cunningham, former Dean of the College of Education at The Ohio State University and a highly regarded expert on schools and race, agreed to serve as the court's special master in the oversight of the desegregation remedy process. He established excellent working relationships with school officials, who were very professional, and he worked to effectively administer the planning and execution of the many complexities of teacher and parent orientation, student assignments, transportation, extracurricular activities, finances, and many other matters attendant to the remedial order.

The Columbus business community and other civic leaders formed the Metropolitan Columbus Schools Committee (MCSC). The committee had as its mission peaceful desegregation and maintenance of quality education in Columbus. The committee was chaired by Rowland Brown who was wise, hardworking, and dedicated to fairness. MCSC's efforts were outstanding. Unfortunately, this commission was ended, shortly after the remedy was in place.

One school board member stated, "What we must do, we must do well." No court orders were disobeyed; no compliance hearings were required; the remedial process was effectively conducted in good faith. The district was peacefully and thoroughly desegregated.

In 1981, the Columbus defendants requested that the injunctive orders be withdrawn—basically claiming that they had faithfully complied with court orders. The request was denied. A few years later the request was made again. Plaintiffs' counsel vigorously resisted relinquishment of jurisdiction claiming that jurisdiction should be continued until all vestiges of segregation are removed "root and branch," citing *Green v. County Board of New Kent.*[10]

Four years later, on April 11, 1985, an order was entered dissolving the injunctions remaining in the case. The defendants had implemented

8. The Ohio State Board of Education and the Ohio Superintendent of Public Instruction also were defendants. They were found then liable for the constitutional violation. The state's failure to prevent or protect intentional segregative local public school policies renders the state directly liable for such discrimination and accordingly the state must bear a portion of the financial cost incurred pursuant to the desegregation order.

9. *Penick v. Columbus Board of Education,* 519 F. Supp. 925 (S.D. Ohio), *aff'd,* 663 F. 2d 24 (6th Cir. 1981), cert *denied.* 455 U.S. 1018 (1982).

10. 391 U.S. 430 (1968).

the remedial plan in good faith. Prior concerns about student discipline, mobility, retention, extracurricular activities, academic achievement and participation had been addressed in a fair and unbiased manner. I felt the *Green* standard had sufficiently been met. The decision to terminate court oversight was extremely challenging. However, I believe that equal protection school desegregation law does not contemplate perpetual court oversight.

Later, in 1991, a majority of the Supreme Court, in *Board of Education Oklahoma City Public Schools v. Dowell*,[11] announced that the standard for the dissolution of remedial injunctions requires a finding that all vestiges of past discrimination have been removed *to the extent practicable*. Although I had reached a theoretically similar conclusion earlier, I find no comfort in a position contra to the dissent of Justice Marshall in Dowell. The narrowing language *to the extent practicable* set forth in the majority opinion, does not really provide much guidance in deciding a motion for the dissolution of injunctions. Deciding what is practicable is fact-driven and always difficult but even more so in school desegregation matters where so many factors and issues are in play.

A factually demonstrated school segregation constitutional violation certainly can be subject to court-ordered remedial action such as student reassignment and transportation, faculty and staff reassignment, orientation, extracurricular matters, academic adjustments, and increased pedagogical resources. Accordingly, over time it is practical and reasonable to identify and purge a number of vestiges of school segregation.

Brown's broader projection is a promised goal of the achievement of egalitarian social justice without regard to race. It is this altruistic promise that courts with limited remedial powers, absent other government and private participation, find so difficult to keep. The Third Branch simply cannot issue orders to bring reality to the promise of curing all the social injustice caused by school segregation. Certain vestiges of segregation are subtle and complex, and it is difficult to establish that they resulted from discrete life experiences. In a society where for so many years racial segregation has been and continues to be alive and active in public and private life experiences, it was impossible to identify all the negative vestiges essentially flowing from school segregation. Some vestiges of school segregation are combined with others resulting from non-school segregated experiences. Other vestiges are mental, emotional, and difficult to identify and remove.

Brown and its precedential aftermath show that judicial mandate can

11. 498 U.S. 237 (1991).

be a powerful force for social justice. However, the social justice for students promised by *Brown*—including the removal of all vestiges of school segregation, particularly the emotional ones—possibly may never be achieved, and probably not in the foreseeable future. My experience with a school desegregation case compels me to believe that the Dowell "practicable" standard is appropriate but not easy to apply. In the reality of contemporary urban dynamics, when desegregation remedial injunctions are dissolved, there is a very high risk of resegregation. In dissenting in *Dowell*, Justice Marshall wrote: "Similarly, avoiding reemergence of the harm condemned in *Brown I* accounts for the Court's insistence of remedies that ensure lasting integration of formerly segregated systems."[12] When the court injunctions were removed, I was hopeful that the Columbus Board would not act to return to a substantial system of student assignment based on neighborhood residence which would result in resegregation. The Columbus metropolitan area is a very livable community. It has a history of good government, a steady diverse economy, great institutions of higher education, active civic organizations, and a significantly less than majority African American population. This platform provided a basis for hope for a positive long-term desegregation result.

For a period of time after the injunctions were removed in 1985, the basic student assignment plan, which had been ordered, remained substantially in effect. However, in 1990, the board appointed a citizen's committee whose mission was to recommend a plan which would reduce transportation while maintaining as much racial balance as possible.[13] The committee was composed of distinguished citizens of Columbus—fourteen African Americans, thirteen whites and three Asians. The committee met, received legal advice, held public meetings, studied demographic trends, reviewed transportation cost data, and procured a public opinion survey.

12. *Board of Education Oklahoma City Public Schools v. Dowell.* 498 U.S. 237, 112 L. Ed. 2d 715, 736.

13. It is interesting to note the committee's transportation status report:

C. *Current Transportation Status.* The specifics of current student transportation are unknown to most Columbus residents. Most would be surprised to learn that 41.4% of Columbus students walk to school. In the 1989–90 school year approximately 64,000 students were enrolled in Columbus Schools. Of those, 26,500 walked to school. Forty- five (45) percent of elementary students and fifty-nine (59) percent of middle and high school students ride buses to school. Of the students bused, 37% are transported for health, safety, distance or other reasons, 17% are bused to alternative schools, 13% are bused for special education and 4% are adjustment transfers and English as a Second Language students. Twenty-nine (29) percent are bused for racial balance purposes.

The committee worked diligently and thoroughly and reported to the Board at page 5 of its statement: "The Committee believes, from all it has learned, that the Board has two options: retain the current plan with modifications to bring all schools within racial balance parameters or design a new plan compromising on racial balance and time distance criteria." The board chose the latter option. As a result, it is fair to say that since early 1996, the district has been substantially resegregated and, arguably, that this was lawfully accomplished. Such an outcome is not in the best interests of our schools or community.

With hindsight and in agonizing reappraisal, I question whether lifting the injunctions was premature. Perhaps holding on longer would have prevented resegregation. School desegregation oversight is complex and concerns many areas of school administration and pedagogy. The authority and efficiency of courts is limited. For example, the *Milliken v. Bradley* suburban safe harbor has an abundance of new residents. Coterminous school districts not found liable of intentional segregation cannot be included in a remedial order.[14] In his excellent book, *Getting around Brown, Desegregation, Development, and the Columbus Public School,* Gregory S. Jacobs writes:

> I will argue that the desegregation of the Columbus, Ohio, public school system failed to ensure equal educational opportunity not because it was inherently detrimental to learning, but because it was intrinsically incompatible with the city's steady geographic and economic growth. Even before the first buses rolled in 1979, the threat of desegregation had redefined the parameters of single-family home building in the city, essentially turning the boundaries of the Columbus school district into a residential development redline. The myriad resources that typically follow new housing were both exiting and avoiding the city schools by desegregation's implementation; busing simply solidified and intensified this already extant process.

He also concludes that "Between 1970 and 1980, the city school system had gone from being essential to residential development in Columbus to being incompatible with it."[15] It is interesting to note that Jacobs

14. 418 U.S. 732

15. Ohio State University Press 1998, 177. It is also interesting to note, Jacobs relates that "I was a fifth grader in the Columbus schools when desegregation began in 1979, and I can still recall being ordered to evacuate Olde Orchard Elementary one gray October morning. At the time, I did not fully understand that what appeared to be an unexpected recess was actually

observes: "Private schools, vouchers, charter schools, home schooling all provide legal plays to end run court desegregation remedial order."[16]

As twenty-first-century America becomes more racially diverse, many large cities become populated with more minority residents. For instance, in Franklin County, Ohio, where Columbus is located, the white population continued to decline, even after the transportation to achieve racial balance had been abandoned.[17] Looking forward, if such trends continue, there may well be no nonminority group left in town with whom to integrate.

Even with the benefit of hindsight, I doubt that a longer term of oversight of the Columbus schools would have removed all of the vestiges of segregation or abated the resegregation of the schools through state, local and private acts or omissions.

III

Almost all citizens attest to the belief that school children should be accorded social justice. However, the great majority did not wish to make the changes necessary to accomplish school desegregation and integration. Many citizens did not want it to be successful. Others believed that the process was not worth its trouble. These days there is little articulated support for separate but equal, but in practice many people continue to hold on to that illusion.

Professor William W. Wayson's 1966 comments in a letter to the editor of a local Columbus newspaper ring true:

> Desegregated schooling allows the public or fair-minded educators to effect more improvements than segregated education does. The educational weaknesses of segregated schools are inherent in the segregation. They cannot be corrected in the segregated setting. The so-called deficiencies of desegregation—even the real ones—could all have been overcome if school personnel, school boards, city fathers,

---

something far more serious: a bomb threat directed at Tracey Duncan, my classmate and the daughter of the district court judge who had ordered the schools desegregated." Two persons were convicted of a criminal conspiracy to bomb the school.

16. Ibid, xv.

17. From 2000 to 2004 the white population of Franklin County declined from 798,787 to 782,107. The African American population increased from 207,222 to 227,204; the Latino population increased from 24,753 to 33,691 and the Asian population increased from 38,833 to 44,379. *Columbus Dispatch.*

and the nation's movers and shakers had sincerely intended to educate children who are poor, who are not white, who live in desperate circumstances neither they nor their parents created or control. [Noted *Time* magazine columnist] Jack White says it well: before we gave up on integration, we should have tried it. The weaknesses of desegregated schools result from lack of will and skill—both of which can be changed and both of which are gradually changed by the dynamics of the setting even if no one is committed to the improvement.

IV

Since school segregation continues to exist, is it predictable that America will experience another round of K through 12 school desegregation lawsuits?

The ability of skillful legal tacticians to produce new approaches to legal problem solving should never be underestimated. However, existing legal precedent and social indicators do not point to new large-scale lawsuits to desegregate K through 12 urban public schools. Civil rights organizations and civil rights lawyers have taken their efforts and resources to struggles on other fronts. So school desegregation is now, more than ever, merged with a host of other social issues that contend for solutions. Our country's rapidly increasing diversity, the diminution of the middle class, extensive poverty, high crime rates among people of color, inadequate health care, and other issues have merged and desperately impact those who have been subject to a history of racial injustice.

Generally, Supreme Court case law presents formidable challenges for those who seek racial justice advocating constitutional violation. In 1973, the Supreme Court in *Rodriguez v. San Antonio Independent School District*[18] undervalued the national criticality of education, holding that gross disparities in funding among school districts did not violate the Fourteenth Amendment, concluding that education was not a fundamental right. This result contributes to the institutionalization of inequality of funding of school districts which negatively affects poor people.

The Supreme Court ruling in *Regents of the University of California v. Bakke* was a devastating blow. Justice Blackmun's opinion in *Bakke* stated in part: "In order to get beyond racism, we must first take account of race. . . . There is no other way. And in order to treat some persons

---

18. 411 U.S. 1 (1973). See Educational Equity and Quality; Brown and Rodriguez and Their Aftermath. Excerpts from Lee Bollinger's Speech at College Board Annual Forum, New York 2003, *The College Board Review* 201 (Winter 2003–4).

equally, we must treat them differently. We cannot—we dare not—let the Equal Protection Clause perpetuate racial supremacy."[19] Such fundamental logic in my judgment is sound, but it did not carry the day. The *Bakke* holding requires that remedial race-based state action must be reviewed with strict scrutiny and found to serve a compelling state interest. Thereafter, the concept of "neo-color-blindness" took on a snowballing hubris for those who seem to be threatened by racial equality. While I am grateful that Justice Powell's diversity rationale kept the door open for some consideration of race in higher education, unfortunately it did not save the day. Other post-*Bakke* jurisprudential commitments have established foreboding standards of proof for historical racial discrimination.[20] In addition, the Supreme Court has constrained the scope of school desegregation remedial orders.[21]

My perception is that the African American community remains divided on the academic and social appropriateness of further efforts to avoid predominantly one race schools. In Columbus, currently there is no active initiative to take action regarding school desegregation. It does not look good for a new round of urban school desegregation lawsuits.

V

Harvard Professor Gary Orfield comments on the value of a desegregated education: He says, in an increasingly pluralistic society, lack of familiarity with others' perspectives will limit the ability of students of all races to compete successfully and live harmoniously when they are adults. "We need to talk to parents. We need a vigorous campaign to tell white parents in particular about why their kids are disadvantaged if they attend a segregated school. We need to give the public a lot of information about why we need this—the benefits of desegregation," says Orfield.

That reframing of the issue, from the rights of minority students to the best interests of all students, and of society at large, is key to jumpstarting the dormant desegregation enforcement system, says Orfield. He cites the Supreme Court's decision in *Grutter v. Bollinger*, 539 U.S. 306 (2003), as indicative of the shift in thinking. In *Grutter*, the court recog-

19. *University of California v. Bakke*, 433 U.S. 265 (1978); See *Becoming Justice Blackmun*, L. Greenhouse, p. 135.

20. *Richmond v. Croson.* 488 U.S. 469; *Adarounod v. Pena*, 515 U.S. 200 (1995); *Hopwood v. Texas.* 248 F. 3d 1141 (5th Cir. 2001)

21. *Bradley v. Milligan*, 418 U.S. 717 (1974); *Pasadena City Bd. of Ed. v. Spangler*, 427 U.S. 424 (1976); *Board of Education Oklahoma City Schools v. Dowell.* 498 U.S. 237 (1991); *Freeman v. Pitts*, 503 U.S. 467 (1992); *Missouri v. Jenkins.* 515 U.S. 70 (1995).

nized a compelling interest on the part of school authorities for diversity in the classroom in upholding an affirmative action admissions policy at the University of Michigan law school.[22]

In *Grutter v. Bollinger,*[23] the Court showing deference to the judgment of the law teachers and administrators found permissible the use of race, among other personal and group attributes, in enrolling a "critical mass" of minority students, as necessary for an appropriate educational experience. While I believe that reasoning is sound, I am uncertain of its reach. Is it only another iteration of Justice Powell's diversity concept set forth in *Bakke?* Or is it a signal of the recognition that the diversity road can lead to social justice?

Judge Harry T. Edwards, in an excellent article in the *Michigan Law Review,* related his hope:

> Fifty years after *Brown,* it is apparent that the rejection of "separate but equal" was not enough to fully realize the ideal integration. Nor were the strategies of assimilation or affirmative action. We can only hope that diversity, broadly conceived, will give the pursuit of integration new integrity and vitality in the years to come.[24]

I share his hope—but my hope light is dim. Born in the 1920s, I have seen major unforeseen positive change in race issues, but we are not even halfway home yet. In the complete history of America viewed in context, achieving racial equality has not even made it anywhere near the top of the agenda of problems that must be addressed with urgency. Perhaps in the twenty-first century a more diverse America, a more diverse Columbus will raise the priority.

22. *ABA Journal* 90 (April 2004).
23. *Grutter v. Bollinger.* 539 U.S. 306 (2003)
24. *Michigan Law Review* 102, no. 5 (March 2004): 944, 978.

CHAPTER 8

A Bi-Generational Narrative in the *Brown v. Board* Decision

ADIA M. HARVEY AND WILLIAM B. HARVEY

Part I—Life as a *Brown* Baby, by William B. Harvey

It would be a slight exaggeration to say that I clearly remember the *Brown v. Board of Education* decision, since I was only six years old at the time this landmark legal edict was handed down. But precocious child that I was, I was about to complete second grade, and, like every other little colored child in the state of North Carolina, I was in a racially segregated school at the time.

What made school a special place for me was that it was across the road from the campus of Elizabeth City State Teachers College, which was the alma mater of my second grade teacher, and most of the other teachers in my town, including my father. We didn't actually go on the college campus very often—sometimes there was a special field trip to see a play or listen to a debate. But most of the time, we just stared in awe and admiration at those cool college kids who dashed here and there, back and forth, in a world that we could only imagine.

Just seeing those earnest young men and women inspired some of us to reach for similar heights. A college education was a rarity in North

Carolina at the time, even for white people. So being in such close proximity to an institution of higher learning—one that I could legitimately aspire to attend—provided me with a sense of the possible that shaped my life at a very early point.

Even at six, though, I was keenly aware of segregation and what it meant. Our world, though nurturing and supportive, was also very tightly defined. Having attended kindergarten and first grade in a Catholic school that was two blocks from our house, I had been taught by white nuns. I remember them as being nice to me, encouraging and supportive, which is pretty important when you are the smallest person in your class. I also remember, however, that in the parent-teacher meetings, when my mother went to check on the progress of my sister and me, the interaction pattern was just a little different with the nuns than it was with the other people in my neighborhood.

It was the same interaction pattern that I noticed when, with my mother, or father, or even my grandmother, we ventured out of our neighborhood to go downtown or to the supermarket—circumstances when we would encounter white people, who I noticed were always in charge. Southern children, especially colored children, were brought up to be polite and always respectful of their elders. When we addressed them, we said sir and ma'am as an acknowledgement of their age and experience. It confused me then, when on a trip to the five-and-ten with my grandmother, she endeavored to get the attention of the white girl behind the counter by raising her hand and saying to her, "Please ma'am, could you give me some help."

Of course I didn't say anything at the time—it wouldn't have been proper—but on the walk home, I asked Grandma why she said ma'am to someone so much younger than she, someone who according to the rules of respect that I had been taught, should have been saying ma'am to her. In her own inimitable way, my grandmother explained that was just the way it was between white people and colored people, but she declared that it wouldn't always be that way—of that she was absolutely certain.

Her assurances notwithstanding, it sure looked and felt like it was always going to always be that way. The next school year came and went, and so did the next one and the next one and the one after that, and there were no noticeable changes in school attendance patterns, or in the world that I knew. In fact, the existing state of affairs was vividly confirmed when I was in the sixth grade. My uncle had built a new house in a different part of town, and he lived immediately adjacent to a white neighborhood. This certainly wasn't unusual in the South, and not too long afterwards, Moses, a friend of mine from school, moved into the same neighborhood.

Right after Moses and his family moved into their house, construction began on a new school building directly across the street. Since the school that we attended was about two miles from where Moses lived, the question on all of our minds was whether he would be able to attend the new school when it was completed, since most of the people in the area were white. About a year later, the city fathers provided the answer, and it was a resounding NO. Every morning, Moses had to get up, leave his home, pretend that the school for white children wasn't there, and walk or ride his bike to the school that, by virtue of his race, he was forced to attend. The segregation laws may not still have been on the books in the state of North Carolina, but the practice clearly had not changed. The year was 1958, four years after the *Brown v. Board* decision.

I had an epiphany of sorts the next year on a school field trip. Our teachers had organized a trip to the University of North Carolina planetarium in Chapel Hill, which one day a month allowed the little colored children of the state to visit the facility. My classmates and I witnessed various kinds of astronogical phenomena and I was quite taken by the experience, until it was time to go. As we walked back across the campus to our school buses, it occurred to me that I could not be a student at this wonderful institution, which was supported by taxes paid by my parents. I wondered then, what the learned professors were saying to their students, in political science, and ethics and history, about the incredible duality that existed outside the windows of the classroom. I didn't wonder long because I knew that they weren't saying anything at all about it. They were quite content with their lives in a world and a nation that provided liberty and justice for some. I had met some of the professors at Elizabeth City State, who always told us that knowledge overcomes ignorance and was the best weapon in the fight against injustice. This was the first time that I clearly understood that the white higher education community—the academic elite, people who were clearly smart enough to know better—were just as much in support of segregation as the most ignorant, unschooled racists. It was a bitter pill to swallow.

The next year, 1960, was a turning point in my life. After attempting for several years to find a teaching position in the North, my father was finally successful. He had resolved to move his family out of the South, into the promised land of the North, and a job offer in New Jersey finally made that happen. Prior to our move in August, however, four brave students at North Carolina A & T University in Greensboro, North Carolina decided to sit-in at a local lunch counter in the spring of that year to protest segregated facilities in that city. This activity was incredibly courageous, as it easily could have resulted in their deaths, and it was replicated by African American students at other institutions, including those at Elizabeth City State Teachers College.

Rather than change their practice of refusing to serve African Americans, the local Woolworth's decided that it would simply wait the students out until the end of the academic year when they would leave for summer vacation. In turn, the leaders of the African American community instituted a boycott of Woolworth's and other downtown stores that practiced racial discrimination. The Civil Rights movement had arrived. The South was going to change, as my grandmother had predicted, but as it turned out, my family wasn't going to be around long enough to benefit from it.

Segregation was mean and ugly and humiliating. It was a state of affairs that made you know your place and that kept you in your place. And if you were colored or Negro or Black or African American, your place was at the bottom. I remember separate toilets and water fountains, being excluded from municipal swimming pools, movie theaters, and amusement parks. I remember reading from books that had been sent over from the white schools when they received new ones. Sometimes this seems like it was a million years ago; sometimes it seems like it was yesterday. Anyway, I confess to being amazed but not amused when we moved to New Jersey, because the neighborhood that we lived in was just as segregated as the one we left in North Carolina. And while the local high school that my older sister and I went to was racially integrated, the neighborhood grammar school that my younger sister attended was all Black, except for the principal. Apparently the people in the North didn't know about *Brown v. Board* either.

When I took the placement tests to start at my new school, the guidance counselors were rather surprised that I did well enough to qualify for a college prep curriculum as a twelve-year-old coming from North Carolina. They had no sense of the unwavering expectations of the African American teachers in my former community that I do well in my studies, and the loss of this phenomenon might be the only negative aspect that is associated with the ending of segregation. The only opportunities that African American teachers had, even those with advanced degrees and preparation that sometimes far exceeded their white peers, were in the colored schools.

So these teachers prepared us well, motivating and inspiring us to be ready for the time when we would be able to compete directly, head to head, against whites. And while they urged us to look forward to that time, they also warned us to be very careful because whites were known to be small-minded and violent. That was evident in the way they conducted themselves. My high school experience, in an integrated setting, was most valuable for confirming what my teachers had told me repeatedly: the color of your skin doesn't determine what kind of person that you can become.

It was twenty-three years before I returned to North Carolina for a significant period of time. We had made occasional visits for family events, but for the most part we had all willingly and easily adjusted to living in the North. In that intervening period, I had finished graduate school, married, and started a family. My spouse, who is from Philadelphia, was less than enthused when I suggested that we move from New York to North Carolina so I could accept a position on the faculty at one of the predominantly white institutions. The "New South" was supposed to be booming, having shed much of its racist trappings, and clearly the opportunity to be a professor at an institution where, because of my race, I most likely would not have gained admission as a student, was evidence of a major change in the cultural patterns and values of the region.

When we went to enroll my daughter in the local public schools, we found them to be completely integrated among whites and African Americans, and they even had a few Asians and Hispanics. In a kind of generational, reverse déjà vu, the school authorities at first were a little reluctant to enroll my daughter in the gifted program. After all, she was transferring in from New York, and the quality of education in that part of the world was considered to be a bit suspect. But when her test scores were analyzed, the doubts were settled and she went on to receive an education that prepared her well enough to receive a bachelor's degree from Spelman College and ultimately a doctorate from Johns Hopkins University. My father had retired in New Jersey after completing his career, and when he visited us in North Carolina and attended my daughter's school on grandparents day, he was completely amazed. A school in his home state where the color of the students was not an issue was something that he thought he would never see.

So, fifty years after *Brown,* some progress has been made, but not nearly enough. In some urban centers, particularly in the North and Midwest, schools are as segregated, and sometimes even more so, than they were before the decision was rendered. An incredible amount of work still must be done in changing attitudes and changing practices if the spirit of this landmark ruling is going to be realized. Policy makers, opinion shapers, and community leaders must work hand-in-hand to make certain that every child receives the best education possible. This is a legacy that we must leave to those who have struggled before us, as well as for those who will come after us.

Part II—*Brown v. Board of Education:* A Contemporary Analysis, by Adia M. Harvey

The last half of the twentieth century has been marked by unprecedented social change. Various underprivileged groups have made rapid advances toward social equality over the last fifty years of the twentieth century. African Americans in particular are one group that has experienced drastic changes in their economic, legal, political, and social rights during the close of the century. Perhaps no legal milestone illustrates these changes better than *Brown v. Board of Education,* the landmark Supreme Court case that ruled that "separate but equal" was a fallacy.

Growing up in the 1980s and 1990s, my educational experiences were shaped in a decidedly postsegregationist world, but one that still wrestled with issues of integration, race relations, equality, and the consummate challenge of untangling all these complicated but interconnected issues in the context of the educational system. My generation was not the one that faced the daunting task of integrating schools while white students threw rocks and the National Guard stood outside. I was not a member of the first generation to be bused from segregated neighborhoods to predominantly white schools. I was not part of the cohort who transitioned from Black schools where teachers knew their names, families, backgrounds, and the nature of their communities, to school environments where white teachers ridiculed these Black schools and their students in accordance with prevailing racial stereotypes.

My generation began our journey through the educational system well after the brave students who faced hostile and irate white students, parents, and teachers who were fundamentally opposed to integration. But we faced a different set of issues, many of which are reflected in the contemporary research that examines the current picture of race and education in the United States. This essay attempts to connect personal experiences to more general issues around race and education, and to place both in the context of growing up in the aftermath of the *Brown v. Board* decision.

One of the issues raised in the aftermath of integration is that one advantage of segregated environments disappeared as a consequence of integration. Specifically, in all-Black settings, students were surrounded by teachers who appreciated their circumstances and did not believe that their race made them intellectually inferior. Despite poverty and disadvantages, Black students were taught by educators who believed in their intelligence and capacity for learning. In contrast, integration placed Black students into classrooms with teachers who frequently doubted their intellectual acuity and, overall, their ability to learn. While the facilities were better in integrated schools, Black students were often thrust into learning environments that ranged from dismissive to outright hostile.

I began elementary school in 1982, almost thirty years after the *Brown* decision. While I didn't enter an integrated school system that held the same vestiges of overt racism and segregation that existed in the late 1950s and early 1960s, it is noteworthy that my interactions with teachers and peers still bore some tinges of racial bias. Isolated incidents still stand out: the teacher who told me that my mother was not to check over my homework anymore because it would give me an "unfair advantage," the sixth grade teacher who openly doubted that I had really written my essay because it seemed too articulate. The unfortunate implication here is that in both cases, teachers failed to display the encouragement and to promote a learning environment that expected that an African American child could and should succeed.

Another related issue that stems from integration is that of cultural isolation, of Black students coming from all-Black schools to being the only Black student in their school. This can produce a sense of alienation and cultural isolation which can adversely affect Black students even as they are in school systems with superior resources and opportunities. In her memoirs, cultural critic bell hooks discusses experiencing this sense of isolation at the college level, when she left her all-Black neighborhood to attend Stanford University. Though hooks describes this experience at the college level, the sense of feeling isolated from familiar faces or from one's cultural background can exist at all levels.

My own experiences from elementary to high school reflect this. Often the lone Black student in classes, I experienced many of the post-integration issues that routinely fall to Black students: being called upon by teachers to testify about my race, expected to refute (or conform to) stereotypes about Blacks, to answer questions that begin with the ubiquitous phrase, "Why do Black people . . . ," or refuting erroneous or racially biased comments. I faced a barrage of these comments and questions from all sides. In institutions where there had rarely existed a critical mass of Black students to promote the equal contact that has the potential to minimize stereotypes and misunderstandings, these sorts of questions and the underlying cultural displacement they produce are commonplace.

Another major issue that has been given attention in the post-*Brown* educational environment is the issue of an oppositional culture among Black students that undermines academic achievement. Fordham and Ogbu (1986) first popularized this concept with their case study of Black students in a Washington, DC high school. Fordham and Ogbu argued that among Black students, an oppositional culture existed wherein scholastic success and educational attainment were viewed as "acting white." Consequently, Black students eschewed educational success in deference to the oppositional culture that derided academic achievement. This argument has been further expanded to suggest that specific cultural factors among African Americans explain their educational disparity with whites; in short, that if Black Americans do not succeed academically to the same extent as their white counterparts, perhaps cultural norms that stigmatize educational attainment are to blame.

This type of rhetoric holds particular importance in a post-*Brown* environment. Its subtle "blame the victim" implications suggest that if Black students are not succeeding at this point, after schools have been integrated, after they have the same opportunities as their white peers, then perhaps the best explanation for the deficit lies in cultural causes. This thinking masks the inequalities that are still inherent within integrated social settings, such as the school system, the workplace, the economic structure, and so on. It is also erroneous to generalize by suggesting that gaps between Black and white educational achievement can be blamed on cultural deficiencies, when all Black students do not have the advantages of well-financed integrated schools, and when historically, Blacks have always stressed educational attainment as a means to economic and social advancement. Perhaps the biggest problem with the oppositional culture explanation is that it masks the reality that American culture, at large, is an anti-intellectual one. Consider that President George W. Bush won a great deal of his popularity from the fact that he did not appear to be too smart, and noted in a debate that his wife "speaks English better than I do."

My personal experience with this issue refutes Fordham and Ogbu's assessment of the oppositional culture. Among my classmates, some Black students were in fact taunted for "acting white," but these were students who rarely associated and even avoided interacting with other Black students; rather they attempted to curry favor with popular white students, not those who were academically successful regardless of their race. Black students recognized that some Black students did well in school, others did not. Furthermore, in informal discussions it became clear that some Black students' interpretations of differential academic success among Black students were attributed to class rather than racialized differences. In other words, many students felt that middle- and upper-class Black students who did well in school had a better chance of advancing than those from working-class backgrounds. This type of analysis reflects a rather sophisticated analysis that for Black students with economic means, educational attainment was a more reliable path for social mobility.

A final issue that has been linked to the passage of *Brown* has to do with the degree of relevance of historically Black colleges and universities (HBCUs). Before *Brown,* these schools were where many Blacks went to obtain higher education. Due to segregation, few Blacks had access to predominantly white colleges and universities, even when they were academically qualified and could afford the tuition. With the *Brown* decision, however, we see the enrollment numbers of students at HBCUs dropping dramatically. Now that Black students have the opportunity to attend Harvard, Yale, Stanford, Princeton, Brown, and other Ivy League universities, some are less likely to see a need to attend Spelman, Morehouse, Hampton, Howard, Xavier, and others. With access to the formerly restricted schools that comprise the upper echelon of the academic elite, there is, among some Black students, a perception that HBCUs have outlived their usefulness.

For me, this debate underscores one of the key paradoxes of the *Brown* decision. While it is true that enrollments for HBCUs are declining, these schools have higher retention rates than their white counterparts in graduating Black students. More importantly, the majority of Black Americans who pursue terminal degrees—PhDs, MDs, JDs—are graduates of historically Black undergraduate institutions. So while a deceptively small number of Black students attend these schools, those who do are disproportionately more likely to gain advanced degrees.

I would argue that the continued success of HBCUs in successfully educating Black students speaks to one of the major issues that exist in the aftermath of *Brown*. That is, even as schools are increasingly racially integrated, the vestiges of inequality still linger in these environments. Integration has not erased fundamental social inequality. Merely placing Blacks in white schools has not erased perceptions that Blacks are intellectually inferior, less able to learn, and, ultimately, marginal members of society. While integration has had its advantages, it has not dismantled the racist thinking that is embedded in many social institutions, of which the educational system is just one.

It was this awareness that compelled me to attend an HBCU. My experience in integrated schools from kindergarten to twelfth grade had a direct impact on my determination to attend a historically Black college. The culmination of the sense of cultural alienation, the frustration of being the only Black student in academically gifted courses, the weariness that stemmed from being expected to explain Black people to curious but disengaged white students and teachers, the absence of courses and course material that examined diverse racial perspectives and addressed the complexity and diversity of Black Americans—all these factors took their toll.

I enrolled at Spelman College and became, for the first (and probably only) time in my life, part of the majority. Here, no one expected me to speak for Blacks as a group. No one expected that as a Black student I would be unable to meet the rigors of the curriculum; in fact, professors often expected more from me than I thought was fair or reasonable. At Spelman, courses about Black people, particularly Black women, were not only part of the curriculum, they were required for graduation. It is a testament to the paradoxes of *Brown* that my experiences in an integrated though still unequal school system drove me to derive the comfort, support, and familiarity that students in segregated pre-*Brown* environments took for granted.

The main point I want to offer from this essay is that years after *Brown,* school integration has become an accepted fact of life in the U.S. Despite the fact that many schools remain segregated, *Brown* ensured that the stark racial separation that characterized the educational system up to 1954 was no longer constitutionally defensible. What needs to occur at this point is a continued dismantling of the structural, institutional inequalities that continue to exist in integrated schools. Integration itself is not sufficient for creating racial equality. Within educational institutions, we have to erode the continued remnants of racial inequality that prevent integration from reaching its potential of being an equalizing force.

References

Feagin, J. 2000. *Racist America: Roots, Current Realities, and Future Reparations.* New York: Routledge.

Fordham, S., and J. U. Ogbu. 1986. "Black Students' School Success: Coping with the 'Burden of Acting White.'" *The Urban Review* 18, no. 3: 176–206.

Harvey, W. 2003. *20th Anniversary Annual Status Report on Minorities in Higher Education.* Washington, DC: American Council on Education.

Harvey, W., et. al. 2004. "The Impact of the *Brown v. Board of Education* Decision on Postsecondary Participation of African Americans." *Journal of Negro Education* 73 (Summer): 338–39.

hooks, b. 1997. *Wounds of Passion: A Writing Life.* New York: Henry Holt and Company.

CHAPTER 9

Why All Deliberate Speed?

Using Brown *to Understand* Brown

john a. powell

Brown v. Board of Education[1] is one of the most cited and studied cases in United States history. While a substantial majority considers it to be one of the most important cases in this country, there are others who demur. But even the detractors are forced to acknowledge *Brown,* if only for the purpose of dismissing it. Like many historic events of this magnitude, the meaning and significance of the case is not easy to settle. This is because the meaning is constantly being redefined, reinterpreted, and contested. There are few icons in our nation's history as significant as *Brown.* It should not surprise us, then, that 2004 was a year in which there were literally hundreds of events to celebrate or, for those who might take a more modest view of the accomplishments under *Brown,* to commentate, or even to mourn *Brown.* My purpose in this chapter is not to revisit the importance of *Brown* or to try to resolve what the Court "should have said." The doctrinal debate over *Brown* is well-rehearsed and need only delay me briefly before I examine some other, less well-considered aspects of the case.

1. 347 U.S. 483 (1954).

Brown v. Board of Education (No. II)[2]

(Brown II) turned fifty on May 17, 2005, a year after *Brown I* reached the same age.[3] But unlike *Brown,* there were few who took note of the anniversary of *Brown II.* Without editorials, books, or reenactments, *Brown II*'s birthday quietly came and went. In this chapter, then, I will break this "covenant of silence" and discuss its importance. I believe that *Brown II* is important in its own right as the remedy stage of *Brown.* I also believe that one cannot adequately understand *Brown* without *Brown II.* When read together, along with their history, the challenge that the Court believed it was confronting in this nation becomes clearer. This understanding is relevant for us today as we continue to live with the reality of segregation.

I will make three claims in this chapter. First that *Brown* cannot be understood without considering its relation to the remedial decision known as *Brown II.* Many commentators think of *Brown II* as a bad afterthought to *Brown* where the Court limited or backed away from its more expansive language of *Brown.* I argue in this chapter that *Brown II,* in spirit if not in content, was decided either before or contemporaneously with *Brown*—certainly not afterward. My second claim is that the Court anticipated but underestimated the degree of change that would be necessary to desegregate our schools and society at large. In the process, I will also examine how the conflation of the terms segregation and integration has made an already difficult process even more so. Finally, I will argue that the realization of a more profound vision of *Brown* requires a radical shift in the meaning of "whiteness" and an understanding of how whites are injured by segregation and "white space."[4]

This chapter will not be a dense examination of legal doctrine based on either *Brown* or *Brown II.* I am more interested in suggesting how we might move beyond the current "failures of integration" discussion. I salute the work of those who have already weighed in on *Brown,* with a special acknowledgment to those who challenge the false nostalgia of

---

2. 349 U.S. 294 (1955).

3. Hereafter, I will refer to *Brown I* as simply *Brown,* as is customary.

4. In a number of respects, I join the Honorable Judge Robert Carter in the claim that segregation is not the illness but a symptom, *Michigan Law Review* 86 (May 1988): 1083, 1095, but I differ from Judge Carter in that I feel that while segregation may indeed be the symptom and not the disease, like a number of symptoms, it can kill us in its own right.

For a more extensive discussion on white space see john a. powell, "Whiteness: Some Critical Perspective: Dreaming of a Self beyond Whiteness and Isolation," *Washington University Journal of Law and Policy* 18 (2005): 13–45.

segregation such as Sheryl Cashin, not only for her treatment of our failures related to integration but for her willingness to introduce the concept of integration back into the segregation discussion. Recognition must also go to Gary Orfield, Jonathan Kozol, Douglas Massey, Nancy Denton, Richard Ford, and others.

Reading *Brown and Brown II* Together

We are in a strange place as a country. Seldom does a week go by that we do not lament the failure of our "urban" education system. It is not surprising that most of the failing school systems are both majority low-income and majority minority.[5] So, even while we celebrate *Brown* and the apparent success of ending racial discrimination and segregation, we continue to live a somewhat disturbed and muted existence with this persistent racial, and now economic, segregation. This might make sense if we were no longer concerned with education in our society, but nothing could be further from the truth. Given our fears and anxieties about globalization and the blossoming of the information age, we insist, loudly and incessantly, that education is more important now than it has ever been to secure us against what appears to be a frightening and uncertain future.

There is a good deal of disagreement today about the importance of *Brown* and what it meant or means. There are those who still think that *Brown* is wrong because integration, or at least the premise associated with *Brown,* is both wrong and racist. This position has been associated with Justice Clarence Thomas and other soft black nationalists. The premise of this position is that a black child does not need to sit next to a white child in order to learn, and to think otherwise is a form of racism toward the black child. Of course, this is a misstatement of what is at issue and is particularly disturbing coming from the sole black member of the current Supreme Court. He and other like-minded Justices, energized by Republicans from Reagan on, have been bent on reversing civil rights that are inconsistent with middle-class white prerogative.

Jack M. Balkin and Brace A. Ackerman, in their interesting volume on *Brown,*[6] rehearse several of the multiple positions on *Brown.* These argu-

5. I think that the term minority is very problematic. It is not a value-free concept nor is it necessarily very accurate. See Michel Laguerre's *Minoritized Space: An Inquiry into the Spatial Order of Things.* However, I will use it in this chapter for lack of a well-accepted alternative.

6. Jack M. Balkin and Brace A. Ackerman, eds., *What* Brown v. Board of Education *Should*

ments run the gamut. Some assert that *Brown* hurt the goal of ending segregation by galvanizing whites against integration and that without it we
may have achieved greater integration than we have today. Others argue
that *Brown* has been a great achievement despite the disappointment in
the educational context. And, of course, there are those who argue that
the current state of schools provides no meaningful comment on *Brown*
because the sole purpose of *Brown* was to eliminate *state-sponsored* segregation, not segregation itself. To that end, *Brown* has been a success.

Compared to its better known cousin, not much has been written
on *Brown II*. Much of what has been written treats *Brown II* as a bad
afterthought, a problem or a mistake in relationship to its more honorable cousin. The dominant story is that the Court, for whatever reason,
blinked after *Brown*. The position of Loren Miller, a lawyer and historian,
is not uncommon: "The harsh truth is that the first *Brown* decision was a
great decision; the second *Brown* decision was a great mistake."[7] But the
truth is not that simple.

Consider the history of *Brown* as reported by Richard Kluger in *Simple
Justice*.[8] The Justices understood the importance of *Brown,* and the Court
was badly divided over whether to reverse *Plessy v. Ferguson*,[9] uphold it,
or find for the plaintiff on some narrow ground that avoided the issue
of segregation. The Court was also concerned that a divided opinion in
such an important case would fail to settle the issue and could hurt the
Court's credibility. Justice Felix Frankfurter had a stroke of genius—
delay. The Court could avoid deciding the case and send it back down
for rehearing. However, the rehearing had to be done in a way that did
not have the appearance of delaying. So, the Court developed a set of
questions that were to be answered by the lower court hearing. During
this delay, Chief Justice Vinson, who was reluctant to overturn *Plessy,*
died.

Earl Warren was appointed as Chief Justice of the Supreme Court to
replace Vinson. He had never served as a judge but had been the governor and attorney general of California. The new Chief Justice was against
segregation and made that clear after *Brown* was reargued in 1953. But he
also felt strongly that a divided court could render a decision ineffective

Have Said: The Nation's Top Legal Experts Rewrite America's Landmark Civil Rights Decisions (New
York: New York University Press, 2001).

7. Derrick Bell, *Silent Covenants:* Brown v. Board of Education *and the Unfulfilled Hopes for
Racial Reform* (Oxford University Press, 2004), 18.

8. Richard Kluger, *Simple Justice: The History of* Brown v. Board of Education *and Black
America's Struggle for Equality* (New York: Knopf, 1976).

9. 163 U.S. 537 (1896).

and hurt the status of the Court. He believed that it was important that any decision be unanimous. Justice Douglas believed that the principle in the case was straightforward—racial segregation was wrong. He would have left the details to be worked out by the lower courts. He believed that in order to get close to a majority in *Brown,* there would have to be a *Brown II.* Additionally, according to Kluger, *Brown* would have to be crafted to give society "a good deal of latitude and enough time to respond in as painless a fashion as possible."[10] The case would have to be carefully crafted to temper and not inflame or blame segregationists, especially in the South, while proclaiming that the time for segregation was over.

Those who know of *Brown II* are most likely to know it for the now famous and disturbing phrase "all deliberate speed." This statement could suggest both that there was a time during which segregation was appropriate and that there is a need to go slowly in reversing this arrangement. Indeed, in the memos back and forth between the Justices, both of these positions were made explicit. There would be an end to segregation in schools, but it was to happen over an extended period of time. This would not be the first time that the country would insist on the gradual implementation of a remedy for injustice, even while recognizing the injury visited on black people. For example, as many states began to reject slavery, a number of them adopted its gradual ending, which would leave slaves in servitude for at least another generation.[11] These situations reflect concern about the institutional complexity of simply doing the right thing. In the case of slavery, there was the concern about the loss of property for the slaveholder and the apparent need to garner white acceptance and support. Similarly, in *Brown II,* the Court was concerned about the innocent segregationist and the embedded nature of segregation—institutionally and culturally—as well as a concern for avoiding a violent rejection of desegregation by whites.[12] In both situations, there was much less concern expressed about the needs and interests of blacks than those of whites. Too often, the cost associated with racial justice is shifted to blacks.[13] Even though black subjugation may be viewed as wrong in the imagined future, there is often only a weak recognition

10. See supra note 9, p. 682.

11. See supra note 6, pp. 50–52.

12. Balkin and Ackerman, *What* Brown v. Board of Education *Should Have Said,* 29–35.

13. Lani Guinier makes the observation that the cost of desegregation, when it finally occurred, was on the back of poor whites. More affluent whites were spared the cost and inconvenience. This arrangement would ultimately undermine the goal of stable integration. See Lani Guinier, "From Racial Liberalism to Racial Literacy: *Brown v. Board of Education* and the Interest-Divergence Dilemma," *The Journal of American History* 91, no. 1 (June 2004): 92–110.

that there was wrongdoing in the real present and past. One reason for the country's continued failure to address racial injustice is the inability to recognize the relationship between racial subornation and whiteness. The goal then becomes the impossible task of achieving racial justice without substantially disturbing whiteness.[14]

The need for gradual desegregation was voiced by a number of the Justices prior to their willingness to sign on to *Brown*. Justice Frankfurter, who was both one of the intellectual giants on the bench and one of the Justices most concerned about overturning *Plessy*, had been strongly courted by Warren for his intellectual as well as general support. As Frankfurter warmed to the idea of overturning *Plessy*, he wrote a memo setting out some of the necessary elements of an opinion overturning that decision. Specifically, he wrote about the limitations of the Court to remedy past wrongs. "When the wrong is a deeply rooted state policy the court does its duty if it decrees measures that reverse the direction of the unconstitutional policy so as to uproot it 'with all deliberate speed.'"[15] Justice Frankfurter was not writing abstractly. He was telling the Court not to expect too much too quickly. Indeed, he and others were to make it clear that one of the preconditions for getting a unanimous decision on *Brown* was that the remedy would have to be pursued "with all deliberate speed."

Alexander Bickel, who clerked for Justice Frankfurter and remained close to him, stated that, "There is little doubt in my mind that at whatever conference the decision was taken in 1954, Justices Frankfurter, Black and Jackson left the room with a mutual understanding of the general form the eventual decree (*Brown II*) of the court would take—that it would provide for a gradual enforcement and not forthwith as was the usual practice."[16] Justice Reed, a Southerner, was the last holdout to the unanimous opinion. While Frankfurter was more likely to write a separate opinion if he did not get what he wanted in the majority opinion, Reed was set to write a dissent up until the last minute. Chief Justice Warren approached him and asked him to think about what was good for the country. According to his law clerk at the time, Reed put aside his basic beliefs. The only condition he extracted from the Chief Justice was a pledge that segregation would be dismantled gradually.

14. See Thomas Ross, "Innocence and Affirmative Action," *V and. L. Rev.* 43 (June 1990): 297; see supra note 4. john a. powell and George Lipsitz, *The Positive Investment in Whiteness* (Philadelphia: Temple University Press, 1998).

15. See supra note 9, p. 686.

16. Ibid., p. 695.

When one looks at the discussion of *Brown* and *Brown II,* they are often treated as two separate opinions. However, history requires that they be read as an interactive whole. If that is done, it makes little sense to think of *Brown II* as a great mistake in relation to *Brown.* Instead, *Brown II* can be seen as a precondition of *Brown.* Chief Justice Warren had a number of challenges before him. The obvious one was to get a unanimous opinion from the Justices who disagreed. But the disagreements were not for the same reason. Some, including Justice Reed, thought segregation and *Plessy* were right. Others, such as Justice Frankfurter, thought segregation was wrong but were not sure of the constitutional bases for challenging it. And almost all of the Justices were concerned with the response of the entrenched South and the harm that the Court might suffer if its order was effectively rejected by whites. This last issue was by far the most significant, and the Court simply would not have found that segregation was unconstitutional without having first addressed it.

If the Court were to find segregation unconstitutional, a number of preconditions would be required. One was not to blame the South for segregation. It might be wrong in the future but it was not wrong in the past. There is circularity in the Court's reasoning. The very fact that segregation was extensive and institutionally embedded was a powerful indication that it is not wrong. This is the very logic the earlier Court used to constitutionalize segregation in *Plessy.* This logic also put anti-segregationists and anti-racists in the position of sounding incoherent in talking about past wrongs: If there were past wrongs, it is not because of past wrongdoers (with a few notable exceptions), and certainly not the average white person. Another precondition was to avoid immediate enforcement of the significant changes that an end to segregation would require. The Court went to great lengths to mollify the South. One of the reasons for having a separate hearing on the remedy was to give the South some time to get used to the idea. The language was specifically chosen to be noninflammatory. And there would need to be ample time to enforce the remedy. Those Justices who were most sure that segregation was wrong were also most sure that the Court could do little to enforce a remedy and, therefore, called on the Court to do virtually nothing to enforce it. They also wanted the Court to treat the case as an individual harm that would have to be enforced individually against one school district at a time. Some of the Justices who were less sure about the rightness of the decision believed there must be some enforcement, but only gradual. *Brown II* adopted parts from the various camps. The remedy would be individually enforced, but it would be enforced with all deliberate speed. Of course, an individualistic response was inconsistent with the concern that segregation was deeply embedded in our institutions and culture.[17]

The Court also framed the remedy in the negative. There was no promise of integration but only a promise that the state would not sponsor segregation. There was no one on the Court pushing for a more expansive structural remedy with immediate impact. In all fairness, even this reading may not be as narrow as it seems today. Much of the South was organized under state-sponsored segregation, so even ending just this was no small matter.[18] But the Court did recognize the embedded nature of segregation and would later more explicitly recognize its institutional relationship and arrangement. But, more often than not, this would be used as an excuse to relieve the Court of any duty. The large contours of remedy were worked out before *Brown* was ever announced. It is difficult, then, to be critical of *Brown II* without implicating *Brown*. They cannot be so easily separated.

Underestimating the Degree to Which Change Is Necessary

The condition of blacks in urban schools is both separate and unequal. Justice Thomas and others who romantically embrace the efficacy of racial segregation have not mounted even a modest challenge to these realities. Professor Derrick Bell, a prominent black law professor, makes a similar argument against *Brown* and integration, although based on a more complicated set of reasons. He argues that the way integration has occurred has not served poor blacks and that the effort to integrate was bound to fail because it conflicts with white interests. He argues that there was a short period of time when, because of international conditions and the interests of the elite, whites supported *Brown* and the ideal of integration. Bell does acknowledge that low-income black children attending more integrated schools do better than nonintegrated blacks based on a number of indicators. What Bell really seems to be saying is that the push for integration has not produced integration and what has been produced is largely harmful to poor blacks. He also argues that the integration that would benefit poor blacks would more likely occur

17. See supra note 9. Also see Kluger, *Simple Justice*.
18. Kimberle W. Crenshaw, "Race, Reform, and Retrenchment: Transformation and Legitimization in Antidiscrimination Law," *Harvard Law Review* 101 (May 1988): 1331, 1359–60.

if the schools were first equalized. Without this, we have a system that continues to hurt low-income blacks.[19]

Like Bell, Professor Lani Guinier also believes that the way we implemented desegregation was problematic. But she draws very different inferences. While Bell would have avoided efforts to integrate schools, Guinier would have focused on integrating black children into high-performing, low-poverty schools. Not only would this have resulted in the best educational outcomes, but it would have also restructured white working-class interests so that there would not be the kind of polarization between low-income blacks and working-class whites that took place.[20]

There are a number of problems with the way we think about *Brown*. Many of these positions require that *Brown* necessarily stand for one thing. While some arguments may be more defensible than others, it is an error to assume that there is a single connotation for what *Brown* meant or should mean. The question is a combination of hermeneutic, normative, and political issues. While it is important to think about what the Court thought it was doing and the context of its actions, this should be the beginning of the inquiry, not the end. I have already suggested in other writings that while the prominent issue before the Court appeared to be embodied in *Plessy,* the actual issue was represented more directly in *Dred Scott.* The issue in *Scott* was whether blacks could be full members of the political community. In *Scott,* the Court made it clear that the answer was no. *Plessy* can be thought of as an extension of *Scott* despite the fact that it was decided after the Civil War. It is clear that the Civil War Amendments were designed in part to overturn *Scott.* But the Court demurred, asserting in the *Slaughter-House Cases*[21] that implementing the Civil War Amendments, and particularly the Fourteenth Amendment Privilege and Immunities clause, would require a radical restructuring of our national and state institutions and social structures to robustly redefine participation and include the freed slave in the community of all citizens.

The very institutions that the Court did not want to disturb were the institutions that came into being under the heavy influence of a slave

---

19. See supra note 8 and Derrick Bell, "Serving Two Masters: Integration Ideals and Client Interests in School Desegregation Litigation," in *Critical Race Theory: The Cutting Edge,* Richard Delgado and Jean Stefancic, eds., 236–48 (Philadelphia: Temple University Press, 2000).

20. See supra note 14. See also j. a. powell (2005): "A New Theory of Integrated Education," in *School Resegregation: Must the South Turn Back?* J. C. Boger and G. Orfield, eds., 261–80 (Chapel Hill: The University of North Carolina Press, 2005), and Shelby Steele, *A Dream Deferred* (New York: HarperCollins Publishers, 1998).

21. 83 U.S. 36 (1873).

society where white supremacy and exclusion remained unquestioned.[22] It is interesting to note that *Brown* faced much of the same problem. While the *Slaughter-House Cases* argued that the Fourteenth Amendment could not have intended such a radical institutional shift, the Court in *Brown* recognized that the Fourteenth Amendment might indeed mandate such an institutional shift, but they were not confident that the Court could effectively order such a shift. One reading of *Brown II* is that because segregation, and by extension white supremacy, was so culturally and institutionally embedded, it could not be fundamentally addressed by the Court or anyone else. The exclusion of blacks and other nonwhites, not just from schools but from every aspect of society where citizenship and benefit were to be conferred, could only be modestly disturbed and even then only with the permission of the offending "innocent" whites. To do otherwise would require a substantial set of institutional rearrangements that seemed to be beyond the competence and practical authority of the Court. The question before the Court in *Brown* was not simply whether *Plessy* or segregation was wrong under the Constitution, but how deeply embedded segregation was in our institutions and national identity, especially in the South. To deal with this substantial challenge, the Court had to narrow the question and the scope of the answer.

The Court's treatment of institutional arrangements and structures has been, at best, confusing and inconsistent.[23] On the one hand, the Court's behind-the-scene musings during *Brown* make it clear that it was aware that successful implementation of the decision would require significant institutional and cultural shifts. At times, it treated these arrangements as opaque and mysterious. At other times, it treated these arrangements as natural and transparent.[24] Both approaches support a false position that the Court cannot or should not significantly disturb the status quo. Consider the Supreme Court's opinion in *Milliken*.[25] In that case, the Court

22. Alberto Alesina and Edward Glaesar, *Fighting Poverty in the U.S. and Europe: A World of Difference* (Oxford University Press, 2004). Sheryll Cashin *The Failures of Integration: How Race and Class Are Undermining the American Dream* (New York: Public Affairs, 2004).

23. See supra note 20 for a good discussion of localism and school and housing link. Sheryll Cashin, *The Failures of Integration: How Race and Class Are Undermining the American Dream* (New York: Public Affairs, 2004). Kimberle Williams Crenshaw, "Race, Reform, and Retrenchment: Transformation and Legitimation in Antidiscrimination Law," in *Critical Race Theory: The Key Writings That Formed the Movement*, Kimberle Williams Crenshaw, ed., 101–22 (New York: New Press, 1995). Richard Thompson Ford, "The Boundaries of Race: Political Geography in Legal Analysis," in *Critical Race Theory*, 449–65. Jared Diamond, *Guns, Germs, and Steel: The Fates of Human Societies* (New York: W.W. Norton, 1997).

24. Richard Thompson Ford, "The Boundaries of Race: Political Geography in Legal Analysis," in *Critical Race Theory*, 449–65.

25. *Milliken v. Bradley*, 418 U.S. 717 (1974).

treated municipal and school board boundaries in the Detroit areas as natural, sacred, and beyond the power of the Court. Yet the issue of local control and local boundaries had been raised many times before. Indeed in *Brown,* the issue was raised by the government, and the Court easily brushed aside the concern of localism in favor of the plaintiffs' rights and the need to end segregation.[26] At the appellate level in *Milliken,* the court had ordered a remedy that included the suburbs, noting that to do otherwise would create the conditions for overturning *Brown.*[27] It noted that local control was not a sufficient concern to stand in the way of a constitutional mandate to desegregate. The Supreme Court did not show the same concern when establishing the foundation for *Brown;* instead, in *Brown II* it all but constitutionalized localism, lessening the concern for desegregation and civil rights.

While asserting that local control was natural, the Court asserted that the cause of housing segregation was opaque. When looking at the patterns of housing segregation that were central in supporting segregation between the city of Detroit and the suburbs, the Court noted that it did not know, and perhaps would never know, why housing was segregated in Detroit. This is an amazing story that the Court and the nation would return to many times despite overwhelming evidence that the cause of housing segregation is not only knowable, but is largely traceable to government action and inaction and even substantial public expenditures.[28]

What the Court and the nation have done is to allow institutional arrangements and racial meaning to obstruct the deeper potential of *Brown* to reach institutional structures. But it is worse than this. The Court has actively participated in supporting the structures that are used to frustrate *Brown*'s ability to challenge the underlying meaning of *Scott* and *Plessy.*

One of the debated meanings of *Brown* is the promise of integration and its ability to alter institutional arrangements. I will not restate the debate here, but will simply point to a prior issue that must be addressed before joining the integration discussion. What do we mean or should we mean by integration; what is the relationship between segregation, desegregation, assimilation and integration? It is surprising how little attention has been paid to these questions, even as policy makers and Justices stake

26. Supra note 9, p. 675.

27. *Milliken,* 418 U.S. 745–6.

28. Douglas S. Massey and Nancy A. Denton, *American Apartheid: Segregation and the Making of the Underclass* (Cambridge, MA: Harvard University Press, 1993).

out positions on what is appropriate. Under close examination, these seemingly simple questions turn out to be quite complex. I believe that before we can make the kind of change that a multiracial democracy calls for, we must first engage these questions. Let's take a brief look at some of these concepts and their relationship to each other.

Segregation means the separation of people or groups, in our context, by race and by class. Racial segregation is the issue that *Brown* was designed to address. Today we are often more sensitive to the class segregation inherent in racial segregation. Some scholars assert that it is really class or "economic segregation" that creates disadvantages for black people. In some respects, there is merit in this claim. For example, putting all low-income students in the same school—when all of a poor student's classrooms are also poor—creates a substantial educational burden for the students. The effect of this economic segregation is different, however, than the family condition of a given student. In fact, a number of studies have asserted that a student from a middle-class background attending a high-poverty school will, on average, do worse academically than a low-income student attending a middle-class school.[29] A story in the *New York Times* focuses on a school district in Wake County in North Carolina that limited the poverty level of each school to no more than 40 percent of students on free and reduced lunch. The impact on the test results of low-income students of color was very significant.[30]

It is interesting that there has been much less challenge to the assertion that economic segregation creates a pedagogically difficult learning environment for students than the assertion that racial segregation produces a similar negative environment for the disfavored group. There are a number of observations that are worth pointing out in this context. The first is that in talking about segregation there is often a false sense of symmetry. This false symmetry is more likely to come up in the racial than the class context. So there will be some who suggest that there is symmetry between whites who are segregated from blacks and blacks who are segregated from whites. Under this rubric, the most racially isolated group is middle-class suburban whites.

A Wisconsin study noted that if an area was 90 percent black, it would be considered segregated, but if it were 9 percent white it would

29. R. D. Kahlenberg, *Can Separate Be Equal? The Overlooked Flaw at the Center of No Child Left Behind* (New York: The Century Foundation, 2004).

30. Alan Finder, "As Test Scores Jump, Raleigh Credits Integration by Income," *New York Times*, Sept. 25, 2005.

not be.[31] Does this suggest that whites are segregated and therefore suffering all the attendant harm associated with segregation? The obvious answer is no. The reason the question might even seem reasonable is because of our failure to seriously examine the nature of segregation. The Kerner Commission Report noted that the segregation of blacks was imposed for the benefit of whites. Marilyn Frye has noted similarly that prisons keep some people in and some people out.[32] Yet even the most extreme formalist would not confuse the lack of symmetry in this example.

Segregation, then, should not be thought of just as the separation of people in some neutral formal sense. It has a value and meaning that goes beyond just the separation. It is more useful to think of segregation as relating to the distribution of opportunity both in a relative and a more objective sense. The purpose of segregation is to separate a group not just from another group but from relative opportunity itself.[33] The failure to see this is to repeat the failure and false promise of *Plessy*. Because there is a differential in benefit, segregation can only be achieved by the exercising of power by one group over another. I am not suggesting that whites are not injured by segregation—they are. There was a claim in some *Brown* cases that whites were injured by segregation. Despite this, we have failed to seriously consider how whites are indeed injured by segregation even when they have more than nonwhites. But this issue was not acknowledged at the Supreme Court level. While there is certainly a need for this examination, it should not be conflated with the injury that blacks and other people of color suffer from segregation.

31. A 2003 study by Quinn and Pawasarat critiques the use of the dissimilarity index as being racially-biased and based on a white majority view of segregation. The authors contend that the dissimilarity index considers any majority African American neighborhood as segregated, but finds most majority white neighborhoods to be integrated, due to the methodological constraints of the index. As stated by Quinn and Pawasarat, "The index, is based on a one-way concept of desegregation where blacks are expected to move into white areas, but whites are not expected to move into majority black areas." See Quinn and Pawasarat, "Racial Integration in Urban America: A Block Level Analysis of African American and White Housing Patterns." Employment and Training Institute, School of Continuing Education. University of Wisconsin-Milwaukee, January 2003. (page 1). Available on-line at: http://www.uwm.edu/Dept/ETI/integration/integration.pdf.

32. Marilyn Frye, *The Politics of Reality* (Trumansburg, NY: Crossing Press, 1983).

33. john a. powell, "Opportunity-Based Housing," *Journal of Affordable Housing and Community Development Law* 12, no. 2 (Winter 2003): 188. For a discussion on the relational harm between groups where all may be above some objective standard of deprivation, see Amartya Sen, *Development As Freedom* (New York: Knopf, 1999). See also john a. powell, "The Legitimate Needs of Members in a Democratic State," *Santa Clara Law Review* 44, no. 4: 969, where I argue what is needed are the goods and status to effectively participate in a democratic society.

One of the ways that we have tried to reconcile our ideological commitment to equal opportunity and colorblindness with persistent segregation and resegregation is to claim that segregation today is not imposed, that it is a function of choice. The choice argument, or justification, tries to maintain that separation between the races, and by extension classes, is either natural or self-selected by the disfavored group. Although there are increasing numbers of African Americans and Latinos who have begun to express the possible benefit of choosing segregation over integration, this should not distract us from understanding the function of segregation as it is imposed by the dominant group. There can be a number of benefits that come from a group being allowed to form both a group consciousness and a strategy to challenge the dominant group. But this is still a defensive action in response to a strategy by the dominant group to subordinate the less-favored group. Even some of the apparent supporters of segregation acknowledge that if segregation stops being a benefit to the dominant group, the dominant group is much less likely to support it. Segregation must be understood in terms of domination, power, and the uneven distribution of burdens or benefits to a group.[34]

Earlier, I touched on the difference between racial and economic segregation in the educational context and our different responses to the two forms of segregation. It may not surprise the knowledgeable reader to find that there is a high correlation between racial and economic segregation. Much of the literature on concentrated poverty shows that low-income black children are significantly more likely to live in a low-income, high-poverty neighborhood and go to a racially isolated high-poverty school. There is little claim that the parents of these children have a choice of whether to send their children to such schools nor does research dispute that the children going to such schools, even middle-class children, face added challenges. In this context, there is a consensus that this situation is externally imposed with a heavy cost on nonwhites. But this de

---

34. There is no instance of black flight because a few whites move into a neighborhood or school. Consistent research shows a strong willingness for African Americans to live in integrated neighborhoods, with most preferring neighborhoods that are racially mixed. See Maria Krysan and Reynolds Farley, "The Residential Preferences of Blacks: Do They Explain Persistent Segregation?" *Social Forces* 80, no. 3 (2002): 937–80. In addition, research suggests that African Americans prioritize neighborhood opportunities and school quality more than racial preferences when selecting neighborhoods. In surveys conducted in the Washington D.C. region, nearly 60 percent of African Americans identified school quality as important in neighborhood selection, while only 3 percent felt neighborhood racial composition was important. See Greg Squires, Samantha Friedman and Catherine Saidat, "Housing Segregation in the United States: Does Race Matter?" Lincoln Institute of Land Policy Conference Paper (2001).

facto segregation is often seen as de jure desegregation, with little effort expended to even recognize, let alone remedy, this condition.

De jure desegregation, at least under federal law, has come to mean that segregation is not deliberately imposed by the state, or more accurately, that plaintiffs cannot prove it under increasingly greater burdens required by the courts. It is not clear that either *Brown* or *Brown II* requires this understanding. Indeed, it was not until the Warren Court had been replaced by a much more reactionary Court that this understanding would emerge. Some state courts have rejected this assumption, ruling instead that de facto segregation as well as de jure segregation violates the law.[35] The harms and disabilities associated with segregation are present regardless of whether it is explicitly state imposed or not. While there may be some disagreement over whether the harms are the same, virtually no research suggests that there is not significant harm regardless of how the segregation came to be. When advocates fight for school desegregation, it is doubtful they intend to fight de facto but not de jure segregation. Adding to this confusion, some use the term desegregation as a synonym for integration.

When advocates fight for school integration, they are challenging segregation without the legal distinction between de facto and de jure segregation.

But what is meant by integration? How is it different from desegregation? The Rev. Dr. Martin Luther King Jr. delineates between the terms this way:

> The word *segregation,* represents a system that is prohibitive, it denies the Negro equal access to schools, parks, restaurants, libraries and the like. *Desegregation* is eliminative and negative, for it simply removes these legal and social prohibitions. *Integration* is creative, and is therefore more profound and far-reaching than desegregation. Integration is genuine intergroup, interpersonal doing. Desegregation then, rightly, is only a short-range goal. Integration is the ultimate goal of our national community. Thus, as America pursues the important task of respecting the "letter of the law," i.e., compliance with desegregation decisions, she must be equally concerned with the "spirit of the law," i.e., commitment to the democratic dream of integration.[36]

35. *Scheff v. O'Neill,* 238 Conn. 1, 678 A. 2d 1267 (1996).
36. "The Ethical Demands of Integration," in *A Testament of Hope: The Essential Writings and Speeches of Martin Luther King, Jr.,* James M. Washington ed., 118 (San Francisco: Harper, 1986).

Much of our conversation about integration is not helpful. As I have suggested, we sometimes use integration to mean no more than desegregation. At other times it is used to mean that students of color are attending the same schools as white students, but not that they are in the same classrooms or getting the same level of instruction. Many "integrated" schools have nonwhite students tracked in remedial classes in the basement, while the AP and college preparatory classes are virtually all-white and located on the upper floors. Some of the attacks on integration are based on this kind of reality. A more subtle, but still problematic form of "integration" occurs when nonwhite students are placed in the presence of white students, but the curriculum and class environment are still oriented toward the white students. There is an assumption that the nonwhite student must assimilate into the white structure and curriculum as an invited guest. This arrangement, which harms both white and nonwhite students, is not true integration and is not good education.

There are other problematic ways of thinking about integration such as putting poor black and Latino students in a school and calling it integrated. Another problematic example is putting poor black and poor white students together. While this might achieve a degree of racial integration, the class segregation can still limit the life chances of the students.

You will recall that Justice Thomas asserted that segregation is not the problem and that the insistence on having a black child sit next to a white child is racist. Maybe, maybe not. The obvious question not asked by Thomas is why whites, with the support of the state and the courts even after *Brown,* continued to resist sitting next to, or for that matter, living next to blacks. Is that racist? Would Thomas also assert that the call for economic desegregation or integration is classist? Justice Thomas's assertion only makes sense in the abstract. In the real world, black students attending segregated schools are not just separated from white students, they are also separated from most middle-class students, qualified teachers, AP classes, and other factors associated with an adequate education. Segregation aids in reproducing the ideology of racial inferiority for blacks and an ideology of racial superiority for whites. But segregation is more than an ideology. It has cultural meaning and it has consequences for the sorting of material benefits.

What desegregation has come to mean, at least in law, is that there is no affirmative state or government sponsored segregation that can be proven. So desegregation can be consistent with de facto segregation. In *Brown,* the Court is fairly clear that even where segregation is not state imposed, there is an injury.[37] But today the Court either rejects that there is injury or maintains that there is no federal constitutional violation if the segregation is de facto.[38] What the Court is asserting is that as long as there is no intentional state requirement, there is no segregation in law. And indeed, some members of the Court today have asserted that the promise of *Brown* is "desegregation," not integration.

So, what do we mean by integration? Some have used integration interchangeably with assimilation. I have asserted that in the U.S. both segregation and assimilation can only be understood in the context of white supremacy.[39] Even what is called self-segregation by black Americans can only be understood in this context. But in what way are assimilation and segregation (de jure or de facto) predicated on white supremacy? Let's consider segregation first. It is predicated on both the "purity theory" and the debasement of blacks. The assumption is that there is something wrong with the "racial other" and, therefore, he must be physically separated from whites. There is a fear that blacks will contaminate both the blood and culture of white society if they are allowed to mix. This message is found in many of the early discourses on race, even by some that supported the end of slavery. Thomas Jefferson was of the opinion that if slavery ended, blacks would have to be sent back to Africa. Benjamin Franklin was concerned about not polluting this white nation. Abraham Lincoln thought it was ridiculous to talk about the mixing of the races.[40] In many respects, the segregation imposed and tolerated by the Court in *Plessy* was already very much a part of the national consciousness and certainly expressed in *Scott. Plessy,* and a number of other cases heard after the Civil War and even today, ignored the fact that the Civil War and the Civil War Amendments were designed to give birth to a new nation.

Segregation is not just an expression of white supremacy; it is also one of the mechanisms for its creation and reproduction. The harms of segregation are bound up with both material consequences and with

37. 347 U.S. at 493–4.

38. I assume that the Court might very well know there is an injury. What they are more likely saying is that they are willing to protect whites and whiteness from having to be polluted by nonwhites. If this seems too strong, consider how careful a more liberal Court was in taking care of the perception and interest of white segregationists and how little concern and attention is paid generations of inner-city children who almost everyone acknowledges are being miseducated.

39. See Steve Martinot, *The Rule of Racialization: Class, Identity, Governance* (Philadelphia: Temple University Press, 2003).

40. Barry Schwartz, "Collective Memory and History: How Abraham Lincoln Became a Symbol of Racial Equality," *The Sociological Quarterly* 38, no. 3 (Autumn 1997): 469–96.

the message that segregation conveys. Judge Robert Carter has said that he was mistaken when he asserted that segregation was the major problem; instead, he indicates that segregation is simply a symptom of white supremacy.[41] This is only partially right. Segregation is both a symptom and a cause. We increasingly accept the notion, if only partially, that race is socially constructed, but how is it constructed? Martha Mahoney notes that after the end of Jim Crow, segregation provided not only a way to distribute material benefits to whites but also a means of constructing white identity. Segregation, then, functions both in the construction of racial identity and in the racialized distribution of material and cultural benefits.

Before leaving this discussion, two caveats are important to note. The first is that there is no single practice or structure that supports racism and white supremacy. As important as segregation is for our current arrangement of white supremacy, there is not an entailment between the two. Nor is racism only an internal or external process.[42] For racism to be sustained there must be both material condition and social meaning to support this arrangement. But the end of Jim Crow should teach us that as the world changes, practices and structures can change and adapt to new conditions giving us new expressions of racism. Each change in a racist condition and justification is likely to produce a different iteration of racism and racist expression.

Like segregation, assimilation is also an expression of white supremacy. The segregationist asserts that there is something wrong with the racial other; he must be either contained or regulated when in "white space." The assimilationist asserts that there is something wrong with the racial other but, instead of just being contained, the racial other must be fixed to become more like the dominant race. Think of the "melting pot" as it applied to eastern and southern Europeans; the burden was on them to become like "normal" Americans. When measured against this white American norm, these immigrants came up short and defective. There was no similar scrutiny of "Americans."[43] This may be considered a softer

41.   Robert L. Carter, "A Reassessment of *Brown v. Board of Education*," in *Shades of Brown: New Perspectives on School Desegregation*, Derrick Bell ed., 23 (New York: Teachers College Press, 1980).

42.   See supra note 43, pp. 175–80.

43.   The argument for assimilation and its supremacy implication are made clear in such work as Samuel Huntington's *Who Are We?: The Challenges to America's National Identity* (New York: Simon & Schuster, 2004). In the book Huntington asserts that we are not an immigrant country but a settler country, the difference being that in a settler country the norms, values and rules are set by the original founders. All others must assimilate to these norms or be excluded.

form of white supremacy. The harder segregationist believes that there is something wrong with the racial minority, while the assimilationist says the same thing but does not believe it to be immutable. But to both, the racial other is inherently defective.

When we look at the efforts and meanings associated with integrating schools, they are likely to be associated with either desegregation, which still allows for de facto segregation, or assimilation, where nonwhite children are invited into "white space" as guests and are expected to behave and assimilate.[44] Many of the attacks on integration by detractors like Bell and Justice Thomas are really an attack in large part on the notion that the racial other must be fixed in accordance with a predetermined set of white norms. If there is a need to be fixed, it must extend to the white population as well as the racial other. In many respects, most critics of integration fail to distinguish integration from assimilation, or to develop a true sense of integration. But rejecting assimilation does not entail embracing segregation, either self-imposed or imposed by others. What then would true integration look like? I will provisionally offer the following definition. Integration in the school context requires that students meet in the learning environment as equals and in a process that supports mutual interaction and reciprocity as equals. The environment must both support and respect the learners. Recognizing that much of the learning process occurs between the students themselves and not just between student and teacher, the environment must encourage, facilitate, and reward meaningful interaction among all students. The environment must reflect the needs of the students as both individuals—whole complex beings—and members of multiple groups, all this while being sensitive to the cognitive, emotional, spiritual, individual, and social needs of the learners. Learners should be brought together in an environment where there is the appropriate "critical mass" of different groups, when possible, for optimum learning to take place. The structure, curriculum, and the norms of the classroom and the building must be consistent with this mission. Integration must be affirmatively valued and pursued. Isolation of students by race, class, or other categories that would undermine the learning of true integration or that would support the learning of inferiority or superiority must be avoided. I also suggest that our understanding of integration and the conditions necessary to actively support integration will continue to evolve. Integration, like democracy, must be seen as a process. We may not get to our goal, but its pursuit should shape our practices.

44. See supra note 5.

Shifting the Meaning of Whiteness

It is not simply that race is socially constructed; in our society it is constructed to support the notion of inferiority and superiority. As suggested above, there is more than one reading of *Brown*. One is the very limited reading that *Brown* was not meant to desegregate schools and certainly not designed to integrate schools. It was meant only to be symbolic, and it has done that. Bell and others make this assertion. A second reading is that the Court blinked; that after deciding *Brown,* the Court got cold feet and took back much of the spirit of *Brown* in *Brown II.* The third reading is that the Court was contemplating something much more profound but did not have an adequate understanding of how to achieve it. It mistakenly thought that time, and little else, would help them bring about a real transformation. They were wrong, but well-intentioned. I assert that the third reading is the best.

The first meaning of *Brown* is reflected in Justice Douglas's position. But it was not accepted by Chief Justice Warren or the Court. The second position need not delay us long. This position views *Brown II* as an afterthought. It was not. Knowing that a radical restructuring was needed to implement *Brown,* the Court had the broad contours of *Brown II* worked out before deciding *Brown.* This reading is also supported by later actions of the Warren Court when it finally rejected the "deliberate" part of *Brown II* and went on to assert a sweeping, but still inadequate, vision of what must be done.

Brown and *Brown II* can more aptly be seen as a profound vision of integration and a multiracial and multiethnic democracy. It is the vision of a society without a superior class. This reading is a rejection not just of *Plessy* but also of *Scott.* It is the call for the nation to break from its racist past and embrace a transformative vision. But this break requires both a restructuring of our institutions and a rethinking of our national meaning.[45] What the Court was concerned about in *Brown* was how to get there, understanding that there would be resistance to the profound social change required. On this, the Court was right. What the Court failed to do was to explicitly talk about and openly explore these profound changes. Some members of the Court thought the resistance would be too strong. It is interesting to note that the members of the Court who

45. In *A New Birth of Freedom,* the late law professor Charles Black argues that the goal of the Civil War Amendments were to usher in a new set of institutional arrangements, and the failure to do this continues to undermine our efforts for a racial democracy. Charles Black, *A New Birth of Freedom: Human Rights, Named and Unnamed* (New Haven: Yale University Press, 1999).

were most clear that segregation was wrong were also most skeptical about the possibility of real change.[46] Some members who were less sure about ending segregation and worried about the Court's legitimacy in overturning *Plessy,* nonetheless believed that it was imperative for the Court to say something about the process for implementing desegregation. They took the position that the South would need to be treated fragilely and given sufficient time to get used to the idea.[47] This was the view that prevailed in *Brown II* and, by extension, in *Brown.*

Where the Court failed was in correctly identifying, or even seriously investigating, what was necessary for this radical transition to work. This was not to be the first time that, as a nation, we have made this mistake. After the Civil War, the North failed to put into place what was necessary to truly end white supremacy and domination in the South and, by extension, in the entire country. The failure was not just in how the country dealt with recalcitrant whites but also the failure to seriously address the needs of black people, to secure their place as full citizens and repudiate *Scott.* In both *Brown* and *Brown II* and Civil War reconstruction, there was an assumption that time, with little else, would do the work. At some point, the country and the Court would reinterpret the goals of *Brown* and the Civil War to be consistent with white dominance based on a different set of institutional arrangements and cultural meanings.

If we are to take seriously the more profound reading of *Brown* and *Brown II* as well as the Civil War Amendments, we must be more explicit about the vision and the process necessary to achieve it. I have already suggested that I think this vision is quite radical, and yet it is deeply connected to our early dream of an American nation as reflected in the Declaration of Independence.[48] That vision is for an inclusive democracy without racial hierarchy, dominance, or subordination. The Court, in its behind-the-scenes musings, recognized that the realization of this vision would require a new set of institutional arrangements and indeed a new kind of black American.[49] What the Court failed to seriously consider is the new kind of whiteness that would be necessary to support this vision. To require blacks to change and prove themselves worthy without recognizing what is required of whites is both wrong and backward. This position reflects the assimilation model in which blacks are seen as damaged and in need of repair before they are allowed into white schools, white

---

46. See supra note 9, pp. 680–85.
47. Ibid.
48. See supra note 50.
49. See supra note 9, pp. 700–5.

neighborhoods, and white society as equals. While this language might seem odd when explicitly stated today, it was espoused by a number of blacks and whites—Booker T. Washington, for example. Of course, it was a less offensive position than the segregationists' view that blacks and whites could never live as equals.

These underlying currents are still very much with us today in less explicit language. While I am not opposed to looking at how a radical vision of inclusion and democracy calls for a change in black America, the heart of the problem must be located in white America. A group of people forced to live in slave conditions are likely to adopt behaviors and norms that would not be appropriate if they were full members of a free society. Similarly, people forced to live in "ghettoes" and conditions of concentrated poverty will likely adopt behaviors and norms inconsistent with living as full members of society. The Kerner Commission recognized this reality almost forty years ago. But in a slave society and a society based on white hierarchy that turns its back on democratic ideals, the problem is with the slavemaster and those who support slavery—not with the slave. The conditions of slavery and segregation are not endogenous, and that is one of many serious errors in understanding racial hierarchy today. If there is a culture of poverty in the poor black community, and there might well be, it is largely created and maintained by those outside of that community for their own benefit. What the Court and others have recognized is that racial justice, and in this case integration, will not likely happen if there is strong resistance from large numbers of whites. One of the ideas that at least some members of the Court relied on was that improving conditions for blacks over time would reduce white opposition. Bell, while being at best ambivalent to the possibility of racial justice and equality, does suggest that if the condition of blacks were to improve, there would likely be less resistance to equality and integration.[50] This may be correct for some whites, but there are reasons to believe that it may be difficult to reach the critical mass necessary to make the radical break I have been discussing. Indeed, one has to wonder why, despite some substantial gains in the size of the black middle class and improvement in racial attitudes, so many of the old norms of Southern racism seem to resonate with so many Americans. Some have suggested that the road to building a majority party is a thinly veiled form of Southern racism.

A number of authors have argued that when racial justice issues run up against white prerogative, racial justice loses. This is Bell's "interest

50. See supra note 8.

convergence theory," or Lipsitz's "possessive investment in whiteness," or Ryan's "middle-class prerogative" in school desegregation. A pessimistic interpretation of this phenomenon is that we will never achieve racial justice, and some of the authors take this position. What I am suggesting is that *Brown* and *Brown II* anticipated a similar problem but arguably took a more optimistic view. The authors of these cases believed that whites could change.

It is to this view that I now wish to turn. But first, let me state it more forcefully. There are two parts to this proposition. The first is that in order to achieve racial justice in our society, mere must be a different kind of whiteness. The second is that this new white space must be perceived as a benefit to people who are currently in the old white space. It is important to note that I am not talking just about people who are phenotypically white. There are a number of reasons for this. Who is classified as a legitimate member of this white space has changed before and will continue to change. As I have suggested above, the goal of assimilation is to expand in some fashion who is legitimately in this space. I asserted above that the assimilation goal is racist because it defines those outside of this space as deficient. They only become sufficient by becoming like whites and only then may they be welcomed in.

Definitionally, those who are not permitted in white space are those labeled as "black." Again, I am not speaking of how people look. Whiteness was defined early on as nonblack.[51] While the definition has changed and will continue to change, there is little to suggest that the nonblack meaning of white space will change. Indeed, there are some suggestions that it will harden.[52] When individual blacks are invited to this white space only to recoil, it is this contradiction that they are often reacting to. When James Baldwin respectfully declined an invitation as a wonderful literary black, he stated that the "price of the ticket" was too high.[53] Leave your "blackness" at the door, if you can. This demand had been made and accepted by a number of Europeans in the history of ethnically nonwhites becoming white. Of course, if all blacks or even large numbers are invited in, and there is not a "new black," white space might cease to operate. But this offer has never been extended. I am also asserting that the goal should not be to get into this space, but to dismantle it.

51. See supra note 43, pp. 65–70.

52. George Yancey, *Who Is White?: Latinos, Asians, and the New Black/Non-black Divide* (Boulder, CO: Lynne Rienner, 2003), 149–55.

53. James Baldwin, *The Price of the Ticket: Collected Nonfiction, 1948–1985* (New York: St. Martin's Press, 1985).

But there is also a problem from the position of those who are dependent upon white space for identity and power—specifically whites. The foundation and the function of this space is exclusion and domination, but because whiteness is relational, it is understandable that after the Civil War whites were anxious and confused about who they were. And in this context, the relationship is one of domination, exclusion, and fear. So assimilation is a problem not just for those who would come in but also for those who are already in this white space. Justice Thomas's skepticism about the need to enter this white space to be successful is understandable. The solution, however, is not to stay outside the space or to leave the space undisturbed. The goal of racial justice is not just to free nonwhites but to free whites from this white space.

What I am suggesting is that there is something problematic for those who inhabit this white space as well as a problem with the space itself. To understand this, we must first look carefully at this space. The space of whiteness, of course, has changed and will continue to change. It is a contested space.[54] But a number of its underlying principles change only in degree. It is a negative space, that is, it is defined in part by who and what is kept out. So it is a space of exclusion and domination. This is because those excluded are already present.[55] The exterior and the interior are radically interdependent and unequal. This sets up a dual relationship that undermines the principles of democracy. Justice Harlan suggested as much when he talked about the Constitution not recognizing dominate or subordinate classes. Creating such a distinction makes a mockery of the democratic norm. Harlan, however, did not go far enough. Even while he was unwilling to accept the constitutional acknowledgment of a racial caste system, he thought such a system was natural and inevitable in the social sphere. He was wrong on both counts. He also failed to recognize the role of law and other public institutions in creating this apparently natural space.

Whites who occupy this space feel both a sense of power over and a sense of danger from the other. There is the constant threat of pollution and annihilation of the other. This fear must be policed, yet the other is needed. But the other is not just in the physical space; the other is also in the psychic space. The space is maintained not just by denying the other

54. Michael Omi and Howard Winant, "Racial Formation," in *Race Critical Theories,* Philomena Essed and David Theo Goldberg, eds., 123–45 (Maiden, MA: Blackwell Publishers, 2002).

55. See supra note 3. Michel Laguerre, *Minoritizing Space: An Inquiry into the Spatial Order of Things* (Institute of Governmental Studies Press and the Institute of Urban and Regional Development, University of California, Berkeley, 1999).

"out there," but, more problematically, by denying the other in the self. The psychological, material, and spiritual damage to those in this state of fear has not been adequately explored.[56] After the Civil War, there was an opportunity to embrace true democracy and a more whole self. But this also required a new kind of whiteness. The failure to produce this radically new white space and white identity under the post-Civil War conditions left many whites adrift, confused, and angry. This anger was used after Reconstruction to develop another space maintained through fear and violence. This white space is a space of spiritual death. We are now in danger of losing the opportunity presented by the civil rights movement as we continue to live under the shadow of *Scott*. To capture this opportunity, we must deepen our understanding of social justice and fundamentally restructure our institutional and cultural arrangements to support a space without masters or servants. This is the unfulfilled promise of our democracy.

It might be too much to expect that the Court would take all this on. This white space emerged over several decades and is supported by many of our institutions and our national ethos. But there is another part of our history and a dream that we must redeem. We must first have our own truth and reconciliation, not just for blacks but for whites. What the Court might have done was to have an experiment that explored the damage to whites caused by segregation and a false sense of superiority. What the court might have done was to push for a better definition of the need for creating a holistic citizenry in our growing democracy. Too often there has been the assumption that nonwhites are defective, and the goal is to move them to the unstated, and sometimes even stated, norms of whiteness. That is why the Civil Rights Act of 1866 could talk about blacks getting the same rights and benefits as whites. We still talk in such terms when we assume that the goal is equality, meaning nonwhites are equal to whites without a more careful examination as to what this means. We must remember that the Civil War Amendments promised the end of slavery and the right of full citizenship before it spoke of equality. It is not that equality is not important—it is. But what must we be equal to?

Whites are not likely to give up white space or participate in its destruction unless they see both how they are harmed by it and that there is a better alternative. It is not simply a question as to whether we can move forward in opposition to white prerogative but whether we can

56. Toni Morrison, *Playing in the Dark: Whiteness and the Literary Imagination* (Cambridge, MA: Harvard University Press, 1992).

gain support for the development of a new kind of white prerogative, a new kind of white being that is not in opposition to the other. There are also signs that the ability to pay the racial bribe for whites to continue to defend white space may be coming undone.[57] There are many shortcomings to *Brown* and *Brown II*. There are also a number of radical readings of these cases. They are both available to us. But I suggest that if we fail to enliven the more radical view of *Brown* and call for a different radical vision of whiteness and eradicate the harms experienced under the present structures, it is more our failure than theirs.

In looking at the injuries that this system inflicts, we must not fall into a false sense of symmetry and assume that the injury to those outside and inside is the same.[58] Nonetheless, we have still not had the analogy of the doll experiment for whites. Maybe there is none. But we must seriously explore the question, what has this white space done to those inside the space—as well as those outside of it?

While an exclusive conception of white space has kept nonwhites out, it has also trapped whites within. By defining themselves as what they are not, whites have prevented themselves from creating a more positive image for themselves. Ultimately, this definition by exclusion, in a world that is increasingly finding value in the multicultural expression of many groups, must leave those trapped within white space feeling increasingly insecure and defensive about their own identity. Future research might focus on any connections between a lack of white identity and the erosion of community supports within suburban America and its effects on predominantly white social problems, such as teenage suicide.

Segregation harms whites and nonwhites, but in very different ways. If whites can begin to see that segregation and its underlying mindsets is more harmful to them than any perceived benefits it provides to them, then true integration may finally become possible. Once whites are able to create a self-identity that is not based on exclusion, then white space as we know it will cease to exist and different races will be able to interact on an equal level. Then, and only then, will segregation have come to an end in America.

---

57. Andrew Barlow, *Between Fear and Hope: Globalization and Race in the United States* (Lanham, MD: Rowman & Littlefield, 2003). Barlow argues that globalization threatens many of the benefits associated with whiteness and thereby may offer a ray of hope. See also Alberto Alesina and Edward L. Glaesar, *Fighting Poverty in the United States and Europe* (New York: Oxford University Press, 2004). Here the authors compare the development of social citizenship in the United States and Europe and find that race has retarded development in the U.S.

58. See supra note 3.

CHAPTER 10

Brown's Legacy

The Promises and Pitfalls of Judicial Relief

DEBORAH JONES MERRITT

Brown v. Board of Education (1954) is one of the greatest achievements of the American judicial system. It decisively declared racial segregation in the schools unconstitutional, inaugurating the modern civil rights era. Citizens around the world, not just in the United States, view *Brown* as a twentieth-century political landmark.

In addition to advancing equality, *Brown* initiated a new type of judicial decision making. After *Brown,* courts increasingly used the federal Constitution to achieve progressive social ends, and they issued detailed orders to implement those goals. Desegregation, busing, prison reform, environmental protection, and many other judicial actions stemmed from *Brown*'s inspiration. The period from 1960 through the present has been an era of judicial policymaking, quite distinct from the New Deal era that preceded it and that relied primarily on legislation to achieve social ends.

This era of judicial supremacy has many advantages. The impact of *Brown* was magnificent. Christian prayer was unlikely to leave our schools without judicial intervention. Some state courts have achieved more equitable school financing systems, a result that would have been highly unlikely from elected legislators. Policies that benefit political minorities of any type often are easier to wrest from the courts than from legislatures.

Appellate courts also appear more receptive than legislatures to serious economic, moral, legal, and constitutional arguments. Legislative caucuses, senate hearings, and statehouse floors do not promote serious study or discussion. Focused litigation often is easier and cheaper than mobilizing grassroots support for legislative change. And there is something very moving—and quintessentially American—about the image of a single individual standing up for his or her rights, taking that case to court, and prevailing on a principle that reshapes public policy.

But the dominance of courts during the last half century has a downside as well. As political scientists have pointed out, judicial power can serve the interests of elites by helping to marginalize more democratic forms of policymaking. Matthew Crenson and Benjamin Ginsberg (2002) recently tagged this trend the "downsizing" of democracy. While paying lip service to democratic participation, Crenson and Ginsberg argue, elites increasingly govern through courts, regulatory agencies, and other means that require little consensus building or democratic support.

Although courts have vindicated both the downtrodden and the powerful during the last fifty years, three factors make them particularly attentive to elites. First, elites understand the obscure customs of judicial process and are comfortable invoking that process. Second, elites can afford to hire the lawyers needed to navigate legal channels. And, finally, judges respond well to the highly intellectual arguments that elites compose. For all of these reasons, *Brown's* legacy is double edged. It promises relief to racial minorities and other disempowered groups in some cases, but also gives elites the power to evade democratic controls.

Crenson and Ginsberg offer the recent tobacco settlements as a compelling example of elites governing through the courts. In the settlements, tobacco companies agreed to pay state governments more than $230 billion over the *next* twenty-five years. Those revenues substantially eased budget crises in many states, allowing some states to cut taxes on the middle classes and wealthy. Relatively little of the revenue has gone to antismoking programs; one study suggests that only 5 percent of the settlement revenues have been used that way (Crenson and Ginsberg 2002, 161). Instead, well-off taxpayers have been the primary beneficiaries of these settlements.

Tobacco companies have also benefited. The companies have passed through the cost of the settlement to smokers: largely working-class and lower-middle-class smokers who are addicted to nicotine. These individuals now pay both the health and financial costs of their addiction, with little in the way of government programs to assist their addiction or prevent their children from becoming addicted. On the contrary, state governments have now become tacit allies of the tobacco industry. If tobacco revenues fall, then the states won't collect future settlement payments and will have to raise taxes.

Viewed in this way, the tobacco settlement was a way for elites to shift rising healthcare costs off themselves and onto low-income smokers, with several billion dollars for wealthy trial lawyers thrown into the bargain. The state litigants and their lawyers may not have plotted the scenario that way, but they secured this result because only elites (state governments on one side, tobacco companies on the other) participated in the settlement negotiations. Low-income smokers had no adequate representation in the tobacco litigation.

Our national debate over racism and affirmative action has begun to show some of the same unhealthy focus on litigation, with elites benefiting from that strategy. White elites increasingly have turned litigation in this area to their advantage, crafting constitutional arguments that paint affirmative action as reverse discrimination and deflecting claims that the Constitution should remedy de facto housing segregation or economic inequalities in education. These conservative arguments withstand scrutiny only in the sterile world of appellate courts and constitutional theory; in the real world of persistent racism and increasing inequality, they would be unpersuasive. Elites have succeeded on these issues in the courts precisely because they have been able to exclude the reality of racism from the discussion.

Even the recent judicial victory for affirmative action in higher education (*Grutter* 2003) has troubling implications. The decision endorsed a labor-intensive admissions process that is most suitable for selective, elite colleges rather than large state universities. The process, moreover, rewards students who can eloquently portray diversity of any type. White children from wealthy families, raised with designer backgrounds and tutored by pricey admissions counselors, benefit from the admissions processes endorsed by this decision as much as the most disadvantaged minority students will.

The case was telling in terms of the outpouring of support it generated from both liberal elites and more conservative corporate and military elites. The litigation generated a record number of amicus briefs. Faculty members and students held rallies and teach-ins around the country; many journeyed to Washington when the case was argued. The case appears to have been one of the top ten political events of 2003; on campuses, it may have attracted even more attention than the Iraq war did.

The support for affirmative action in *Grutter* was admirable, and may even have helped tip the balance of decision. But where are the same academic, corporate, and military elites when states cut funding for elementary schools in poor, predominantly minority districts? Or refuse to overturn property tax funding for education? Or reject stronger laws against housing discrimination? Why don't elites march on statehouses as readily as they march on courthouses?

An unhappy possibility is that elites are comfortable with affirmative action in higher education but would be challenged by more direct remedies for racism and inequality. When universities implemented affirmative action plans in the late 1960s, they concurrently began to expand the size of their classes (Merritt 1998, 1060). More white students have gained admission to selective colleges, law schools, and medical schools after affirmative action than before it. Despite the constant griping of white applicants rejected by some universities, whites have suffered relatively little from affirmative action in higher education (Kane 1998; Bowen and Bok 1998).

At the same time, these elites have been able to assure themselves that they are enlightened, tolerant people who live in an integrated society. Selective colleges have just the "right" mix of white and minority students, enough African American and Latino students to give the campus an urbane, cosmopolitan air without threatening the white campus majority. Whites have also benefited from affirmative action by learning to work compatibly with minorities and by grooming enough well-educated minorities to serve as business and military leaders, keeping rank-and-file minority workers complacent. The *Grutter* briefs themselves stressed these benefits of affirmative action.

Since the Supreme Court decided *Grutter* in June 2003, public discussion of racism and affirmative action has declined dramatically. The issues barely surfaced in the 2004 presidential campaign. From the public debate, one would think that deaths in Iraq, increasing poverty, cuts in stage budgets and social programs, widening inequality, and election fraud are all race-neutral trends. Even the fiftieth anniversary of *Brown* did little to awaken serious discussion of ongoing racism and racial disparities.

It seems that, having secured the racial comfort of their campuses, officer corps, and corporate recruiting programs—a comfort, I hasten to add, that allows only modest participation of racial minorities—the professors, generals, and CEOs have gone back to their libraries, maps, and budgets. No one is wrestling seriously with the deep inequalities and persistent racism that mark our society.

Nor will the courts solve those problems. The courts have steadfastly refused to recognize constitutional principles that would address the difficult issues of endemic racism. And, in truth, these are problems that require broader societal solutions than courts can supply. Without real democratic pressure and concerted action, we will not resolve the roots or racism.

The elites, however, have already obtained the remedy they sought—affirmative action in higher education—from the courts. What will bring them back into the political process to fight alongside the disadvantaged for greater equality? Lawsuits do not require the bargaining that the legislative process entails. Elites can obtain their desired ends from the courts without promising, in return, to support the agendas of their allies. This is the dark side of relying primarily on courts for social change: in the end, the courts may serve the ends of elites without requiring those elites to include less empowered citizens in their social agenda.

Brown is not to blame for these troubles. The decision was a true watershed in racial equality, a beacon for all the world to follow. It capped a brilliant litigation strategy that justifiably inspired others. But we have forgotten since the triumph of *Brown* that elites have an uncanny ability to assert themselves. During the last fifty years, they have done so in part by seizing the coattails of *Brown* itself.

Brown's Legacy

In sum, as we celebrate *Brown,* we must also look to new forms of political engagement to develop *Brown's* full legacy. The civil rights leaders who built the strategy behind *Brown* chose the right strategy for their time. It was essential that the United States Supreme Court declare the fundamental principle of equality and begin enforcement of that principle. Today, the times demand a different tactic. Courts may still play a role in finishing the battle that *Brown* began, but grassroots politics, community organizing, elected officials, and even global networks of protesters will play a more essential role. These are the new political forces with the power to challenge elites.

References

Bowen, W., and D. Bok. 1998. *The Shape of the River: Long-term Consequences of Considering Race in College and University Admissions.* Princeton, NJ: Princeton University Press.

Brown v. Board of Education. 1954. 347 U.S. 483.

Crenson, M., and B. Ginsberg. 2002. *Downsizing Democracy: How America Sidelined Its Citizens and Privatized its Public.* Baltimore: Johns Hopkins University Press.

Grutter v. Bollinger. 2003. 539 U.S. 306.

Kane, T. 1998. "Racial and Ethnic Preferences in College Admissions." *Ohio State Law Journal* 59 (Autumn): 971–96.

Merritt, D. 1998. "The Future of *Bakke:* Will Social Science Matter?" *Ohio State Law Journal* 59 (Autumn): 1055–67.

Smith, G. 2004. *The Politics of Deceit: Saving Freedom and Democracy from Extinction.* Hoboken, NJ: John Wiley & Sons.

CHAPTER 11

The Not So Strange Path of Desegregation in America's Public Schools

PHILIP T. K. DANIEL

Introduction

> The [*Brown*] decision . . . became the archetype of a landmark decision. Landmark decisions are, at bottom, designed through reference to constitutional interpretations and supportive legal precedents to address and hopefully resolve deeply divisive social issues. They are framed in a language that provides at least the appearance of doing justice without unduly upsetting large groups whose potential for noncompliance can frustrate relief efforts and undermine judicial authority. For reasons that may not even have been apparent to the members of the Supreme Court, their school desegregation decisions achieved over time a far loftier place in legal history than they were able to accomplish in reforming the ideology of racial domination that *Plessy v. Ferguson* represented. (Bell 2004)

This passage from the book *Silent Covenants: Brown v. Board of Education and the Unfulfilled Hopes for Racial Reform* by Derrick Bell provides a fitting description of the life of racial equality in America's public schools, and Bell's own early career illuminates the sequence of judicial events. Bell began his legal career in the Civil Rights Division of the United States Justice Department. In the years 1960–65 Professor Bell was an attorney for the NAACP Legal Defense Fund supervising the litigation of desegregation cases for that organization. In 1966 he reunited with the Justice Department, aiding in the enforcement of Title VI of the Civil Rights Act "authorizing the termination of federal funds to school districts . . . in noncompliance" with early federal court desegregation decisions (Bell 2004, 3). Today, Mr. Bell is an ardent critic of those same decisions he helped to enforce, claiming that court-ordered desegregation is a "fiction," that racial discrimination against people of color is as ingrained in American society as apple pie, and that school districts are inappropriate places to seek racial reform.

So goes the journey of school integration as the legal status of discriminatory acts against students on the basis of race is rooted firmly in the United States Constitution, especially the concept of equal protection of the laws found in the Fourteenth Amendment. The journey of desegregation has been circular following the swings of social eras involving more than one hundred and fifty years of litigation. Except for a few significant cases, state and local government officials and members of school boards have been afforded power in determining authority to circumvent desegregation decrees based on the Tenth Amendment of the United States Constitution declaring, "[t]he powers not delegated to the [federal government] by the Constitution . . . are reserved to the states" (U.S. Constitution, Amend. X). Specifically, racial discrimination in schools has had a history largely supported by judicial decisions under the rubric of states' rights.

Those in the racial majority in the South and the North have steadfastly resisted any change in the status quo of student separation. African Americans, more recently, have themselves begun to question judicial intervention that would force students to remain together particularly in the kind of hostile environment that for years accompanied black student attempts at integration. This is the not so strange story; one where the undermining racial rationales of apartheid constitute a closed plane curve in the chronicles of American education.

The Expansion of Judicial Authority to Order Desegregation

The history of education for black children in the United States began with laws making it a crime to teach slaves to read or write (Goldstein et al. 1995). History informs us that pre-Civil War education provided for blacks in the North was often encapsulated by discriminatory laws. In *Roberts v. City of Boston* (*Roberts* 1849), for example, the Supreme Court of Massachusetts held that state law did not require blacks to attend school with whites, and for that matter, did not even require education for black students notwithstanding the fact that black parents were taxed for education at the same rate as whites. Such attitudes and beliefs continued well into the twentieth century and some states had laws against black children attending any school or simply built no facilities in areas for segregated black populations (Daniel 1980).[1] When education was finally provided for black children, state laws required that the races be separated; the direct consequence of such decisions was that black children for many years received an inferior education with substandard instruction and instructional materials (Kluger 1975). Legal separation was a product of a decision announced by the United States Supreme Court in *Plessy v. Ferguson* (*Plessy* 1896). *Plessy* ushered in the doctrine of "separate but equal" in railway and other public accommodations in society; this included education in public schools. It is interesting to note that the Supreme Court in *Plessy* cited as a foundation for its decision the case of *Roberts v. City of Boston* (*Plessy* 1896, 544).

National school desegregation by court order began with *Brown v. Board of Education* (*Brown I* 1954). In that case the United States Supreme Court asked the question: "Does segregation of children in public schools solely on the basis of race, even though the physical facilities and other tangible factors may be equal, deprive children of the minority group of equal educational opportunities? We believe it does" (*Brown I* 1954, 493).

When the Court answered affirmatively, it reversed the separate but equal doctrine of *Plessy* and ruled unconstitutional the legal basis for segregated and dual public school systems under the Equal Protection Clause of the Fourteenth Amendment of the United States Constitution.

For a year *Brown I* was the center of great confusion and even *greater* controversy. In an attempt to clarify its intent and provide direction to the lower courts, the Supreme Court heard further arguments on the question of appropriate relief. In *Brown II* (*Brown II* 1955) the Court

---

1. The decision in *Roberts* was similar to a concurring opinion rendered by Associate Justice Clarence Thomas in the recent desegregation case of *Missouri v. Jenkins,* 215 U.S. 70 [1995] (*Missouri II*), where he stated that black and white children could be separated in school and that all-black public schools were not necessarily the product of constitutional violations.

stated that lower federal courts should consider all relevant factors such as transportation systems, physical conditions of the buildings, difficulties in revising school districts and attendance zones, and other necessary local laws when framing a remedy and considering any plans by the school districts to remedy the illegal discriminatory acts. The Court concluded: "[A]nd the cases are remanded to the District Courts to take such proceedings and enter such orders and decrees consistent with this opinion as are necessary and proper to admit to public schools on a racially non-discriminatory basis with all deliberate speed the parties to these cases" (*Brown II* 1955, 301).

Although school districts, with the help of the federal courts, were supposed to move with "all deliberate speed" toward dismantling of dual school systems, the next ten years saw massive resistance on the part of the public schools and creation of novel schemes by states to avoid the mandates of *Brown I* and *Brown II*. State and local officials at first decided not to follow the dictates of *Brown I*. These included terminating state support of education and closing of schools (*Griffin* 1964). Feigned compliance came after Brown *II,* however, and one of the reasons for this quick turnabout was the message of the Supreme Court itself. After expressing the hegemony of federal law and the Supremacy Clause (U.S. Constitution, Article VI) over state law in *Brown I, Brown II*'s decision gave state and local government primary responsibility for defining how desegregation would take place. Changes need not take place immediately, but "with all deliberate speed"; moreover, all corrective efforts could be premised upon the conditions of the region (*Brown II* 1955, 299).

As such, state and local government in both the South and North was generally sanguine about *Brown II*. Two issues were at stake: the meaning of "all deliberate speed" and the court's interpretation of a desegregation remedy. One official in Georgia spoke for many states about the significance of "all deliberate speed" indicating that he had faith that local judges would define the phrase as "one or two hundred years" (Woodward 1974, 153). The remedy could reflect the rationale for the actions of local government. If those actions were said to be race neutral, even if the discriminatory status quo was maintained, courts typically agreed with the remedy. States created pupil assignment laws which on paper eliminated explicit racial placement, but were designed, nonetheless, to maintain segregation. State statutes also permitted students to apply for transfers to adjacent schools based on race-neutral criteria. Those criteria included whether a student would be a good fit relative to intelligence, aptitude, academic preparation, morals, breaches of the peace, and the health of the student (Meador 1959). Under these conditions few students were granted transfers (*Dillard* 1962).

A Brief Desegregative Respite

The Supreme Court, after more than a decade, began again aggressively scrutinizing school districts and their desegregation efforts. As in *Brown I,* during this time, states' rights were viewed as subordinate to the authority of the federal courts. On one level, the federal judiciary had no choice but to increase its involvement in integration. The courts had given public school officials the opportunity to discontinue the use of race in student placement, a chance largely rejected. In *Griffin v. County School Board of Prince Edward County* (*Griffin* 1964), a case decided in 1964, the Supreme Court ruled that the local school district could not close its public school system while providing tuition grants to private all-white schools because this denied African American pupils equal protection of the law. The Court, in requiring Prince Edward County to reopen and desegregate its public schools, gave notice to the states that it would no longer tolerate state-sanctioned devices created to perpetuate a segregated education system.

At approximately the same time that the *Griffin* case was announced, the United States Congress helped to expedite the process of desegregation by enacting the Civil Rights Act of 1964 (Civil Rights Act 1964). Led by President Lyndon Johnson, the United States Congress passed Title VI of the Act requiring educational institutions to operate devoid of racial discrimination (Title VI 2000). Corollary federal legislation was promulgated in the Elementary and Secondary Education Act (ESEA 2000) making federal funds available to states and their school districts. The executive branch of government through the former Department of Health, Education, and Welfare (HEW) also played a prominent role. School officials had to commit in writing to HEW that they were in compliance with federal law. Those school districts found in violation of the legislation were subject to lose the federal set-aside funds. Congress, however, gave HEW no influence over school district compliance other than fund termination. Consequently, to further persuade states to desegregate, congressional legislation granted license to the Department of Justice to initiate legal causes of action against school districts for continued discrimination under Title IV of the Civil Rights Act.

With the three branches of government operating in unison, the federal will could now compel desegregation with both a carrot and a stick. The battle came quickly; three years after the *Griffin* decision the Supreme Court was faced with another scheme to avoid desegregation (*Green* 1968). This time, New Kent County, Virginia had promulgated a "freedom-of-choice" plan in response to pressures that it develop a method to desegregate its public schools. Under the plan, black and white students were free to choose which schools they would attend. In practice, no white students chose to attend the all-black school, and only 15 percent of the black students chose to attend the former all-white schools. Although the Court did not declare "freedom-of-choice" plans unconstitutional per se, it ruled that "if there are reasonably available other ways, such, for illustration, as zoning, promising speedier and more effective conversion to a unitary, nonracial school system, 'freedom of choice' must be held unacceptable" (*Green* 1968, 441). In so ruling, the Supreme Court removed from affected school districts the power to devise plans that would just eventually desegregate dual school systems as *Brown I* and *Brown II* had required. Rather, the districts were commanded to assume the additional task of creating a totally "unitary nonracial system of public education" (*Green* 1968, 436). Any plans that did not have as an immediate goal the elimination of racial discrimination "root and branch," and that were not intended "realistically to work, and . . . realistically to work now" (*Green* 1968, 439) would not be acceptable. The Court further determined that school systems must satisfy seven factors in order to comply with a desegregation order. Known later as the "Green factors," they require that (a) students of all races receive the same quality education; (b) administrator and teacher assignments be race neutral; (c) student assignments be race neutral; (d) all students be given equal access to the school transportation system; (e) all schools receive equitable allocations of resources; (f) school buildings and facilities be of equal quality; and (g) all students be given equal access to extracurricular activities (*Green* 1968, 440). The Court announced that the burden of desegregation was not upon students and parents, but, instead, upon the school district, based on these seven factors. The Court concluded that the district had not satisfied the factors and required New Kent County to formulate a new plan for desegregation which would result in the elimination of racially identifiable schools (*Green* 1968, 442).

The Supreme Court's impatience with dilatory tactics and inadequate desegregation plans was further emphasized in 1969 when it refused to allow certain Mississippi school districts any additional extensions of time to develop acceptable desegregation plans. In *Alexander v. Holmes County Board of Education* (*Alexander* 1969), the Court simply stated that "continued operation of segregated schools under a standard of allowing 'all deliberate speed' for desegregation is no longer constitutionally permissible" (*Alexander* 1969, 20).

The above-cited cases *Green* and *Alexander* established the present standards to which a school district must adhere in eliminating the vestiges of de jure discrimination. In effect, the Fourteenth Amendment is read as requiring the immediate establishment of a unitary, racially heterogeneous school system to replace dual systems or any remnants of such systems.

Busing to Achieve Racial Balance

When the Supreme Court ruled that formerly segregated school systems must not simply adopt a racially neutral policy, but must take affirmative action to assure that any vestiges of a prior discriminatory policy are eliminated, the lower courts were left to devise a variety of remedial plans. The most difficult problems arose in school districts encompassing large metropolitan areas in the South. To meet the desegregation requirements of the Supreme Court, many lower courts ordered major restructuring of attendance zones and intradistrict busing to eliminate "black" and "white" schools. There was a substantial question as to whether the Constitution allowed the courts such wide discretion in remedying past discrimination. This issue was addressed by the Supreme Court in *Swann v. Charlotte-Mecklenburg Board of Education* (*Swann* 1971). In *Swann,* the federal district court had ordered cross-district busing in Charlotte, North Carolina, in order to bring about better patterns of integration within the school district. The federal circuit court reversed on the grounds that massive busing such as that ordered by the district court would place an unreasonable financial and educational burden on the school district and school pupils.

In upholding the district court's busing plans, the Supreme Court sanctioned busing as a legitimate means to remedy the problems caused by de jure discrimination. The Court noted that "bus transportation has been an integral part of the public education system for years, and was perhaps the single most important factor in the transition from the one-room schoolhouse to the consolidated school. . . . [T]herefore we find no basis for holding that the local school authorities may not be required to employ bus transportation as one tool of school desegregation. Desegregation plans cannot be limited to the walk-in school" (*Swann* 1971, 29–30). In fact, the only limitations that the Court placed upon busing plans were "when the time or distance of travel is so great as to risk either the health of children or significantly impinge upon the educational process" (*Swann* 1971, 30–31).

In addition to mandating unitary school systems, the *Swann* decision acknowledged a difference between de jure and de facto segregation. De jure racial discrimination, as defined by the courts in desegregation cases, occurs in public education when the state or its representative agencies classify and segregate students according to race and thereby create dual school systems or racially identifiable schools within a school district. In contrast, de facto segregation in the public schools refers to a racial imbalance caused by such social or economic factors as housing patterns, rather than any official action. The *Swann* Court held that regardless of the type of segregation, where a system evidences a history of statutory segregation, school authorities bear the burden of eliminating vestiges of such discrimination (*Swann* 1971, 15–16).

Although *Swann* was specifically directed toward correcting the problems created by dual school systems that had existed mainly in the South, an upshot of the decision was to focus attention on the "black" and "white" schools in many Northern cities. In *Keyes v. School District No. 1, Denver Colorado* (*Keyes* 1973), a federal district court found that the Denver School District had engaged in de jure discrimination in one part of the district by making decisions concerning such things as attendance boundaries, school placements, and optional attendance zones by considering racial and ethnic rather than educational factors. The district court ordered the desegregation of the area affected by de jure discrimination, and in addition ordered integration of the core city schools because they provided an "inferior education." The United States Court of Appeals for the Tenth Circuit upheld the desegregation order as it applied to those schools affected by racially motivated decisions, but reversed the order's application to the core city schools, concluding that schools segregated solely because of housing patterns or other factors not caused by the state should not be subject to desegregation orders. The Supreme Court agreed with the district court and court of appeals as far as the desegregation order concerning those schools where de jure discrimination had occurred. But the Court went further than either of the two lower courts by imposing upon the school district a burden to show that discrimination had not occurred throughout the whole system if discriminatory actions were found in a part of the system. The Court was cautious to note that it was still addressing itself to de jure discrimination, but the effect of the *Keyes* decision was to put school districts in all areas of the country on notice that they are not immune from desegregation orders and court-ordered busing if discriminatory acts were found to have adversely affected any part of the school system.

A Shift in Judicial Activism

The *Brown I, Green, Swann,* and *Keyes* cases resulted in federal courts retaining a great deal of authority over public school systems. But the Supreme Court only briefly strayed away from the dominance of states' rights over the field of public education. Beginning in 1974 the Court, in an abrupt departure from previous rulings, removed much of the remedial authority it had granted to the lower courts.

The busing orders considered by the Supreme Court up to 1974 dealt only with intradistrict busing. But in order to devise remedies to correct problems caused by racial discrimination, especially in large metropolitan areas where many of the core cities are occupied almost exclusively by blacks, some lower courts ordered busing across district lines. The Supreme Court was asked in *Milliken v. Bradley* (*Milliken* 1974) to decide whether an interdistrict busing order affecting the Detroit school district and fifty-three outlying districts met constitutional requirements. The facts as determined by the district court showed that de jure school segregation had occurred in the Detroit school district, but that there was no evidence that other school districts included in the plan had failed to operate unitary school systems or had engaged in acts of intentional segregation, the specter of white flight notwithstanding. Chief Justice Warren Burger began the unraveling of desegregation remedies found in previous Supreme Court decisions by claiming that federal courts had become pseudo school superintendents and had exhibited de facto legislative authority in holding for plaintiffs in such cases. He reemphasized states' rights, finding that such inappropriate judicial roles would "deprive the people of control of schools through their elected representatives" (*Milliken* 1974, 744). In holding that the lower courts' remedies were too broad, the Supreme Court set forth the applicable constitutional standard:

Before the boundaries of separate and autonomous school districts may be set aside by consolidating the separate units for remedial purposes or by imposing a cross-district remedy, it must be shown that there has been a constitutional violation within one school district that produces a significant segregative effect in another district. Specifically, it must be shown that racially discriminatory acts of the state or local school districts, or of a single school district have been a substantial cause of interdistrict segregation. . . . [W]ithout an interdistrict violation and interdistrict effect, there is no constitutional wrong calling for an interdistrict remedy. (*Milliken* 1974, 744–45)

The Court rendered its support of attendance policies for schools established by school officials, independent of discriminatory motive or result, and stated that lower-court judges were not in a position to supplant the decisions of school board members or licensed school administrators. Such a preemption, according to the Court, would produce problems involving pupil assignments, transportation, and tax-based financial support. For this reason lower-court decisions sanctioning an interdistrict remedy were found to unconstitutionally abolish local control and the Court refused to impose a desegregation remedy without extant evidence that suburban, mostly white, school districts had participated in intentional segregation.

Milliken represents a movement away from active judicial intervention in school desegregation so typical in cases from *Brown I* to *Keyes*. Subsequent rulings followed *Milliken* in finding no constitutional violation in desegregation disputes. In *Pasadena City Board of Education v. Spongier* (*Pasadena* 1976) the Supreme Court held that a district court exceeded its authority when ordering that school officials adopt a desegregation plan that required annual adjustments of attendance zones to avoid a majority of either black or white students in any school. The new trend continued in *Dayton Board of Education v. Brinkman* (*Dayton* 1977), where the Supreme Court in vacating and remanding the judgment of a federal appeals court held that a system-wide remedy imposed to eliminate racial discrimination in the operation of the Dayton, Ohio, schools, following the school board's repudiation of previous resolutions for desegregation, could not be justified. Directly following its *Milliken* decision, the Supreme Court held that there should be a system-wide remedy for segregation only if there has been a system-wide segregative impact from constitutional violations. This means that school district boundary lines matter when crafting a remedy. Those boundaries must be respected; as in the early desegregation decisions the Court had returned to state and local control as the locus of its opinion.

Dowell, Freeman, and Missouri III

The most recent and meaningful school desegregation cases heard by the Supreme Court have involved school districts attempting to extricate themselves from federal court supervision of desegregation obligations. In *Board of Education of Oklahoma City Public Schools v. Dowell* (*Dowell* 1991) the Supreme Court addressed what it considered to be the proper standards for declaring a former segregated school district unitary by a federal district court. The Oklahoma City schools had been declared unitary in 1977. African American plaintiffs, however, claimed resegregation and attempted to reopen the case in 1985. Plaintiffs' rationale for claiming resegregation related to a new school reassignment plan introduced in 1984 which effectively returned many previously desegregated schools to one-race schools. In response to the plaintiffs' complaints, the school district sought an end to federal judicial oversight of the schools. In a sharply divided opinion, the Supreme Court held that judicial control of public school desegregation efforts should be temporary if there is a finding that the district has cooperated with existing decrees and has eliminated past discrimination as much as practicable. The Court reasoned that federal supervision of local school districts was intended to be a temporary measure to remedy past discrimination. It repeated the *Milliken* Court's emphasis on local control of education; if a school district has complied with court conditions for a reasonable period, dissolution of a judicial desegregation decree recognizes the importance of states' rights. The decision established a good-faith standard whereby school districts need only demonstrate "that they had eliminated the vestiges of past discrimination, 'to the extent practicable,' rather than make a more definite showing of compliance" (*Brown-Nagin* 2000, 791).

This now meant that "de jure segregated school district[s] that had been found unitary could return to assigning students to neighborhood schools, even if such schools would be racially segregated" (*Brown-Nagin* 2000, 785). In this case the Court declared that school officials needed only to establish that they were operating within the Equal Protection Clause and that it was "unlikely [they] would return to [their] former ways" (*Dowell* 1991, 247). Such a showing would demonstrate "that the purposes of desegregation litigation had been fully achieved" (*Dowell* 1991, 247). The Court retreated from much prior litigation in making it clear that lower-court jurisdiction should cease once a school district is unitary, since at that point the purpose of litigation would be accomplished. The mandate of Supreme Court precedent before *Dowell* requiring school districts to remove all vestiges of past discriminatory practices was overruled. The Court now only required the removal of discriminatory vestiges to the extent practicable. The Court, however, offered no insight on how "practicable" a school district's effort toward the elimination of discriminatory vestiges had to be.

This trend was followed in *Freeman v. Pitts* (*Freeman* 1992), where the Supreme Court refined the guidelines to be used by lower federal courts in determining how to relinquish authority over school desegregation to school authorities. In a case directly influenced by the findings in *Milliken,* the Supreme Court held that resegregation of schools does not have constitutional implications if the resegregation results from private choices rather than state action. A local school system in Georgia sought a final release from judicial supervision for its desegregation efforts. School officials claimed that private residential decisions by parents caused resegregation in the area; this was remarkable since racial separation had been the issue before the desegregation decree. Moreover, while the desegregation plan in place required busing for students wishing to transfer schools, school leaders budgeted no funding for this kind of transportation. The school district asserted that a plan had been created that satisfied some, but not all, of the factors necessary for achieving unitary status. A federal district court held that the district had achieved unitary status in some but not all relevant areas. The court released the school district from judicial control in those areas that had been found unitary. The United States Court of Appeals for the Eleventh Circuit reversed, holding that full judicial control should be retained until unitary status is achieved in all areas.

In reversing the decision of the appellate court, the Supreme Court restated its holding in *Dowell* that judicial control of a district's desegregation efforts was intended to be temporary and that the ultimate objective was to return control to local authorities. In another divided opinion, the Supreme Court declared that lower courts may relinquish control of school systems in incremental stages before full compliance is realized (*Freeman* 1992, 488). The Court also indicated that racial imbalance in schools was only to be remedied if there were constitutional implications (*Freeman* 1992, 469). Specifically, courts are under no obligation to remedy racial imbalance in schools caused by private demographic decisions.

The recent triumvirate of Supreme Court decisions undermining desegregation and further compromising the education of African American students includes *Missouri v. Jenkins* (*Missouri III* 1995). The state of

Missouri had incorporated laws fostering de jure segregation and agreed to follow the desegregation mandate of *Brown,* but only after several years of legal complaints by Black parents. The Supreme Court considered the validity of three desegregation remedies that a lower federal court had imposed on the Kansas City, Missouri school system. The remedies consisted of salary increases for all personnel, the creation of a remedial quality education program in the form of a city-wide "magnet" school district, and additional state funding for the purpose of increasing student achievement scores of African American students to those approaching national norms. All of the remedies were designed to make the school system attractive enough to avert white flight and to encourage some suburban children to seek education in the city.

The Supreme Court, in yet another sharply divided opinion, reversed and held that the district court went beyond its remedial powers when it fashioned this novel set of remedies for the school district. Namely, courts must only order remedies that "restore the victims of discriminatory conduct to the position they would have occupied in the absence of such conduct" (*Missouri III* 1995, 70). In this case salary increases would make the district more attractive and contribute to the impermissible goal of inducing white students from outside the school district to return to Kansas City. Such a remedy was outside the district court's remedial authority because the Court found no constitutional violation that could be attributed to any school district outside the city (*Missouri III* 1995, 70). This was also true of the magnet school remedy; it too focused on bringing nonwhites back into the city (*Missouri III* 1995, 71–72). Finally, the Supreme Court questioned the propriety of ordering additional state funding for the purpose of bringing the achievement scores of Kansas City school children to that approaching national norms. The Court found that disparities in test scores did not justify a continued desegregation order in that *Brown* signified an educational opportunity for all students, not a commensurate outcome. Differences in test scores between blacks and whites was said to be an insufficient basis for continuing a court order. Such an endeavor was not an appropriate remedy under a desegregation order as it was not necessary to achieve partial unitary status (*Missouri III* 1995).

Conclusion

The circle of racial segregation in schools has completed itself based on the more recent Supreme Court cases pervasively weakening the welfare of African American and other students of color as regards an appropriate education. The tenor of the federal courts, though at one ten-year period in the 1960s and 70s serving as a champion of equal educational opportunity rights, has now determined that the vehicle for supporting those rights, a desegregation decree, may not operate in perpetuity. The lawsuit has a short locus of points and soon after state and local control of schools must be restored. This legal phenomenon is not a new one. As noted above, southern state officials were sanguine about the language of *Brown II,* decided in 1955; changes could be arranged at the pace decided by the wrongdoers themselves and corrective efforts could be premised upon the social and economic conditions of the region.

The three branches of government, legislative, executive, and judiciary, once a trio to enforce desegregation decrees, later banded together to circumvent such activities. For example, part of the return to judicially supported segregation in education occurred in the 1980s when the Justice Department during the administration of President Ronald Reagan offered its assistance to school boards, particularly in the South, to help end federal judicial supervision of decrees (Boger 2003). Finding solace in this presidential approach, the three primary cases of *Dowell, Freeman,* and *Missouri III* offer persuasive arguments that the judiciary will interpret *Brown v. Board of Education* as standing for an opportunity for an education, not protection of education, and certainly not a right to racial desegregation. The three decisions indicate a willingness to defer to state and local authorities even if a consequence is the resegregation of mostly one-race schools. With local control as a constitutional imperative, courts cannot issue remedial orders for interdistrict remedies for de jure segregation absent findings that all of the school districts in the order deliberately participated in discrimination that affected other school districts. Furthermore, segregation is constructively sanctioned by the courts when that separation is deemed to be caused by private actors.

The courts have accepted the provision of a return to one-race schools due to choices of domicile causing self-segregation. Justice Antonin Scalia, for example, in his concurring opinion in *Freeman v. Pitts* determined that "[r]acially imbalanced schools are . . . the product or a blend of public and private actions, and any assessment of a particular one of those factors[,] is guesswork" (*Freeman* 1992, 503). This legal fiction informs us that discrimination in education can almost never be the fault of government. Such a position not only introduces forgiveness for the initiation of discrimination, but also perpetuates its longevity since private choice is the eternal and indefinite culprit. A casualty of this philosophy is the achievement of students of color who today, statistically as a group, lag behind their white counterparts. The courts have found that poor student achievement that might be occasioned by these private choices is not remediable under the Fourteenth Amendment equal protection clause when no state actor is implicated.

While *Brown I, Green, Swann,* and *Keyes* required compliance in realistic time, states' rights notwithstanding, the more recent Supreme Court decisions have engaged in local authority restoration, thereby excusing failure or intended desire not to achieve desegregation. Lower courts have gotten the message, and have been quite willing to dismiss school desegregation lawsuits. Local control is returning. One ten-year study of district court opinions and the appeals of these opinions demonstrated that nearly every request for unitary status was granted (*Parker* 2003). They note that while unitary status is a goal, and not a conditional precedent, a return to local control is the intended outcome. Protection from the invidious effects of a segregated education, hence, is bounded by local control of education.

References

Alexander v. Holmes County Bd. of Education. 1969. 396 U.S. 19.

Bell, D. 2004. *Silent Covenants: Brown v. Board of Education and the Unfulfilled Hopes for Racial Reform.* London: Oxford University Press, 8–9.

Boger, J. C. 2003. "Education's 'Perfect Storm'? Racial Resegregation, High-stakes Testing, and School Resource Inequities: The Case of North Carolina." *North Carolina Law Review* 81, no. 2: 1375–1462.

(*Brown I*) *Brown v. Board of Education.* 1954. 347 U.S. 483.

(*Brown II*) *Brown v. Board of Education.* 1955. 349 U.S. 294.

Brown-Nagin, T. 2000. "Toward a Pragmatic Understanding of Status-Consciousness: The Case of Deregulated Education." *Duke Law Journal* 50, no. 1: 753–886.

Civil Rights Act of 1964. 1996. 42 U.S.C. Sec. 2000(c)(d).

Daniel, P. T. K. 1980. "A History of Discrimination against Students in Chicago Secondary Schools." *History of Education Quarterly* 20, no. 1: 147–65.

Dayton Board of Education v. Brinkman. 1977. 433 U.S. 406.

Dillard v. School Board of City of Charlottesville. 1962. 308 F.2d 920 (4th Cir.).

(*Dowell*) *Board of Education of Oklahoma City Public Schools v. Dowell.* 1991. 498 U.S. 237.

Elementary and Secondary Education Amendments of 1966. 2000. 20 U.S.C. Sections 6301 et. Seq.

Freeman v. Pitts. 1992. 503 U.S. 467.

Goldstein, S., E. G. Gee, and P. T. K. Daniel. 1995. *Law and Public Education.* Charlottesville: Michie Law Publishers.

Green v. County School Board of New Kent. 1968. 391 U.S. 430.

Griffin v. County School Board of Prince Edward County. 1964. 377 U.S. 218.

Keyes v. School District No. 1, Denver Colorado. 1973. 413 U.S. 189.

Kluger, R. 1975. *Simple Justice: The History of Brown v. Board of Education and Black America's Struggle for Equality.* New York: Vintage Books.

Meador, D. 1959. "The Constitution and the Assignment of Pupils to Public Schools." *Virginia Law Review* 45, no. 1: 517–63.

Milliken v. Bradley 1974. 418 U.S. 717.

(*Missouri III*) *Missouri v. Jenkins.* 1995. 515 U.S. 70.

Parker, W. 2003. "The Decline of Judicial Decisionmaking: School Desegregation and District Court Judges." *North Carolina Law Review* 81, no. 3: 1623–57.

Pasadena City Board of Education v. Spangler. 1976. 427 U.S. 424.

Plessy v. Ferguson. 1896. 163 U.S. 537.

Roberts v. City of Boston. 1849 59 Mass. (5 Cush.) 198. (The decision in *Roberts* was similar to a concurring opinion rendered by Associate Justice Clarence Thomas in the recent desegregation case of *Missouri v. Jenkins,* 515 U.S. 70 [1995] [*Missouri II*] where he stated that black and white children could be separated in school and all-black public schools were not necessarily the product of a constitutional violation.)

Swann v. Charlotte-Mecklenburg Board of Education. 1917. 404 U.S. 1.

Title IV of the Civil Rights Act of 1964. 2000. 42 U.S.C. Sec. 2000d-1.

Title VI of the Civil Rights Act of 1964. 2000. 42 U.S.C. Sec. 2000d-1.

U.S. Constitution, Amendment X. U.S. Constitution, Article VI, Cl. 2.

Woodward, C. V. 1974. *The Strange Career of Jim Crow.* 3rd ed. Oxford: Oxford University Press.

CHAPTER 12

The Big Disconnect
between Segregation and Integration

VINCENE VERDUN

I. Introduction

The hearts and minds of the American people have been won over on the issue of segregation.[1] Flash back over the fifty years since the landmark decision *Brown v. Topeka*,[2] which ended legal school segregation, and reflect on the long and arduous effort to convert attitudes away from the longstanding acceptance of race segregation. It took a monumental civil rights movement, marked by marches, sit-ins, hoses, billyclubs, beatings, dogs, bombings, murders, arrests and the myriad of memories and rememories we hold of the American Civil Rights Movement to achieve widespread acceptance of the ultimate wrongness of segregation.[3]

---

1. Sheryll Cashin, *The Failures of Integration: How Race and Class Are Undermining the American Dream* (New York: Public Affairs, 2004) (demonstrating that while studies show that Americans believe in housing integration, most choose to live in segregated neighborhoods). See also Derrick Bell, *Silent Covenants* (New York and London: Oxford University Press, 2004) (Bell notes that at a Yale graduation in 2002, the audience expressed awe and respect over *Brown* decision).

2. *Brown v. Topeka,* 347 U.S. 483 (1954).

3. For a short but thorough documentary on the American Civil Rights Movement, see "A Time for Justice" produced by the Southern Poverty Law Center, Teaching Tolerance, and

Today, only the most extreme groups, residing on the very fringes of polite society, herald the ideology of segregation of the races.[4] American corporations, in preparation for their role in the global marketplace with an increasingly multiracial consumer base, have been strong supporters of diversity for decades, and many submitted amicus briefs supporting affirmative action in *Grutter v. Bollinger (The University of Michigan).*[5] Recently, in *The New York Times Magazine,* several corporations collaborated on a lengthy article designed to extol the virtues of diversity and integration.[6] Integration has been embraced as an unassailable structure in our society.[7]

The dilemma we confront as a society, is that while an overwhelming majority of Americans would cringe at the idea of a racially segregated America, America remains racially segregated and racial equality is more ideal than real.[8] Even though there is almost no legal segregation in America, most Americans live in segregated neighborhoods,[9] attend

---

accompanying text, "Free At Last" Montgomery, AL (1989).

4. Stephen E. Atkins, *Encyclopedia of Modern American Extremists and Other Extremists Groups* (Westport, CT: Greenwood Press, 2002) (providing the most up-to-date information on 275 of the most influential and significant homegrown extremists and extremist groups that have operated in the U.S. since 1950, and more than 75 percent of the coverage deals with the period since the 1980s, including subjects unavailable in other sources).

5. *Grutter v. Bollinger,* 539 U.S. 306 (2003). For a list of Amicus briefs filed in the *Grutter* case see University of Michigan website on Admissions Laws, http://www.umich.edu/~urel/admissions/legal/gru-amicus-ussc/um.html. Sixty-five Fortune Five Hundred companies joined in one brief supporting race-based affirmative action, under the heading 3M et. al. Several other corporations, including General Motors, filed briefs in the case.

6. See Jason Forsythe, "Winning with Diversity," *The N.Y. Times Magazine,* Sept. 19, 2004, 93–132. The article is a paid advertisement by the corporations featured in the article, with the apparent motivation of promoting diversity among other corporations while building good will for employment, consumer, and marketing purposes.

7. See George Lipsitz, *The Possessive Investment in Whiteness: How White People Profit from Identity Politics* (Philadelphia: Temple University Press, 1998) (offering a very pointed argument that racialized hierarchies in American society are driven by public policy and private prejudice).

8. See generally, Cashin, supra note 1. The Gallup Poll in 1999 showed that 60 percent of Americans believe more should be done for desegregation in public schools (K–12).

9. Michael O. Emerson, George Yancey, and Karen J. Chai, "Does Race Matter in Residential Segregation? Exploring the Preferences of White Americans," *American Sociology Review* 922, no.6 (2001): 66 (finding Asian and Hispanic American neighborhood composition does not affect white Americans' decisions to move into a neighborhood as much as black neighborhood composition).

United Way of Central Ohio, Racial Disparities Report (2003). The residential segregation dissimilarity index, used to measure on the scale of 0–100 the degree to which two groups are spread evenly among census tracts in a given metropolitan area, demonstrates a high level of racial segregation for major cities throughout the country, as designated below:

segregated schools[10] and churches,[11] play on segregated beaches, vacation in segregated hotels and resorts, and many have segregated workplaces.[12] There is an apparent theoretical disconnection in America between the evils of segregation and the virtues of integration. Our society accepts segregation as bad, but it also views forcing individuals to forego any personal liberty for the sake of integration and equity as unfair and illegal. Thus we have the "Big Disconnect"[13] between the legal and social wrong of segregation and the means of achieving integration, whether that comes in the form of school integration plans or affirmative action.

This essay will take a look in broad strokes over the past fifty years at how America has progressed legally, ideally, and actually from the pre-*Brown* society that accepted the legal segregation of the races, to the post-

---

Black/White Segregation* Selected Metro Areas, 2000

> Detroit–84.7
> New York–81.8
> Chicago–80.8
> Cleveland–77.3
> Cincinnati–74.8
> Indianapolis–70.7
> * Pittsburgh–67.3
> * Columbus–63.1
> * San Francisco–60.9
> * Minneapolis–57.8
> * Seattle–49.6
> * Phoenix–43.7
> (*Dissimilarity index, with 100 being most segregated. Ibid., 2–6)

10. Gary Orfield and Susan E. Eaton, "Back to Segregation," *The Nation,* March 3, 2003, 5 (stating that nearly 40 percent of black students in 2000 attended schools that were 90 to 100 percent black—up steadily from a low of 32 percent in 1988. In 2000, about one-sixth of blacks attended schools where 1 percent or less of their fellow students were white).

11. Kevin Dougherty, "How Monochromatic Is Church Membership? Racial Ethnic Diversity in Religious Community," *Sociology of Religion* 64, no. 1 (Spring 2003): 65–85; also available at http://www.findarticles.com/p/articles/mi_SOR/is_1_64/ai_99984518 (last visited Oct. 26, 2004).

12. It is the author's observation in traveling that resorts, beaches, cruise ships, and hotels are racially segregated. Many local minorities use public beaches, while tourists and white people use beach fronts attached to hotel property. In most cases the beaches adjoining the hotels and resorts are public, but nonetheless they are managed as if they were private and therefore restricted.

13. See john a. powell, "Living and Learning: Linking Housing and Education," in john a. powell, *In Pursuit of a Dream Deferred: Linking Housing and Education Policy,* Gavin Kearney and Vina Kay, eds., 16–17 (New York: Peter Lang, 2001) (explaining *Milliken v. Bradley* and *Missouri v. Jenkins* from context of Court's failure to acknowledge responsibility of suburban communities to participate in urban desegregation plans).

Grutter society, which has sacrificed racial integration and accepted racial inequality in the process. The United States Supreme Court (The Court) decisions from the popular affirmative action battlegrounds of education, business, and employment will be used to demonstrate how the law and attitudes of the American people support the perpetuation of a segregated and unequal society, while extolling the virtues of integration. On several occasions in the past fifty years, the Court had opportunities to facilitate integration in schools, colleges, and universities; to promote equal employment opportunities; and to encourage the participation of excluded minorities in the nation's economic growth. Instead, time after time, the Court forfeited that opportunity and rendered decisions that perpetuated a separate and unequal America. I contend that on the many occasions discussed in this article, the Court got it wrong.

II. Why Are Our Public Schools and Society Still Segregated and Unequal Despite the Mandate of *Brown?*

The battleground was set with *Brown*.[14] Frankly, American society was not ready for desegregation in 1954, theoretically or realistically. *Brown* was the beginning of a revolution of thought that did not take root until the civil rights movement was in full force in the late sixties. It took over twenty years for Americans to digest and accept the idea that segregation was wrong, and It was not accepted without significant resistance. The American institution of slavery had been justified based upon the belief in the innate inferiority of African Americans, and that idea was part of the design of the American quilt in 1954. African Americans were still described using subhuman references, which failed to offend the sensibilities of the speaker or listener. It is hard to determine the exact moment of the transition, but minds were changed in the past fifty years and few Americans would openly and overtly resist integration of schools today because of their desire for segregation. Professor George Lipsitz, disagrees with this assertion in his book, *The Possessive Investment in Whiteness* where he argues,

14. See also *Brown v. Bd. of Educ.,* 98 F. Supp. 797 (D. Kan. 1951); *Briggs v. Elliott,* 98 F. Supp. 529 (E.D.S.C. 1951); *Belton v. Gebhart,* 32 Del. Ch. 343 (1952); *Davis v. County Sch. Bd.,* 103 F. Supp. 337 (E.D. Va. 1952). (These cases were combined to form *Brown* and involved four school districts in Kansas, South Carolina, Delaware, and Virginia. All had challenged school segregation and lost. The lower-court decisions found segregation had a substantial negative impact on the education of African American children, but would not order desegregation as remedy due to *Plessy.*)

Whiteness has a cash value: it accounts for advantages that come to individuals through profits made from housing secured in discriminatory markets, through the unequal educations allocated to children of different races, through insider networks that channel employment opportunities to the relatives and friends of those who have profited most from present and past racial discrimination, and especially through intergenerational transfers of inherited wealth that pass on the spoils of discrimination to succeeding generations.[15]

While I agree with Professor Lipsitz that whiteness has economic value, I do not think the decisions that result in segregation in the twenty-first century are made for the purpose of promoting segregation. Rather, segregation is a consequence of decisions made for a variety of reasons that are not directly related to the decision maker's desire to avoid integration. The Court has not found the benefit of integration sufficient to decide cases in a manner that promotes integration when individual decisions promote segregation.

A. The Court will not interfere with the individual choices that result in segregation.

Arguably, the pervasiveness of segregation is due to individual and group choices motivated by well-cloaked, unconscious racism.[16] The charge of racism is as taboo as support for segregation. As a result, legally and socially, racism is denied until it raises its ugly head in the most overt form—such as use of the N word.[17] Individuals are at liberty to make

15. George Lipsitz, *The Possessive Investment in Whiteness: How White People Profit from Identity Politics* (Philadelphia: Temple University Press, 1998).

16. See Charles Lawrence, "The Id, The Ego and Equal Protection: Reckoning with Unconscious Racism," *Stanford Law Review* 39 (January 1987): 317. (This article challenges the doctrine of discriminatory purpose established in the landmark case *Washington v. Davis*, 426 U.S. 229 [1976]. The discriminatory purpose doctrine requires plaintiffs challenging a facially neutral law to prove discriminatory purpose on the part of those responsible for enacting the law.)

17. See generally Randall Kennedy, *Nigger: The Strange Career of a Troublesome Word* (New York: Pantheon Books, 2002). Racism is also ignored or treated as nonexistent until recorded on videotape. See "Videotape: Nissan Fight to End Ties with Car Dealer Accused of Racism Crumpler Vows to Keep His Franchise; Hearings to Resume," *Virginian-Pilot & Ledger Star,* July 27, 1997, A1. (Kentucky Nissan dealership owner was videotaped while referring to an employee of his James City County trailer park as a "nigger"). Beth J. Harpaz, "Texaco Chair Apologizes for Racist Slurs," *The Columbian,* Nov. 7, 1996, D3 (Texaco executives referred to black workers as "niggers" and "black jelly beans," mocked a Kwanzaa celebration and destroyed documents concerning minority hiring).

choices that result in segregation, without supporting segregation or living with the label of racist. Repeatedly, the courts have upheld the exercise of individual liberty even when the result is increased segregation. Dorothy Roberts labeled this legal phenomenon the "priority paradigm" which recognizes that the American value of individual liberty takes priority over racial equality in our laws.[18] The result is that individual choices that result in segregation are upheld when challenged legally, as long as they are facially race neutral.[19]

For example, many white individuals choose to live in exclusive neighborhoods, designed to segregate by economics, if not specifically by race. Since whites earn more money than African Americans and Hispanics, and can afford houses in exclusive, expensive, suburban communities, the schools in those communities tend to be disproportionately white. If individuals are asked their reasons for their choices of community, the responses are facially race neutral. Whites choose to live in expensive suburbs because the school system is better, the structure of house, neighborhood, lot size, etc. was available in the suburb chosen and not in the city, the suburb is safer, and other race-neutral reasons. Many whites choosing the suburbs would be highly offended if their decision was charged with the racist purpose of promoting segregation, even if that is the effect of their choices. Sheryll Cashin made this statement about neighborhood choices and upward mobility:

> Choosing a neighborhood that separates one's family and oneself from "worse" elements farther down the economic scale has become the critical gateway to upward mobility. Like it or not, this is the established path to better schools, less crime, better services, and stable property values. We seem to understand, if not accept, that the opportunities and amenities available in a neighborhood, as well as responsiveness of local government to its needs, are often closely calibrated to its racial and economic makeup. We may not agree with this system. We may even decry its unfairness. But when it comes to

18. Dorothy Roberts, "The Pursuit of Social and Political Equality: The Priority Paradigm: Private Choices and the Limits of Equality," *University of Pittsburgh Law Review* 57 (Winter 1996): 363.

19. Ibid. For example, in *Milliken v. Bradley*, 418 U.S. 717 (1974), the Supreme Court would not order an interdistrict remedy in the Detroit Metropolitan Area because the individuals who fled to the suburbs had not participated in the injury to the Detroit schoolchildren or segregation of the Detroit Public schools. The Court in *Missouri v. Jenkins*, 515 U.S. 900 (1995) protected the right of white residents to live in the suburbs and avoid paying for desegregation plans in the inner city schools.

our personal choices about where to live, our primary motive is to maximize benefits and comfort for ourselves and our families.[20]

However, facially neutral choices are often cloaked racism. When *Brown* ordered the schools desegregated, the national uproar was over quality of education, with most whites in agreement that integration would lower the quality of education. When whites first started making choices to move to the suburbs for better schools, in 1954, the new suburban schools had no track records. What measure was used to distinguish between the suburban school and the newly integrated city schools then? It is quite likely that white was perceived as "better" and integrated was perceived as "worse." Fifty years after *Brown*, urban schools are full of poor people who are less well educated, and there is little doubt that school districts can be compared qualitatively based upon quantitative factors such as test scores, graduation rates, and college matriculation, and it can be safely said that many suburban schools are better than many urban schools. Race may have been more of a factor fifty years ago than it is now in the choice of communities; nonetheless, it is highly likely that race-based choices led to the dual school systems of quality suburban schools and weak urban schools we now have.

Since Americans do not support segregation, and schools are segregated based upon a series of individual choices rather than intentional discriminatory acts by government actors, should Americans tolerate segregated schools? If they are just a consequence of random individual choices, surely we are not powerless to redress the problem? If Americans do not support segregation and segregated schools, we are well posited to design integrated schools and communities. The courts have made it clear that residential segregation without state action will not be sufficient to sustain an action based upon discrimination and result in an order requiring desegregation of schools.[21] Furthermore, the Court of Appeals for the Sixth Circuit made it clear in *Milliken* that suburban school districts could not be made to participate in the remedy for the segregation in the urban communities to which they are related unless the suburban school district also discriminated.[22] Schools segregated

20. See Cashin, supra note 1, p.16.
21. For cases demonstrating that residential segregation provides insufficient basis for school desegregation order, see *Swann v. Charlotte-Mecklenburg Bd. of Educ.*, 402 U.S. 1 (1971) (holding that it must be found that state agents intentionally segregated schools in order for courts to intervene). See also *Keyes v. Sch. Dist. No.1*, 413 U.S. 189 (1973) (holding intent to segregate by school officials is necessary for desegregation order).
22. *Plessy v. Ferguson*, 163 U.S. 537 (1896).

based upon residential segregation stemming from individual choices, are not illegally segregated and cannot be forced to desegregate in Fourteenth Amendment actions.[23] Since individuals who would not support segregation made decisions that resulted in segregated schools, it is up to the decision makers to devise plans to undo the unintended result of segregated schools. While the courts will not order desegregation, an enlightened community that does not support segregation could decide that diversity is important to education, just as corporations are promoting diversity in the twenty-first century because it is the right thing to do and because it is good for business. Colleges and universities fought for and retained diversity in their student bodies despite stiff opposition and legal battles challenging affirmative action.

Americans could decide that integration of schools is important to an excellent education in kindergarten through grade twelve, just as they have in other arenas, and make it happen because it is the right thing to do and better for the entire community.

B. There was no clear mandate in Brown.

While *Brown* overruled the sixty-year-old separate-but-equal rule of *Plessy v. Ferguson*,[24] many agree *Brown* lacked a compelling mandate to the population to act, so it did not. When the issue of enforcement was brought before the court in *Brown II*,[25] the Court used the nebulous language, "all deliberate speed" to define the time frame within which school districts had to desegregate their schools.[26] Ralph Frazier, in a speech at The Ohio State University to Minority Graduate and Professional Students, said African Americans focused on the word "speed" and expected all the students who walked past the white school to get to the African American school to be reassigned to the closer white school in the fall of 1954.[27] On

23. *See* powell, supra note 13, pp. 20–21 (Professor john a. powell discusses the potential of basing school desegregation cases on state constitutional actions, which are based upon "adequacy" not intent to discriminate).

24. *Plessy v. Ferguson,* 163 U.S. 537 (1896).

25. *Brown v. Bd. of Educ.,* 349 U.S. 294 (1955) (Brown was reargued on the question of relief).

26. Ibid. at 298. See also Linda S. Greene, "Race in the 21st Century: Equality through Law?" *Tulane Law Review* 64 (Autumn 1990): 1515, 1537.

27. Ralph Frazier, speech at The Ohio State University Minority Graduate and Professional Students' Welcome Banquet (Sept. 24, 2004). Ralph Frazier and his brother integrated the University of North Carolina (UNC) in 1955 pursuant to court order after winning the discrimination lawsuit, *Frazier v. Board The University of North Carolina,* 134 F. Supp. 589 (Del

the other hand, white southerners designing and implementing desegregation plans focused on the word "deliberate," which meant they took
careful, unhurried, well thought-out action.

Dynamically, the will of the community to resist integration, and the
lack of determination in the message from the Court, merged into an
overriding attitude of laissez faire. Four years after the *Brown* decision,
the Little Rock School District went back to court and sought a post-
ponement of a plan for desegregation adopted by the board because the
extreme public hostility in the community would render integration of
the high school impossible.[28] In Prince Edward County, Virginia, instead
of desegregating schools, all public schools were shut down and public
funds were used to support private schools for whites only.[29] School districts all over the country maintained their segregated schools until they
were specifically ordered to do otherwise. Every step in the process had
to be litigated all the way to the highest court possible, and long delays
were more common than immediate desegregation.[30] That resulted in a
series of lawsuits for the next fifty years challenging dual school systems
all over the nation, or, in turn, challenging continued judicial oversight
of prior court orders.

Columbus, Ohio, for example, maintained a dual and segregated
school system for twenty-four years after the *Brown* decision.[31] Nothing in
the *Brown* decision made the school system feel compelled to integrate.[32]

1955), aff'd, *University of North Carolina v. Frazier,* 350 U.S. 979 (1956). (Although the Court
affirmed Frazier's right to integrate UNC, he and his brother later transferred to the historically
black college, North Carolina Central University.)

28. *Cooper v. Aaron,* 358 U.S. 1 (1958), *aff'd* 257 F.2d 33 (8th Cir. 1958), *rev.g,* 163 F. Supp.
13 (E.D. Ark. 1958).

29. *Griffin v. County Sch. Bd.,* 377 U.S. 218 (1964).

30. See also *Bradley v. Sch. Bd. of Virginia,* 382 U.S. 103 (1965). (The Court noted litigation had been ongoing for several years and further indicated that further delays related to the
desegregation of the schools would be intolerable.) There were other cases where the judicial
system was strategically used to delay desegregation of the schools included.

31. After the *Brown* decision, Columbus changed its laws so that school districts were no
longer changed whenever property was annexed to the city. Prior to *Brown* school districts and
city limit lines were contiguous and when the city annexed land to the city, the school district
lines were simultaneously changed to conform to the annexation. After *Brown,* the school district lines were a separate decision from the decision to annex property to the city. The result
of this practice, over time, is that many Columbus communities have school districts that are
part of a suburban school system. See Ohio Revised Code § 3311.06 (effective Sept. 29, 1955)
(stating "When territory is annexed to a city which comprises a part but not all of the territory
of a school district, the said territory shall become a part of the city school district only upon
approval by the State Board of Education.")

32. Gregory S. Jacobs, *Getting Around Brown: Desegregation, Development and the Columbus
Public Schools* (Columbus: The Ohio State University Press, 1998), 15–51 (describing how the

The city had to be sued[33] and in turn used significant public resources to wage a difficult legal battle to maintain a segregated school system. After only seven years of busing for desegregation, Columbus followed the course of similarly situated school districts and was declared a unitary school system and judicial oversight was withdrawn.[34] Ten years later, the school board adopted a student reassignment plan that was hailed as an end to forced busing.[35] Twenty-five years after *Penick,* 85 percent of the students in Columbus attended schools that were predominantly African American, and public schools in Columbus were still segregated. If the Court had sent a clearer message, and if the named school district of Little Rock had in fact integrated the schools immediately, the response of the rest of the nation, including Columbus, Ohio, might have been different. For example, when the Court of Appeals for the Fifth Circuit (Fifth Circuit) said that race could not be used as a factor in admissions in *Hopwood,* colleges all over the Fifth Circuit redesigned their admission practices immediately and the number of African American and Hispanic students attending those institutions declined dramatically in the incoming class following the decision. The dismantling of affirmative action happened as quickly in the states within the Fifth Circuit's jurisdiction as Ralph Frazier expected the dismantling of segregation to occur all over the nation after *Brown.* Apparently, the speed with which the system worked to implement the court orders depended upon whether white privilege was being infringed upon or preserved.[36]

C. The Court failed to include suburban school districts in the remedy for state supported segregation of urban schools.

School desegregation could have taken on an entirely different character if suburban school districts would have participated in desegregation plans. Detroit attempted to include suburbs in the desegregation plan by order of the district court when the plans submitted were found woefully

---

Columbus School Board and the city maintained a segregated school system until ordered to integrate in *Penick*).

33. The Columbus School desegregation case, *Penick v. Columbus Board of Education,* 429 F. Supp. 229 (1977), was filed after years of effort by African American Board members and community to get the Columbus School Board to voluntarily formulate a desegregation plan.

34. Judge Duncan said the city of Columbus was one of the most desegregated school systems in the country. *Penick et. al. v. Columbus Board of Education et al.,* April 11,1985, at 3.

35. Ibid. at 204.

36. Cheryl I. Harris, "Whiteness as Property," *Harvard Law Review* 106 (June 1993): 1707.

inadequate. The final plan submitted and approved by the district court included Detroit and fifty-three other school districts in surrounding suburbs.[37] The Court of Appeals for the Sixth Circuit agreed the metropolitan plan was correct and that an interdistrict remedy could correct only the wrongful acts by the state.[38] The Court reversed reasoning that since the disparate treatment of white and African American students occurred within the Detroit school system and resulted in no significant segregative effect in suburban school districts, the remedy had to be limited to the Detroit school system.[39]

Milliken proved disastrous to school desegregation, since, as the district court in *Milliken* knew, an intradistrict plan would result in an all African American school system, a prophecy that came true in Detroit and all over the country when intradistrict plans were implemented.[40] Later in *Missouri v. Jenkins,*[41] the Court strengthened the message that the role of the court was not to ensure meaningful integration and certainly not to spend exorbitant amounts of money to achieve that end.[42] Using the same logic as the *Milliken* Court, the Court in *Jenkins* reasoned that the improvements recommended were insufficiently related to past segregation and were therefore beyond the federal court's discretion to implement.[43] The message of *Jenkins* was clear. Not only will we not force white suburbanites to participate in an interdistrict plan, such as the one proposed in *Milliken,* but we will not unduly burden suburban taxpayers with the price tag for improving the quality of the illegally segregated schools, as proposed in the *Jenkins* plan. After *Jenkins,* the federal courts became even further removed from the solution to the school desegregation issue.

Why was *Milliken,* and later *Jenkins,* so devastating to school desegregation? The answer is evident in the district and appellate court's reasons for first demanding, then supporting an interdistrict plan in *Milliken.*

37. *Milliken v. Bradley,* 418 U.S. at 732.
38. *Milliken v. Bradley,* 484 F. 2d 215, 245 (6th Cir. 1973).
39. *Milliken v. Bradley,* 418 U.S. at 747–52.
40. See Cashin, supra note 1, pp. 212–13.
41. *Missouri v. Jenkins,* 515 U.S. 70 (1995).
42. See Cashin, supra note 1, pp. 215–16. ("In the *Jenkins* case, the district court's desegregation plan required every high school, every middle school, and half of the elementary schools in the school system to become magnet schools. The cost of making the schools attractive enough to retain white students had exceeded $200 million annually, and the state legislature that had been ordered to pay the bill was crying out for relief. The Supreme Court emphasized that the goal of district courts is to remedy desegregation to the 'extent practicable' and to restore local authority over the school system.")
43. *Jenkins,* 515 U.S. at 87.

The interdistrict remedy provides an opportunity for actual integration of public schools. The intradistrict remedy inevitably results in an even more segregated urban school system.

As noted earlier, individual choices result in residential segregation. Does that necessarily mean that schools should be segregated also? If schools were segregated by the illegal actions of city and state government actors, reasonable minds certainly could differ on the power of the state and the courts to use any means necessary, including a metropolitan plan or a costly magnet school program, to rectify the ills of such discrimination. The decision in *Milliken* was five to four, which definitely suggests there were persuasive arguments on both sides of the issue. The Court got it wrong and the result is the Detroit Public schools, far from being integrated, were over 90 percent African American in 2004, and the Kansas City schools are still failing their students academically and have not attracted suburban or higher-income students to the district. The decisions sewed the disparity in education received by the rich and the poor into our national quilt, and it has become an embarrassing part of our national legacy. One of the most powerful and richest nations in the world runs a segregated school system and fails to provide a quality education to an alarming number of its African American students who live in urban areas.

D. The Court required intent to demonstrate discrimination.

In *Washington v. Davis*,[44] the Court established the doctrine of discriminatory purpose, which requires the plaintiffs challenging the constitutionality of a law or practice that is race neutral on its face to prove a racially discriminatory purpose on the part of the entity or individual responsible for enactment of the law or practice. For all practical applications, discriminatory purpose is a synonym for discriminatory intent, and the law was well established in 2004, that discriminatory intent is necessary to support the unconstitutionality of a facially neutral law, even if the law has a racially disproportionate impact.[45]

---

44. *Washington v. Davis,* 426 U.S. 229 (1976). (Plaintiff's arguments that disparate impact which is a foreseeable consequence of the action is sufficient to support a constitutional violation was rejected by the Supreme Court. See also *Columbus Bd. of Educ. v. Penick,* 443 U.S. at 464 stating " . . . disparate impact and foreseeable consequences, without more, do not establish a constitutional violation.")

45. Lawrence, supra note 16, p. 318.

In *Keyes v. School District No. 1*,[46] the Court dispelled any doubt that the discriminatory intent rule would be applied to school desegregation cases. Furthermore, the Court did not give any clear indicators of what actions would satisfy the "intent" requirement. As in *Brown,* when the Court used the nebulous language "all deliberate speed" as a guideline for implementing the school desegregation order, the Court in *Keyes* gave little direction to plaintiff's lawyers on what would be required to prove intent. Instead the Court said that the necessary degree of state involvement is incapable of precise definition and as a result there are no per se answers to the question of what or how much action is required.[47]

Fortunately, the Court did recognize that it might be difficult to prove "subjective" discriminatory intent given the unlikelihood that public officials would confess to discriminatory motives in the seventies, with the same liberty they would have been comfortable with in the fifties and before. Discriminatory intent can be inferred from objective evidence, which analyzes the totality of the relevant facts. Despite this concession, of sorts, these questions still need to be asked: "Why require a showing of intent at all? Why does the court need more than disparate impact which is the foreseeable consequence of the action?" It is not clear why intent is the mandate except as a further attempt to exculpate Americans from any guilt associated with racism and the racial inequity that results from it. If we legally define acts as nonracist, then society is free from the burden of the racial inequity that persists in our society today. If the law so narrowly defines racism that only the most overt conduct is included as culpable activity, and the law requires no redress unless intentional individual action is proven, then there is no personal or public responsibility for segregation or its effects. Denial of racism makes it easier to blame African Americans for poor schools, poor academic performance, poverty, unemployment, lack of wealth, and a host of other social ills for which society does not care to accept responsibility.

E. The Court failed to recognize benign discrimination.

University of California v. Bakke[48] paved the way for affirmative action programs in institutions of higher education throughout the nation. Colleges and universities used the diversity rationale in the *Bakke* decision

---

46. *Keyes v. Sch. Dist. No. 1,* 413 U.S. 189 (1973).
47. Ibid. at 215.
48. *Univ. of California v. Bakke,* 438 U.S. 265 (1978).

to shape admissions programs that included race as one among many factors that contribute to establishing a diverse student body, and thereby promote the academic missions of the institutions. The assertion that the Court got it all wrong in *Bakke* might come as a surprise to many colleges and universities who utilize the decision to maintain the legality of their affirmative action plans designed to promote racial diversity.

The Court forfeited an opportunity to recognize benign discrimination in the *Bakke* case. The Court rejected the argument that strict scrutiny should only be used for racial classification when it disadvantages discreet and insular minorities.[49] Instead of holding true to the intent of the drafters of the Fourteenth Amendment, which was adopted to protect the rights of the newly freed slaves, the Court used the law to protect the rights of the beneficiaries of overt legally sanctioned discrimination, and acknowledged the right of a white male to use the Fourteenth Amendment to defeat a program designed to benefit the intended beneficiaries of the Fourteenth Amendment.[50] The Court emphasized,

> [T]he denial to innocent persons of equal rights and opportunities may outrage those so deprived and therefore may be perceived as invidious. These individuals are likely to find little comfort in the notion that the deprivation they are asked to endure is merely the price of membership in the dominant majority and that its imposition is inspired by the supposedly benign purpose of aiding others. One should not lightly dismiss the inherent unfairness of, and the perception of mistreatment that accompanies a system of allocating benefits and privileges on the basis of skin color and ethnic origin.[51]

The Court was more interested in the comfort, outrage, and perception of mistreatment of the white students than in providing opportunities to students who were members of a group that had been historically discriminated against by the institution and the society. In *Bakke,* integration took second fiddle to the hurt feelings of white students.

49. Ibid. at 287–88.

50. In *Wygant v. Jackson Board of Education,* 476 U.S. 267 (1986), Justice Powell reiterated the view taken in *Bakke,* that the standard of review does not change when the challenged classification operates against a group who has suffered historical discrimination. Ibid. at 273. He emphasized that innocent people should not bear the burden of remedying past discrimination. Ibid. at 281.

51. *Bakke,* 438 U.S. at 295.

The Court addressed the benign discrimination issue again in the *City of Richmond v. Croson* case.[52] In *Croson,* the Court held that the standard of review in evaluating equal protection claims would not change when the race of those burdened or those benefited changes. The Court emphasized that it is impossible to evaluate which racial classifications are benign and which are motivated by illegitimate notions of racial inferiority or simple racial politics.[53] It is hard to tell if the Court was concerned about the feelings of white people or minorities when it asserted that all racial classifications bring the threat of stigmatic harm and may promulgate racial hostility and ideas of racial inferiority unless they are only used for remedial purposes.

While I have often heard the "stigma" argument against affirmative action proposed by whites, I have rarely heard African Americans assert that they would rather not have an opportunity to be awarded a government contract, for example, than deal with the stigma of being given an advantage in the bidding process due to an affirmative action program. Although the Court recognized that a "sorry history of both private and public discrimination in this country has contributed to a lack of opportunities for black entrepreneurs,"[54] that sorry history was not enough to recognize benign discrimination and thereby uphold the constitutionality of minority business enterprise programs. Again, in *Adarand Constructors, Inc. v. Pena,*[55] the Court rejected the idea of holding benign racial classifications to a lower constitutional standard of scrutiny. After *Adarand,* it was clear the Court would not recognize benign discrimination in local, state, or federal Fourteenth Amendment claims.

One hundred years after the Fourteenth Amendment was adopted to protect the rights of newly freed slaves, it was used to defeat programs designed to promote racial equity and social justice, because of the burden those programs placed on the majority group that benefited most from the discrimination. When South Africa adopted its equal protection clause, it had the history of affirmative action in the United States at its disposal. The South African constitution specifically provides that the equal protection clause will not be used to defeat programs designed to benefit groups that have been historically discriminated against.[56] Hopefully, the experience of African Americans with the Fourteenth Amend-

52. *City of Richmond v. Croson,* 488 U.S. 469 (1989).
53. Ibid. at 493.
54. Ibid. at 499.
55. *Adarand Constructors, Inc. v. Pena,* 515 U.S. 200 (1995).
56. See generally Constitution of the Republic of South Africa.

ment will not be repeated one hundred years from now when and if the South African equal protection clause is challenged based upon reverse discrimination.

F. The Court made it impossible to prove racism and discrimination.

Bakke also got it wrong because diversity was used as the compelling state interest that justified the use of race in the admissions process. The University of California discriminated against African Americans just as surely as the Court permitted such discrimination in *Plessy v. Ferguson*. Why should the foundation for the Fourteenth Amendment compelling interest be diversity instead of historical race discrimination? The *Bakke* Court rejected the use of race-conscious preferences as a means of remedying past societal discrimination in the absence of evidence of specific, race-based injuries to individuals. Instead, in a split decision, the Court determined that colleges and universities had a compelling interest in a diverse environment for education and race was one factor that could be considered in establishing diversity.

The diversity foundation for the decision has created a host of illogical results, such as the Fifth Circuit decision in *Hopwood*,[57] in which in order to defeat affirmative action in Texas universities and consequently in all of the Fifth Circuit, the Court determined that race did not contribute to diversity.[58] The result in *Hopwood* is as preposterous as the result in *Plessy v. Ferguson*. It is equally as obvious that "separate but equal" does not provide equal protection of the law, as it is that race contributes to diversity of thought. Racial groups, physically isolated by law for hundreds of years, and segregated for the past fifty years by individually protected choices, will necessarily develop different cultures and points of view as a result of the limited interaction with one another, if not for a host of other reasons.[59] The diversity rationale in *Bakke* opened the window of opportunity for a court so inclined, like the *Hopwood* court,

57. *Hopwood v. Texas,* 248 F.3d 1141 (5th Cir. 2001).

58. For discussion deriding benefits of diversity see various articles by Roger Clegg, *National Review Online,* http://www.nationalreview.com. Clegg criticizes the Texas Ten Percent Plan as being inspired by desire to promote racial diversity, and is thereby rendered racially discriminatory. See Roger Clegg, "If College Quotas Are Stuck, Percentage Rule Could Offer New Hopes—And Problems," *Fulton County Daily Report* 114, no. 29 (February 12, 2003).

59. See Vincene Verdun, "If the Shoe Fits Wear It: An Analysis of Reparations to African Americans," *Tulane Law Review* 67 (February 1993): 612–19.

to aggravate the wrong of discrimination, by getting it even more wrong by defining race out of diversity.

One of the fortunate things about *Hopwood* is that it resulted in a race-neutral selection process in Texas that has been copied in other states. The ten percent rule guarantees the top ten percent of students, based upon grades, from high schools all over Texas admission into a state college or university. Many have declared the program a great success since the number of African American and Hispanic students has increased to their pre-*Hopwood* levels. Already, the ten percent system is under attack. Detractors claim that the ten percent rule is just a proxy for race and that many deserving Texans are going out of state for college because their places were taken by the students who were admitted with the ten percent rule. Such criticisms reek with overtones of white privilege and the assumption that white students are entitled to the seats currently taken by minorities.

Hopwood is not the only decision affected by the diversity rationale in *Bakke*. *Gratz v. Bollinger*,[60] the companion case to *Grutter*, ultimately decided the undergraduate admissions program at the University of Michigan, which included a point system, was unconstitutional. The Citizens for Affirmative Action's Preservation, defendant interveners in that case, argued that the undergraduate admissions program should pass constitutional muster because it is a narrowly tailored means of remedying past discrimination by the University of Michigan. The district court addressed the historical discrimination rationale of the interveners in a separate opinion devoted to that issue.[61] The first hurdle the interveners had to jump was whether the admissions policy for the university was, in fact, motivated to redress historical and current discrimination with their policy. That proved difficult to do, because the University of Michigan had adopted the constitutionally safe, *Bakke* diversity rationale to support its admissions programs. Nowhere in their policy had the University of Michigan even mentioned historical or present discrimination. The court concluded that defendant interveners had not met the burden of demonstrating that the real or even shared justification for the admissions policy was discrimination.[62] Most university admissions policies after *Bakke* used the *Bakke* diversity rationale as the justification for their programs. Discrimination was thereby divorced from the remedy. Ironically, throughout the nation, use of the *Bakke* diversity rationale

60. *Gratz v. Bollinger,* 539 U.S. 244 (2003).
61. *Gratz v. Bollinger,* 135 F. Supp. 2d 790 (E.D. Mich. 2001).
62. Ibid. at 794–96.

made affirmative action in college admissions distinct from the pervasive historical discrimination that contributed to the need for affirmative action. The irony is even greater in Texas, where the challenged affirmative action plan did not mention the historical discrimination that surely could have been documented, and instead relied on the *Bakke* diversity test, and the Court found it unconstitutional to use race as a factor in establishing a diverse student body.

The interveners in the University of Michigan case produced significant evidence of historical discrimination. They provided evidence of the miniscule number of African Americans admitted to the university prior to 1969, the refusal to integrate dorms, racist exclusionary clauses in student organization charters, admonitions from the federal government regarding compliance with Title VI, and students' concerns and charges of discrimination documented in several studies over the years. The long history of discrimination was discounted while the Court instead focused on proof of discrimination by the admissions department. The Court defined discrimination as "outright exclusion" and "discriminatory impact" by admissions policies. The Court pointed out that all of the discriminatory activities took place long before the challenged admissions policy was put into place, and further found statistical disparities in state high school graduation rates compared with university enrollment unacceptable as a means of demonstrating current effects of past discrimination based upon the rationale in the *Croson* case. The district court said, "As the Supreme Court has acknowledged, there is no doubt that the sorry history of both private and public discrimination in this country has contributed to the lack of opportunities for African Americans. That observation, however, by itself, is not sufficient to justify race-conscious measures."[63]

It is mind-boggling that it has become impossible to prove discrimination, historical or current, in a society when all agree discrimination was a stark feature in our history and that it still exists. In *Croson,* the Court said the city of Richmond could not admit to historical discrimination, it had to prove it in order to justify the use of race in a city minority business enterprise program designed to increase the number of city dollars spent with minority businesses. The Court went further to indicate that it was not enough to demonstrate a disparity in the racial makeup of the community when compared with the dollars spent with minority contractors. Instead the Court insisted the relevant comparison

63. Ibid. at 801 (citing *Croson,* 488 U.S. at 499).

was between the available pool of minority contractors and the dollars spent with minority contractors by the city. When that measure is considered from a practical perspective it makes no sense. Why would minority contractors make themselves available to do work for the city of Richmond when they are fully aware that the work is not available? How could a pool of contractors prepare themselves for such availability when the trade unions discriminated against minority apprentices which made entry into the industry impossible? By cutting discrimination into little isolated pieces and not connecting the various parts of the puzzle that could lead to lack of an available pool of minority contractors at any given point in time, the Court made it impossible to prove discrimination. It is not clear why any parent would encourage their child to go into contracting, with hopes of gaining work from the city of Richmond at a time when there was little hope of getting a contract because of racial discrimination. Without hope for obtaining work, the available pool of minority contractors would necessarily be nonexistent, which in turn makes discrimination impossible to prove under the *Croson* test.

With mountains of evidence of discrimination in the city of Richmond, the capital of the Confederacy, the Court rejected a finding of historical discrimination as a foundation for race-based affirmative action. With a boatload of evidence of discrimination on the part of the University of Michigan, the district court used the *Croson* rule to find there was insufficient evidence to find historical discrimination or current effects of historical discrimination at the University of Michigan. The courts have made historical discrimination impossible to prove by narrowly defining the wrongdoer so that most evidence is unrelated to the very particularized activity the court is scrutinizing. It was necessary to find discrimination on the part of the Admissions office, not the University as a whole. The city of Richmond must find discrimination in its procurement process, not in the city as a whole. Such narrow definitions of discrimination render using historical discrimination impossible as a foundation for race-based programs, and the court says, too bad, so sad, no remedy for you today.

What is the impact of making racism, known to exist, impossible to prove? Perhaps it eliminates racism altogether from our society. Since the Court says that the city of Richmond did not discriminate, that means it is not guilty. Furthermore, since racism is impossible to prove, all of America is not guilty for historical and continued discrimination, which means that African Americans must be responsible for their plight, not the American society. Inoculation of society from responsibility for the ills of racism leads to arguments that inequities based upon race are because of defects in the race.

G. The Court terminated federal court intervention in school desegregation cases.

After a period of slow desegregation of schools throughout the country, a process that took over thirty years, levels of integration in public schools reached an all-time high in the 1980s.[64] With the speed on full throttle and school districts all over the nation responding to court-ordered monitoring of desegregation plans, the court retrenched.[65] Starting with the landmark case of *Oklahoma City School Board v. Dowell,*[66] the Court ended federal court intervention in school desegregation. *Dowell* and the series of cases that followed it are appropriately called the resegregation cases. Once the district court[67] found the school district had operated within the parameters permissible under the Fourteenth Amendment, the purpose of desegregation was fully achieved and there was no more need for Court intervention.[68] *Missouri v. Jenkins* followed *Dowell* and together the cases sent a new message to school districts all over the nation. According to Sheryll Cashin:

> Within a year of the *Jenkins* decision, school districts across the nation were scrambling to get the benefit of the case's relaxed standard; it was now much easier for school districts to get out from under desegregation orders and to weaken their integration efforts. . . . Researchers found that as federal courts eased oversight of school desegregation

64. Margaret Graham Tebo, "Are Schools Returning to the 1950's," *American Bar Association Journal* (April 2004): 50–51. (Percentage of Black students in majority white schools rose from none in 1954 to 43.5% in 1988. After removal of court oversight only 30.2% of black students attended integrated schools in 2001.)

65. See Bell, supra note 1, pp. 125–27. See also Cashin, supra note 1, p.215 (the retreat from *Brown* started with *Dowell*).

66. *Oklahoma Bd. of Educ. v. Dowell,* 498 U.S. 237 (1991).

67. See 778 F. Supp. 1144 (1991).

68. In *Freeman v. Pitts,* 503 U.S. 467 (1992), the Supreme Court decided the school system achieved unitary status even though it was still segregated upon a showing that racial imbalance was due to demographic changes. In *Missouri v. Jenkins,* 515 U.S. 70 (1995), the Supreme Court sent the clear message that schools did not have to overextend themselves economically to remedy the effects of past de jure segregation.

programs in the early 1990's, the percentage of minority students in schools with a substantial white enrollment fell appreciably. [69]

Once the oversight of a court is removed, after a school system has earned the status of unitary, the school district is then free to reassign students based upon neighborhoods, eliminate busing, and in some school districts, effectively resegregate the schools. After they achieved unitary status, school districts were free to take actions that resulted in resegregation, as long as those actions, when evaluated separately, would overcome a new challenge of constitutionality.

The theory supporting removal of court supervision of schools was that the unconstitutional effects that caused segregation had been cured and the supervision of the courts was no longer needed. A finding that the system was unitary washed the old wrong away. Any new action would have to sustain the *Washington v. Davis* and *Keyes* discriminatory intent standard in order to support a constitutional challenge. The discriminatory intent requirement was much more difficult to demonstrate in 2004 than it was in 1954. Few school districts that had gone through a desegregation lawsuit and years of judicial intervention would be likely to fall prey to a finding of discriminatory intent in the twenty-first century. Lawyers carefully scrutinize laws and actions to make sure they are facially neutral with race-neutral reasons supporting them. The combination of awarding unitary status to school districts and the requirement of finding discriminatory intent in order to support a Fourteenth Amendment violation, dovetailed with the narrow standards now applied to a finding of racial discrimination, means school districts can rest on their laurels after federal supervision is withdrawn. Schools can remain separate and unequal with little likelihood of successful legal challenge in the twenty-first century.

III. Conclusion

We deal here with the right of all of our children, whatever their race, to an equal start in life and to equal opportunity to reach their full potential as citizens. Those children who have been denied that right in the past deserve better than to see fences thrown up to deny them that right in

69. *Cashin,* supra note 1, pp. 216–17 (citing Peter Applebome, "Schools See Re-emergence of 'Separate But Equal,'" *N.Y. Times,* April 8, 1997, A10). See also Gary Orfield, *"Brown* at 50: King's Dream or *Plessy's* Nightmare," Harvard Civil Rights Project (Jan. 2004).

the future. Unless our children begin to learn together there is little hope that our people will ever learn to live together.[70]

U.S. Supreme Court Justice Thurgood Marshall observed twenty-five years after *Brown,* what was clear to him at the time he argued *Brown* before the Supreme Court. There are many benefits of an integrated education, not the least of which is that people learn to live with each other. Fifty years after *Brown,* seven out of ten minority students attend predominantly minority schools and most white students attend schools that are eighty percent white.[71] Given the history of this country, whether school segregation caused residential segregation or vice versa is a chicken-and-egg argument. The roots of separation and the history of inequality run deep in America. In *Brown,* an integrated education system was equated with an egalitarian system. Fifty years after *Brown,* American schools are not integrated and the race of the child is largely determinative of the quality of education a child receives.

This essay began with the assertion that the hearts and minds of the American people have been won over on the issue of segregation. The body of this essay proceeded to describe a series of personal and U.S. Supreme Court decisions that have contributed to our schools and our society remaining segregated and unequal. It would be easy to challenge the sincerity of the first statement, given the series of decisions made by the American people that followed the *Brown* decision. The dilemma is that while Americans truly oppose segregation and would not tolerate the forced separation of the races, Americans have no true dedication to integration. There is a "big disconnect" between segregation and integration. Only the extremists actually want to experience exclusively white or black facilities, whether public or private. On the other hand, individuals make choices that reap an immediate benefit to themselves and their families. Their decisions may not be inspired by a desire to segregate, but segregation is a result.

The reasons for segregative choices are dynamic. It would be too easy to suggest that the reasons are purely economic. For example, people choose homes in neighborhoods that offer qualities they think maximize their enjoyment of their homes. However, it is an understatement to say that white people are wealthier and thereby choose more expensive homes, which exclude African Americans who have less wealth and income as a group. Wealth is a factor in choice, but it does not explain

70. Thurgood Marshall, counsel in the *Brown* case, wrote these words as a justice of the Supreme Court in his dissenting opinion in the *Milliken v. Bradley* case.

71. Cited in Cashin, supra note 1, p. 218.

why African Americans who can afford homes in upper-middle-class white neighborhoods might choose instead to live in upper-middle-class African American neighborhoods, or why whites who can choose between upper-middle-class African American neighborhoods and similar white neighborhoods, choose the white neighborhood.[72]

Furthermore, there is little explanation for why our governments allow economically exclusive neighborhoods to be developed in the first place, when developers and local governments are familiar with the benefits of fair housing and the burdens of poverty-stricken ghettos. Even equipped with knowledge, exclusive communities are being developed as I write these words, despite the detrimental social consequences.

There are a few things we can rely upon when assessing this problem. First and foremost is that the Court will not help us integrate our schools or promote racial justice. Second, forced integration will have limited success and will be met with resistance just as it was after *Brown*. If America is to achieve racial integration, a quality education for all children and racial justice, the people must decide they want those things. That does not mean giving lip service to an idea when a poll is taken. The public must "will" a quality education for all children. The public must "will" integration. The public must "will" racial justice.

Colleges and universities all over the country decided they wanted racial integration of their campuses in 1969. They made it happen through recruitment efforts, affirmative action policies in admissions, and whatever else worked. Nine years after integration began, when the Court let the nation down in the *Bakke* decision, colleges and universities remained steadfast in their resolve to maintain racial integration and adapted their admissions policies to conform to the diversity mandate in *Bakke*. Twenty-five years after *Bakke,* the University of Michigan fought with all its heart to retain the diversity mandate of *Bakke* and won. Even when the Fifth Circuit misinterpreted *Bakke* and common sense, and ruled that race was not a diversity factor, Texas adopted a race-neutral percent rule, which resulted in some level of racial integration. There is a commitment to racial integration in higher education because the entire industry has bought into the concept that it is good, right, just, and perhaps more fun.

Imagine what would happen if the average American citizen, school district, board of education, developer, local and state government actually bought into the concept of racial integration in the same way that

---

72. See generally, j. a. powell, *In Pursuit of a Dream Deferred: Linking Housing and Education Policy,* Kearney and Kay, eds. (New York: Peter Lang, 2001).

colleges and universities have. What if we had counties fighting with all their heart to provide the children in their districts with a racially diverse experience in kindergarten through grade twelve? Could we not develop metropolitan school districts that incorporated suburban and urban schools as was contemplated by the district court and school administrators in the *Milliken* case? If we really wanted to provide every student with a quality education, couldn't we devise a system to pay for education that provided a more equitable distribution of resources than the school district property tax system?

The problem, obviously, is not that the issues are too complex for resolution, it is that we have not won the hearts and minds of the American people on the issue of integration. If Americans were convinced that integration was good for their children, that their children would receive a better education in an integrated environment, that children educated in a segregated environment are less creative, less able to adapt and achieve in an innovative and changing global environment, Americans would fight for integration. Colleges and universities were quick to catch on to the concept of racial integration and its benefits, even before they accepted the concept of diversity on many fronts. We now need to move that concept from higher education to all education, and then perhaps we can have "children who begin to learn together," which provides hope that people will "learn to live together."

CHAPTER 13

Brown v. Board of Education at Fifty

Where Are We Now?

JANINE HANCOCK JONES
AND CHARLES R. HANCOCK

On May 17, 2004, our nation celebrated the fiftieth anniversary of a landmark decision, *Brown versus the Board of Education of Topeka, Kansas*. This U.S. Supreme Court decision was an impressive unanimous vote. In the words of the Court, "We conclude that in the field of public education the doctrine of 'separate but equal' has no place. Separate educational facilities are inherently unequal. . . . It is doubtful that any child may reasonably be expected to succeed in life if he is denied the opportunity of an education" (*Brown v. Board of Education* [1954], 347 U.S. 483). This landmark decision was celebrated in 2004 throughout the country, and it is therefore appropriate that it also be written about in scholarly outlets such as this one. The primary goal of this essay is to build the case that *Brown* was and remains an important watershed moment in U.S. history, especially for those whose job it is to educate the next generations of collegiate Americans in small private institutions of higher learning and large public ones alike. Documentation for this chapter comes from the work of many researchers such as Williams (1988), Betances (1994), Delpit (1995), Suarez-Orozco (1995), Nieto (1996), Tatum (1997), Jacobs (1998), and Tushnet (2001). It is also based on public legal documents from the U.S. courts and other sources.

In 1954, the U.S. Supreme Court struck down the "separate but equal" doctrine of *Plessy v. Ferguson* that the Court had rendered in 1896. Unfortunately, even after this landmark decision, the *Brown I* decision needed to be reinforced in what is known as *Brown II* by an additional clarification in which the Court held that public schools must integrate "with all deliberate speed." Social conditions and failure to integrate public education necessitated follow-up legislation, especially in certain regions of the country where deliberate stalling tactics were widely implemented.

Now, more than fifty years later, a number of important questions must be asked: How far have we come in achieving equity in our U.S. school systems, colleges, and universities? Indeed, what are the implications of *Brown* for those who work in schools, colleges, and universities? Is creating and maintaining a diverse student body a priority value for educational institutions? And if the answer is a predictable "yes," then what are the necessary steps in recruiting, retaining, and graduating a diverse student body at all levels of the educational enterprise? How do contemporary students rate their current teachers and themselves low or high on a diversity climate scale? Is our U.S. society better off because of our collective educational efforts to provide access and opportunity for a solid academic education for all students?

Answers to the above questions can be found, in part, in the work of some of the most widely read social scientists and education writers of the past decade. For example, the works of Delpit, Sleeter, Betances, Jacobs, and Nieto suggest that we "have a long way to go before we can sleep." In other words, the aims of *Brown v. Board of Education* are far from having been achieved in the U.S., despite the half-century and more since the initial legislation was passed.

This essay explores some of the above questions and presents answers, but first a brief historical recap is needed to set the stage for treating such questions. In 1954, the year of *Brown I,*

- Public schools, colleges, and universities were, for the most part, separate for black and whites. By law, in the South, white students and black students attended separate schools [de jure]. By custom, in the North, it was typically the case that school attendance was separated along racial lines [de facto]. In today's U.S. society, of course, public schools cannot legally be separated by race.
- Schools for white and black students were almost always unequal no matter what evaluation measures were used.

- Many held that black students were "deprived of equal educational opportunity" through their "separate but equal schools."

At that time in history, Thurgood Marshall was one of the chief legal advisors for the National Association for the Advancement of Colored People (NAACP). He and other NAACP attorneys had assembled lawsuits from various areas of the country that might eventually be used collectively in a U.S. Supreme Court case to impact school attendance practices. We now recognize the defining case as in *Brown v. Board of Education* (May 17, 1954).

By 1965, some conditions had changed:

- The Civil Rights Act of 1964 had been passed by Congress.
- Restaurants, hotels, and other businesses that served the general public were legally required to serve all people without regard to race, color, religion, or national origin. The Civil Rights Act also banned discrimination in *voting, public accommodations, schools,* and *employment.* Also the Fifth and Fourteenth amendments to the Constitution forbade depriving a person of life, liberty, or property. An important principle of "due process" further mandated that the U.S. government treat each person fairly.

It is also important to note that the Fourteenth Amendment of the U.S. Constitution states, "No state shall make or enforce any law which shall abridge the privileges or immunities of citizens of the United States; nor shall any state deprive any person of life, liberty, or property, without due process of law; nor deny to any person within its jurisdiction the *equal protection of the laws*" (emphasis added). These last few words are the well-known "equal protection" clause that was at the heart of the *Brown* legal argument that swayed the Supreme Court justices and resulted in a unanimous decision in *Brown I.*

In 2001, President George W. Bush signed the No Child Left Behind Act. It required all K–12 schools that receive federal funding to "test students" to measure yearly academic progress, particularly in reading and mathematics. Tests to measure science achievement are predicted as the next set of tests to be developed and mandated. Each state in the U.S. determines which tests to use to measure student achievement, but most states have chosen to implement some type of standardized achievement test as an accountability measure.

With this brief historical recap as a context for the next section of the article, it is important to return to the *Brown I* decision of 1954. In that decision, Chief Justice Warren wrote: "It is doubtful that any child may reasonably be expected to succeed in life if he is denied the opportunity of an education. Such an opportunity is a right which must be made available to all on equal terms. . . . We conclude that, in the field of public education, the doctrine of 'separate but equal' has no place. Separate educational facilities are inherently unequal."

It is appropriate at this point to ask *if the United States is any better off as a result of the* Brown I *and* II *decisions?* And, at first glance, of course, it can be agreed that the country is better off now than it was before the *Brown* decision of 1954. With these decisions, our country removed a legal barrier to fair educational opportunities for all of its citizens, both black and white. However, a closer analysis of the current reality in the U.S. reveals that *Brown* set the stage for fundamental changes, some of which remain unachieved.

Thurgood Marshall was the champion of the cause. Because of his long and hard work, he was not only a key voice for integration in the U.S., including the public schools, but it is also now commonly acknowledged that he was subsequently appointed by President Lyndon Johnson to the U.S. Supreme Court because of his integration work and his strong record in winning cases presented to the Supreme Court. Justice Marshall was the first Black American to receive the honor of being appointed to the U.S. Supreme Court.

Now that fifty years have passed since the first *Brown v. Board of Education* ruling, it is indeed appropriate to celebrate Thurgood Marshall and all the other valiant individuals who fought for better schooling for all of our citizens, both black and white. We honor them today for their groundbreaking civil rights work. But where are we today on the issues that were the focus of Marshall's work and the important *Brown* decision?

One set of answers can be found in publications of the Civil Rights Project at Harvard University which in 2004 released a study showing that public schools, especially in the South, are becoming resegregated at surprising levels. Some scholars believe that *poor black children,* due largely to housing patterns and economics, *may be in a worse condition today* than in 1954 because the *Brown* decision at least guaranteed an equal education: " . . . opportunity of an education. Such an opportunity, where the state has undertaken to provide it, is a right which must be made available to all on an equal basis," wrote Chief Justice Earl Warren, writing for a unanimous Supreme Court in *Brown v. Board of Education.* And when this right was denied, there was a legitimate basis upon which legal action could be taken.

The NAACP with Thurgood Marshall's leadership changed the course of U.S. history. However, today, many ethnic and racial minorities are still trapped in separate and unequal schools. Sadly, *Brown v. Board of Education* is not fully living up to its aims.

Rosenberg (1991) and Reed (2001) have taken differing positions on the impact of *Brown v. Board of Education.* In a somewhat controversial book entitled *The Hollow Hope,* Rosenberg argued that in handing down the *Brown* ruling, the Supreme Court and lower courts achieved very little in terms of impacting the integration of schools. Reed took a different position in his examination of the *Brown* ruling on school funding issues. He has argued that *Brown* helped focus the nation's attention on the "harms of racial prejudice and discrimination" (Reed, 15).

We link these two authors together because Reed took issue with Rosenberg's contention that *Brown* "barely caused a blip in American political consciousness and activity" (Reed, 16). Indeed, Reed has written that his own book, *On Equal Terms: The Constitutional Policies of Educational Opportunity,* is "a rejoinder to Rosenberg" (Reed, 16). In particular, Reed's book demonstrates the meaningful effects the courts, including the Supreme Court ruling in *Brown v. Board of Education,* have had on school finance.

In a recent report entitled *A Multiracial Society with Segregated Schools: Are We Losing the Dream?* Frankenberg, Lee, and Orfield (2003) reported that U.S. schools are becoming more segregated. Nationally, U.S. school segregation is now at a 1969 level in some regions of the country. This is shocking in light of the primordial focus of *Brown v. Board of Education.* Some findings reported in this important study are worth reiterating here:

- In 2000 and 2001, the most segregated groups were white students; they typically attend schools with a student population of 80 percent or more white students.
- Desegregation for black students was increasing until the late 1980s; however, since then, many black students have ended up in segregated schools. Some scholars have identified the conditions in these segregated schools as being "apartheid-like." This is an alarming but largely accurate description.
- In 1967, many suburban school districts were primarily white; and that situation seems to be repeating itself in contemporary settings. For many U.S. communities, housing patterns are currently having a negative impact on school integration. This is,

unfortunately, true for both urban and suburban school districts nationwide, according to the Harvard Report (Frankenberg, Lee, Orfield, 2003).

- According to Frankenburg, Lee, and Orfield (2003), the largest growth in student population is among Latinos. Parenthetically, the authors wish to state that they have intentionally used the term *Latino* in this article, despite the fact that *Hispanic* is also commonly used in the professional literature. Subsequently, the term *Chicana* is used by the authors to denote a female of Mexican or Mexican American origin. These are not unimportant name reference choices by the authors. From 1994 to 2004, Latinos grew 45 percent, from 22.4 million to 32.4 million students. This group is the most segregated group and shows signs of becoming more segregated by language and cultural traditions. Unfortunately, it must be reported that Latinos also have the highest school dropout rates, especially in P–12 school settings. The data show that heavy school dropout rates are increasing for Latino male students, especially young middle school Latino males.

- The fastest trend towards resegregation for black students in the U.S. is occurring in the South, where these students attend increasingly segregated schools. States considered to be in the South are: Alabama, Arkansas, Florida, Georgia, Louisiana, Mississippi, North Carolina, South Carolina, Tennessee, Texas, and Virginia. Schools in the West: Arizona, California, Colorado, Montana, Nevada, New Mexico, Oregon, Utah, Washington, and Wyoming.

In 2003, the Supreme Court decided the now commonly known *Grutter v. Bollinger* case by upholding the University of Michigan Law School diversity policies related to admissions procedures. The Court declared that diversity is a significant state interest. In 2002, school vouchers gave students who attended what were termed "failing" public schools the option to attend private or parochial schools. Also in 2002, President George W. Bush signed into law the No Child Left Behind (NCLB) Act, patterning his education agenda, at least in name, after the work of Marian Wright Edelman of the Children's Defense Fund. Interestingly, however, President Bush's education agenda focuses on testing for accountability, while Dr. Edelman's agenda is well known for its emphasis on helping children. This is not an insignificant distinction.

President Bush announced that NCLB was necessary because "too many of our neediest children are being left behind." He also announced that this law, designed as a basis for education reform, was designed to improve student achievement and change the culture of America's schools. However, the problem with NCLB is that it punishes schools when students do not make "adequate yearly progress" as measured specifically by standardized achievement tests administered at different grade levels, especially in reading and mathematics. The harsh sanctions required by NCLB against so-called "failing schools" are very likely to be counterproductive. Reaction across the country to NCLB is raising serious questions about its merits and the need for greater funding to support NCLB.

Reasonable people and particularly those who care about public schools in this country are also raising serious questions about the plight of children in so-called "failing" public schools identified as part of NCLB. What happens to the children who remain in the so-called "failing" schools? What will happen to these children's education? What quality of education will they receive? Who will assure that we do not create a different type of undesirable segregation, namely, one based on socioeconomic status? In other words, where are the safeguards for all of America's children, including the poorest ones, whether they are black, Latino, Asian, Native American, or white? Answers to questions like these reveal that, despite the *Brown* decision, public schools are currently facing major segregation and resegregation problems. No reasonable person would disagree that a good education is needed for all children and youth. In Chief Justice Warren's words on behalf of the Supreme Court previously cited above, "it is doubtful that any child may be expected to succeed in life if he is denied the opportunity of an education."

It is clear, too, that U.S. schools are still not equal. The goal should not be to focus so heavily on accountability that test scores end up creating further divisions and racial segregation in our public schools. An even more important goal should be to assure that a quality education is offered to every child in spite of their socioeconomic level. After all, participatory democracy is built on the assumption of equality and freedom for all citizens, and that includes educational access. Clearly, there can be no reasonable argument against these rights for all U.S. citizens.

So, why do we need racially and ethnically diverse student bodies in U.S. schools, colleges, and universities? In *Grutter*, Justice O'Connor aptly stated that "Numerous studies show that student body diversity promotes learning outcomes, and better prepares students for an increasingly diverse workforce and society, and better prepares them as professionals" (2003; Justice Sandra Day O'Connor for the U.S Supreme

Court). Our country is composed of a rich mixture of people from vary-ing races, ideals, cultures, and lifestyles. The U.S. Supreme Court con-tinues to celebrate diversity while admitting that racial inequality must be legally eliminated wherever it occurs. And the previously mentioned Civil Rights Project study has indicated a significant problem with the resegregation of U.S. public schools.

Justice O'Connor's words also include references to the value of a diverse workforce when she says, " . . . major American businesses have made it clear that the skills needed in today's increasingly global market-place can only be developed through exposure to widely diverse people, cultures, ideas, and viewpoints."

Beverly Tatum has written an important book that should be required reading for all educators. The book is entitled *Why Are All the Black Kids Sitting Together in the Cafeteria?* As a psychologist and educator, Dr. Tatum has dealt straightforwardly with the sticky issues of race and racial iden-tity, and has encouraged educators as well as parents to have conversa-tions about race and racial issues. She made the claim that if one were to walk into any racially mixed high school or college, one might expect to see black youth seated together in the cafeteria. She also predicted that white, Latino, Asian, and Native American groups would also be clustered together in school settings such as the cafeteria area. Is this self-segregation a problem that should be "fixed," or is it a coping strategy for students that should be supported?

As a reader, what do you think? Of course, on some level, reasonable individuals would agree that people should be allowed to make their own decisions about where to sit and with whom to communicate on a regular basis. But, then, why do we make a concerted effort to integrate the student body, staff, and faculty of our nation's schools if people are going to naturally cluster in racial or ethnic groups as a phenomenon of natural human behavior? Can a person achieve the true benefits of studying and working in a racially or ethnically diverse setting without interacting with people who are from different racial and ethnic groups? In short, is simply sitting next to someone in a class enough, or should one grow educationally by interacting with people whose views may be different than yours? Is Professor Cornell West right when he advocates that "race matters"?

Chapter 8 of Dr. Tatum's book (Tatum 1997) deals with racial identity, not only for blacks but also for Latinos, Native Americans, and Asians. In this chapter, she quoted several college students as very convincing examples of contemporary college students' views:

- Judith, a Chicana (Mexican female) college student stated: "I took a Chicano [Mexican] studies class my freshman year and that made me very militant."
- Cristina, A Puerto Rican college student, stated: "I'm a lot more fluent with English. I struggle with Spanish and it's something I've been trying to reclaim . . . I'm reading and writing more and more in Spanish, and I'm using it more in conversations with other Puerto Ricans."
- Don, a Native American college student, stated: "There is a certain amount of anger that comes from the past, realizing that my family, because they had to assimilate through the generations, don't really know who they are."
- Khanah, an Asian American college student, stated: "Being an Asian person, a person of color growing up in this society, I was taught to hate myself. I did hate myself, and I'm trying to deal with it."
- A Chinese college student asked Mark, a young white college student of Italian ancestry, "What do you know about Asians?" Mark answered: "I'm going to be honest with you. I completely believe the stereotype. Asian people are hard workers, they're really quiet, they get good grades because they have tons of pressure from their families to get good grades. . . . Asians are quiet so people can't have a problem with them."

Dr. Tatum beautifully illustrated a point in her book that America can never be viewed as solely a racially black-white society. "Cultural identities are not solely determined in response to racial ideologies, but racism increases the need for a positive self-defined identity in order to survive psychologically" (Tatum 1997, 165).

And so an important series of related questions arises: Where do we go from here? How are we grappling with some of these tough education issues that are linked both directly and indirectly with *Brown v. Board of Education?* How should the nation deal with issues of assuring a racially and ethnically *diverse* student body in schools and colleges? Assuring a racially and ethnically diverse staff in schools and institutions of higher education? Assuring a racially and ethnically diverse faculty and administration in all school settings? Celebrating our racial, ethnic, and cultural differences? Recognizing that racial and ethnic differences in school settings must not be perceived with connotations of good or bad, but different?

So, why was it important for us to celebrate more than fifty years of *Brown v. Board of Education?* The issues that prompted the *Brown* ruling in 1954 continue to plague us today throughout the U.S. Studies have shown that we are in a state eerily and arguably similar to the pre-*Brown* era. It is indeed crucial that "no child be left behind." However, educators, legislators, and concerned citizens everywhere, especially those who work in educational institutions, need to ensure that the vision of *Brown* is fully realized. We must all work together to make sure not only that the principles of *Brown v. Board of Education* continue to be upheld, but that its ideals become embedded in all of our American institutions, particularly our schools, colleges, and universities "with all deliberate speed."

As Dr. Martin Luther King Jr. told a crowd of about 20,000 college students who were protesting segregation in the 1960s: "Segregation injures one spiritually. It scars the soul and distorts the personality. It inflicts the segregator with a false sense of superiority while inflicting the segregated with a false sense of inferiority." (Washington 1999, 121)

Brown v. Board of Education's fiftieth anniversary is an appropriate time for the nation to pause for a moment and evaluate our achievement of the aims and vision of the landmark 1954 *Brown* decision. If asked to rate the current level of success of *Brown v. Board of Education*, we, the authors of this essay, would assign a grade of C+ at this point in our nation's history. We look forward to the opportunity to assign a higher grade in the future.

References

Betances, S. 1994. "African Americans and Hispanics/Latinos: Eliminating Barriers to Coalition Building." Paper presented a the Ethnic Diversity Roundtable, Chicago Urban Policy Institute and the Joint Center for Political and Economic Studies.

Delpit, L. 1995. *Other People's Children: Cultural Conflict in the Classroom*. New York: New Press.

Jacobs, G. S. 1998. *Getting Around* Brown: *Desegregation, Development, and the Columbus Public Schools*. Columbus: The Ohio State University Press.

Nieto, S. 1996. *Affirming Diversity: The Sociopolitical Context of Multicultural Education*. 2nd ed. White Plains, NY: Longman.

Reed, D. S. 2001. *On Equal Terms: The Constitutional Policies of Educational Opportunity*. Princeton, NJ: Princeton University Press.

Rosenberg, G. N. 1991. *The Hollow Hope*. Chicago: University of Chicago Press.

Sleeter, C. 1994. "White Racism." *Multicultural Education* (Spring): 5–8, and 39.

Suarez-Orozco, C., and M. Suarez-Orozco. 1995. *Transformations: Immigration, Family Life, and Achievement Motivation among Latino Adolescents*. Stanford, CA: Stanford University Press.

Tatum, B. D. 1997. *Why Are All the Black Kids Sitting Together in the Cafeteria? And Other Conversations about Race*. New York: Basic Books.

Tushnet, M.V., ed. 2001. *Thurgood Marshall: His Speeches, Writings, Arguments, Opinions, and Reminiscences.* Chicago: Chicago Review Press, Inc.

Washington, J. B. 1999. *A Testament of Hope: The Essential Writings of Martin Luther King, Jr.* San Francisco: Harper San Francisco.

Williams, R. 1988. *Eyes on the Prize: America's Civil Rights Years 1954–1965.* New York: Penguin Books.

CHAPTER 14

Children of *Brown*

MAC A. STEWART

Readers of these essays may find themselves surprised, as I was, by the number of times that the authors spoke directly and often movingly from their personal experience. I believe that many of these essays turn personal because the issues in *Brown* strike so deeply at the heart of the individual, especially for those who lived a decade or more prior to May 17, 1954, the date the Supreme Court struck down "separate but equal." Manning Marable summarizes the point for this generation when he says, "I am a child of the *Brown* decision, and my own personal journey symbolizes the successes and failures of legal desegregation."

In one way or another, we are all children of *Brown*. Lester Monts, remembering Little Rock in 1957, recounts the pervasiveness of segregation, suggesting the many ways in which African American lives were constricted, making "feelings of neglect and despair . . . rampant in black communities." When desegregation came to Central High School, along with the National Guard and the national media, *Brown* led to violence and injury. Out of that cauldron of terrorism and disorder, there emerged an "ambiance" of "former-foes-now-friends," not only in Little Rock but in many cities and states. This transmutation, decades in the making, affected the social fabric by forcing individuals to confront and assess their personal beliefs relative to their community. A sudden and powerful sense of hope contrasted with an inescapable environment of dread and danger: these conflicting, almost simultaneous, highly emotional experiences deeply imprinted themselves on the entire generation.

But the African Americans who were born and came to social consciousness in the 1960s and later are also children of *Brown,* even though they did not experience the full range of restrictions of segregation. My sons see what is going on today, but they don't realize how far we advanced in the years between the world prior to *Brown* and the world of today. Because of the protracted length of time that passed as communities implemented desegregation, because "all deliberate speed" often meant subterfuge and delay, the promise of *Brown* was widely delayed or denied. Several of our authors have described the slow progress of that promise through Congress and the courts—from the "separate but equal" of Jim Crow, to desegregation, to affirmative action, to diversity. This movement is tied to such landmarks as *Plessy v. Ferguson, Brown I, Brown II,* the Civil Rights act of 1964, and Title IX, among others. Because this movement has been slow and incremental (it is, after all, more than fifty years since the judgment in *Brown*), many contemporary observers lack the perspective to recognize and appreciate the progress that has been made. So it is an important contribution of some of these essays that they bring to life the conditions of segregation for a generation that has not known them at first hand. For since 1954, much has been accomplished *in law,* with consequential changes in daily living. The changes in law have settled into the daily practical consciousness of the country.

If the wider reality seems to lag behind the achievements in the courts, it is in part because *Brown* established the standard against which our contemporary social realities can be measured. That is, prior to *Brown,* equal justice was not in fact an operational goal, because "separate" was everywhere observably more important than "equal." People who idealized equality had to base their hopes in religious belief or in philosophical argument, neither of which has the practical temporal force of the law. But since *Brown,* the goal under law is equality, and the law must operate within the light of that goal. Thus, the impact of *Brown* became the promise of equal justice under the law. And with this promise of equal justice in place, it becomes incumbent to ask, as many of our authors do, has that promise been kept? Or is there evidence that "separate and unequal" is still tolerated in the public venues of American life?

The National Urban League monitors the state of Black America with the "Equality Index," which is described in their literature as "a statistical measurement of disparities or 'equality gaps' between blacks and whites across five different areas"—namely, economic status, education, health and quality of life, social justice, and civic engagement. This index assigns whites a weighted index value of 1 in each of these component areas and calculates a comparative value for blacks on each component. "An index value of less than 1 means blacks are doing worse than whites in a particular category, while a value of 1 or above means they are doing equal or better."[1]

The most recent available data measure equality as of 2006, with the following quantitative results by component area and overall:

Economic	0.56	30%
Health	0.76	25%
Education	0.78	25%
Social Justice	0.74	10%
Civic Engagement	1.04	10%
TOTAL	0.73	

(The final column indicates the weight given to each component as a percentage of the total in the final line.) In short, blacks participate in civic affairs (for example, by voting) to a slightly greater degree than whites. However, on all other components they score well below whites, especially on the economic vector that considers income, home ownership, business ownership, and related matters.[2]

Assuming this general snapshot of the current state of Black America is reasonably accurate, what does it suggest about the extent to which *Brown* has succeeded in changing the real landscape of American society? Arguably the most important component in this Equality Index is education, since it is generally well documented that better education usually leads to better income, as well as to better health and better health care, and to an improved quality of life. Thus, we circle back to *Brown*. It is reasonable to hypothesize that since 1954, greater access to good education has improved African American well-being and narrowed the equality gap. Fortunately, we are not restricted to hypotheses. Careful social scientists have studied the state of black education and the extent of desegregation for nearly all the years since the implementation of *Brown*. That literature is noted in several of our essays and in the bibliography.

1. National Urban League, "The State of Black America 2006," 29 March 2006 press release.

2. For more information, go to www.nul.org.

I turn especially to a study published in 2002 by the Civil Rights Project of Harvard University—namely, "Race in American Public Schools: Rapidly Resegregating School Districts" by Erika Frankenberg and Chungmei Lee. The good news that they report is that, "Nationally, segregation for blacks has declined substantially since the pre-*Brown* era," but this is coupled with the observation that segregation for blacks "reached its lowest point in the late 1980s": "We are now [in 2002] almost fifty years from the initial Supreme Court ruling banning segregation and more than a decade into a period in which the U.S. Supreme Court has authorized termination of desegregation orders. These plans are being dissolved by court orders even in some communities that want to maintain them; in addition, some federal courts are forbidding even *voluntary* desegregation plans" (emphasis added).[3] In short, progress toward universal school integration has been reversed, partly by action of the courts themselves.

The picture is complicated by changing national demographics. For example, for the growing population of Latinos, "the story has been one of steadily rising segregation since the 1960s and no significant desegregation efforts outside of a handful of large districts." Changing birth rates, the growth of charter schools, regionally changing levels of private school enrollment—all these factors are contributing to an emerging trend of rising segregation amid increasing diversity. Studied at the district level, the picture shows that "patterns of segregation by race are strongly linked to segregation by poverty, and poverty concentrations are strongly linked to unequal opportunities and outcomes."[4] Dropout rates have been shown to be highest in segregated high-poverty high schools, report Robert Balfanz and Nettie Letgers.[5] The conclusion is stark: "*virtually all* school districts analyzed are showing lower levels of inter-racial exposure since 1986, suggesting a trend towards resegregation, and in some districts, these declines are sharp" (emphasis in original).[6] This harsh reality contrasts dramatically with the increased diversity predicted by all accounts for twenty-first-century American life, a diversity for which educators almost universally assert that effectively integrated education is the best preparation.

Moreover, it is a fundamental value of American social belief that public schools offer the way up and the way out, that accessible, free,

3. Frankenberg and Lee, 2.

4. See Gary Orfield, *Schools More Separate: Consequences of a Decade of Resegregation* (Cambridge, MA: The Civil Rights Project, Harvard University, July 2001).

5. Cited in Frankenberg and Lee, 3.

6. Ibid., 4.

high-quality education is central to the development of each individual's potential and to the nation's economic well-being, as well (now one supposes more than ever) as its physical security. Enlistment in the Armed Services can remain voluntary only if the citizenry from which volunteers emerge is adequately educated.

Our technological superiority is challenged if quality education falters or is available only to a favored elite. We are in no position to criticize nations that restrict education by gender if we have built a structure that restricts education by race, country of national origin, or family income, especially if there is a high correlation between economic status and race.

In short, while I certainly agree with the authors who demonstrate educational advances made in the wake of *Brown*'s call for integration, I fear the erosion of some of those advances due to changes in recent years, some of which ironically are due to actions by the courts. And I would add a personal observation that as a topic of public dialogue, the conversations about school segregation that we hear in the twenty-first century lack the intelligence and conviction of the public dialogues of the 1960s and 1970s. They lack the articulate ethical leadership of Martin Luther King Jr. and the incisive journalistic commentary of those decades. Even if public awareness were to focus on the issues as they might now be defined, I am skeptical that the public's attention would be held for very long. The culture of "blogging" has replaced sustained public discourse in almost all of our news media. I deeply wish that I could conclude otherwise; however, after reviewing their essays, and the world that presents itself in our current decade, it seems to me that the promise of justice represented by *Brown I* and *Brown II,* and reaffirmed in *Bakke,* illuminates the paths of the righteous. But all the Lord's people are not prophets, and too many still prefer to walk in the dark.

Adams v. Richardson. 1974. Federal District Court of the District of Columbia. Washington, D.C.

Albany Evening Journal. 1857. March 29. Albany, New York.

Alexander v. Holmes County Bd. of Education. 1969. 396 U. S. 19.

Anderson, James. 2004. *The Unfinished Agenda of Brown v Board of Education.* Hoboken, NJ: J. Wiley & Sons.

Bates, D. 1962. *The Long Shadow of Little Rock.* Fayetteville, AR: University of Arkansas Press.

Before Brown, beyond boundaries: commemorating the 50ᵗʰ anniversary of Brown v Board of Education. A publication of the Association for the Study of African American Life and History. Trenton, NJ: African World Press.

Bell, D. 2004. *Silent Covenants: Brown v. Board of Education and the Unfulfilled Hopes for Racial Reform.* 8–9. London: Oxford University Press.

Bell, Derrick A. 2004. *Silent Covenants: Brown v Board of Education and the Unfulfilled Hopes for Racial Reform.* New York: Oxford University Press.

Betances, S. 1994. "African Americans and Hispanics/Latinos: Eliminating barriers to Coalition building." Paper presented at the Ethnic Diversity Roundtable, Chicago Urban Policy Institute and the Joint Center for Political and Economic Studies.

Boger, J. C. 2003. "Education's 'Perfect Storm'? Racial Resegregation, High Stakes Testing, and School Resources Inequities: The Case of North Carolina." *North Carolina Law and Review* 81, no. 2 (August): 1375–1462.

Bowen, W., and D. Bok. 1998. *The Shape of the River: Long-term Consequences of Considering Race in College and University Admissions.* Princeton, NJ: Princeton University Press.

(Brown I) Brown v. Board of Education. 1954. 347 U.S. 483.

(Brown II) Brown v. Board of Education. 1955. 349 U.S. 294.

Brown-Nagin, T. 2000. "Toward a Pragmatic Understanding of Status-Consciousness:

The Case of Deregulated Education." *Duke Law Journal* 50, no. 1 (December): 753–886.

Brunner, E. 1945. *Justice and the Social Order.* Trans. by Mary Hottinger. New York and London: Harper & Brothers.

Buber, M. 1955. *Between Man and Man.* Boston, MA: Beacon Press. Originally published in 1947.

Byrne, Dara N. 2005. Brown v. Board of Education: *Its Impact on Public Education, 1954–2004.* Brooklyn, NY: Word for Word Publishing Co.

Cheryl J. Hopwood et al. v. State of Texas. 1996. No. 84–50569 U.S. Court of Appeals for the Fifth Circuit.

Civil Rights Act of 1957. 1957. U.S.C.

Civil Rights Act of 1964. 1964. U.S.C.

Civil Rights Act of 1964. 1996. 42 U.S.C. Sec 2000 (c) (d).

Clark, Kenneth Bancroft. 2004. *Toward Humanity and Justice: The Writings of Kenneth B. Clark, Scholar of the 1954* Brown v. Board of Education *Decision.* Westport, CN; New York: Praeger.

Cottrell, Robert J. 2003. Brown v. Board of Education: *Caste, Culture, and the Constitution.* Lawrence, KA: University Press of Kansas.

Crenson, M., and B. Ginsberg. 2002. *Downsizing Democracy: How America Sidelined Its Citizens and Privatized Its Public.* Baltimore: John Hopkins University Press.

Cushman, Clare. 2004. *Black, White and Brown: The Landmark School Desegregation Case in Retrospect.* Washington, D.C. CQ Press.

Cushman, R. 1947. *Leading Constitutional Decisions,* 8th ed. New York: F. S. Crofts & Co.

Daniel, P. T. K. 1980. "A History of Discrimination against Black Students in Chicago Secondary Schools." *History of Education Quarterly* 20, no. 1 (Summer): 147–65.

Davis, H., and R. Good, R, eds. 1960. *Reinhold Niebuhr on Politics.* New York: Charles Scribner's Sons.

Dayton Board of Education v. Brinkman. 1977. 433 U.S. 406.

Delpit, L. 1995. *Other People's Children: Cultural Conflict in the Classroom.* New York: New Press.

Dillard v. School Board of City of Charlotteville. 1962. 308 F.2d 920 (4th Cir.).

(Dowell) Board of Education of Oklahoma City Schools v. Dowell. 1991. 498 U.S. 237.

Elementary and Secondary Education Amendments of 1966. 2000. 20 U.S.C. Sections 6301 et. Seq.

Executive Order No. 3 C.E.R. 1961. Establishing the President's Committee on Equal Employment Opportunity. The White House.

Feagin, J. 2000. *Racist America: Roots, Current Realities, and Future Reparations.* New York: Routledge.

Frankenbuerg, Erika, and Lee Chungmei. *Race in American Public Schools: Rapidly Resegregating School Districts.* Cambridge, MA: Harvard University, 2002.

Franklin, J. H. 1974. *From Slavery to Freedom.* 4th ed. New York: Alfred. A. Knopf.

Franklin, J. H., and A. A. Moss Jr. 1994. *From Slavery to Freedom: A History of African Americans.* 7th ed. New York: McGraw-Hill, Inc.

Freeman v. Pitts. 1992. 503 U.S. 467.

Friedman, Leon. 2004. Brown v. Board: *The Landmark Oral Argument before the Supreme Court.* New York. New Press.

Goldstein, S., E. G. Gee, and P. T. K. Daniel. 1995. *Law and Public Education*. Charlottesville: Michie Law Publishers.

Green v. County School Board of New Kent. 1968. 391 U.S. 430.

Greenberg, Jack. 2004. *Brown v. Board of Education: 1968. Witness to a Landmark Decision*. New York: Twelve Tables Press.

Griffin v. County School Board of Prince Edward County. 1964. 377 U.S. 218.

Grutter v. Bollinger. 2003. 539 U.S. 306.

Harvard Classics, The. 1938. *American Historical Documents*. New York: P. F. Collier and Son.

Harvey, W. 2003. *20th Anniversary Annual Status Report on Minorities in Higher Education*. Washington, DC: American Council on Education.

Harvey, W., et al. 2004. "The Impact of the *Brown v. Board of Education* Decision on Postsecondary Participation of African Americans." *Journal of Negro Education* 73 (Summer): 338–39.

hooks, b. 1997. *Wounds of Passion: A Writing Life*. New York: Henry Holt and Company.

Jackson, John P. 2005. *Science for Segregation: Race, Law, and the Case against* Brown v. Board of Education. New York: New York University Press.

Jacobs, G. S. 1998. *Getting around* Brown: *Desegregation, Development, and the Columbus Public Schools*. Columbus: The Ohio State University Press.

Kane, T. 1998. "Racial and Ethnic Preferences in College Admissions." *Ohio State Law Journal* 59 (Autumn): 971–96.

Keyes v. School District No. 1. 1973. Denver, CO, 413 U.S. 189.

Kushner, H. S. 1981. *When Bad Things Happen to Good People*. New York: Schocken Books.

Lau, Peter. 2004. *From the Grassroots to the Supreme Court: Brown v. Board of Education and American Democracy*. Durham: Duke University Press.

Logan, R. 1997. *The Betrayal of the Negro*. New York: Da Capo Press.

Meador, D. 1959. "The Constitution and the Assignment of Pupils to Public Schools." *Virginia Law Review* 45, no. 1 (May): 517–63.

Merritt, D. 1998. "The Future of *Bakke:* Will Social Science Matter?" *Ohio State Law Journal* 59: 1055–67.

Miller, L. 1966. *The Petitioners: The Story of the Supreme Court of the United States and the Negro*. New York: Pantheon Books.

Milliken v. Bradley. 1995. 418 U.S. 717 1974.

(*Missouri III*) *Missouri v. Jenkins*. 1995. 515 U.S. 70.

National Urban League 2006. "The State of Black America 2006." Press release, 29 March.

Nichol, G., 2004. "A Great Decision Rescued the Court." *The News & Observer*, May 9.

Niebuhr, R. 1932. *Moral Man and Immoral Society: A Study of Ethics and Politics*. New York: Charles Scribner's Sons.

Nieto, S. 1996. *Affirming Diversity: The Sociopolitical Context of Multicultural Education*. 2nd ed. White Plains, NY: Longman.

Ogletree, Charles. 2004. *All Deliberate Speed: Reflections on the First Half Century of* Brown v. Board of Education. New York: W. W. Norton & Co.

Orfield, Gary. "Schools More Separate: Consequences of a Decade of Resegregation." Cambridge, MA: The Civil Rights Project, Harvard University, July 2001.

Parker, W. 2003. "The Decline of Judicial Decisionmaking: School Desegregation and District Court Judges." *North Carolina Law Review*. 81, no. 3 (August): 1623–57.

Pasadena City Board of Education v. Spangler. 1976. 427 U.S. 424.

Patterson, J. T. 2001. *Brown v. Board of Education.* New York: Oxford University Press.

Philogene, Gina. 2004. *Racial Identity in Context: The Legacy of Kenneth B Clark.* Washington, D.C.: American Psychological Association.

Plessy v. Ferguson. 1896.163 U.S. 537.

Pritchett, C. H. 1959. *The American Constitution.* New York: McGraw-Hill Book Company, Inc.

Rawls, J. 2001. *Justice as Fairness.* Cambridge, MA: Harvard University Press.

_____. 1971. *A Theory of Justice.* Cambridge, MA: Harvard University Press.

Reed, D. S. 2001. *On Equal Terms: The Constitutional Policies of Educational Opportunity.* Princeton: Princeton University Press.

Rhode, Debra. 2004. Brown *at 50: The Unfinished Legacy: A Collection of Essays.* Chicago: American Bar Association.

Roberts v. City of Boston. 1848. 59 Mass. (5 Cush.) 198.

Rountree, Clarke. 2004. Brown v. Board of Education *at Fifty: a Rhetorical Perspective.* Lanham, MD: Lexington Books.

Rosenberg, G. N. 1991. *The Hollow Hope.* Chicago: University of Chicago Press.

Salisbury, David. 2004. *Educational Freedom in Urban America:* Brown v. Board *after Half a Century.* Washington, D.C.: Cato Institute.

Sleeter, C. 1994. "White Racism." *Multicultural Education* 1, no. 4 (Spring): 5–8, and 39.

Smith, G. 2004. *The Politics of Deceit: Saving Freedom and Democracy from Extinction.* Hoboken, NJ: John Wiley & Sons.

Stone, R. H., ed. 1968. *Reinhold Niebuhr: Faith and Politics.* New York: George Braziller.

Suarez-Orozco, C., and M. Suarez-Orozco. 1995. *Transformations: Immigration, Family Life, and Achievement Motivation among Latino Adolescents.* Stanford: Stanford University Press.

Swann v. Charlotte-Mecklenburg Board of Education. 1971. 404 U.S. 1.

Tatum, B. D. 1997. *Why Are All the Black Kids Sitting Together in the Cafeteria? And Other Conversations about Race.* New York: Basic Books.

Telgen, Diane. 2005. *Brown v. Board of Education.* Detroit: Omnigraphics.

Tillich, P. 1960. *Love, Power, and Justice: Ontological Analyses and Ethical Applications.* New York: Oxford University Press.

Title IV of the Civil Rights Act of 1964. 2000. 42 U.S.C. Sec. 2000d-1.

Title VI of the Civil Rights Act of 1964. 2000. 42 U.S.C. Sec. 2000d-1.

Tushnet, M.V., ed. 2001. *Thurgood Marshall: His Speeches, Writings, Arguments, Opinions, and Reminiscences.* Chicago: Chicago Review Press, Inc.

U.S. Census Bureau. 2001. *Statistical Abstract of the United States.* Washington, D.C: U.S. Government Printing Office.

U.S. Constitution, Amendment X.

U.S. Constitution, Article VI, Cl. 2.

Walton, H., Jr., and R. C. Smith. 2003. *American Politics and the African American Quest for Universal Freedom.* 2nd ed. New York: Addison Wesley Longman, Inc.

Washington, J. B. 1999. *A Testament of Hope: The Essential Writings of Martin Luther King, Jr.* San Francisco: Harper San Francisco.

Williams, R. 1988. *Eyes on the Prize: America's Civil Rights Years of 1954–1965.* New York: Penguin Books.

Willie, C. V. 1978. *The Sociology of Urban Education.* Lexington, MA: Lexington Books.

Willie, C. V., R. Edwards, and M. J Alves. 2002. *Student Diversity, Choice and School Improvement.* Westport, CN: Bergin and Garvey.

Woodward, C. V. 1974. *The Strange Career of Jim Crow.* 3rd ed. Oxford: Oxford University Press.

SAMUEL DUBOIS COOK is a political scientist whose specialty is political philosophy. A native of Griffin, Georgia, he is also a civil and human rights activist. He is president emeritus of Dillard University. After completing his A.B. degree in history at Morehouse College, he earned his Master's and Ph.D. degrees at The Ohio State University. Dr. Cook began his professional career as a teacher after a short stint in the U.S. Army. He taught political science at Southern University in Baton Rouge, Louisiana, then moved to Atlanta University where he also became politically active. He worked on black voter registration and served as youth director of the NAACP. Professor Cook later taught at other colleges and universities, including the University of Illinois, the University of California, Los Angeles, and Duke University. Cook became the first African American professor at Duke University. He was also the first African American to hold a regular faculty appointment at a predominantly white university in the South.

PHILIP T. K. DANIEL is the William Ray and Marie Adamson Professor of Educational Administration/Higher Education at The Ohio State University, where he is also adjunct professor of law. Dr. Daniel was president of the Education Law Association in 2003–04 and a member of its Board of Directors from 1999 to 2005. He has taught at the university level for more than thirty-three years. He received Ohio State's Alumni Award for Distinguished Teaching and was inducted into the Ohio State Academy of Distinguished Teaching in 1993. He is a member of the

Author's Committee of *West's Education Law Reporter* and serves on the editorial boards of the *Brigham Young University Journal of Law and Education,* the *Journal of Education and Urban Society,* and the *Journal of the South African Society for Education.* Professor Daniel is a well-known presenter at national and international conferences and has authored and co-authored a number of scholarly articles. He is co-author of the books *Education Law and the Public Schools: A Compendium* and *Law and Public Education.* He is currently writing two other books entitled *Law, Policy and Higher Education* and *Legal Research for Educators.*

ROBERT M. DUNCAN is currently the chair of the board of trustees at The Ohio State University, a position which culminates a lifetime career in law and justice. After completing his undergraduate and law degrees at Ohio State, he worked for more than thirty years in public service—as Chief Counsel to the Attorney General of Ohio, as judge in the Franklin County Municipal Court, as a Justice in the Supreme Court of Ohio, as judge and chief judge in the United States Military Court of Appeals, and as judge in the United States District Court for the Southern District of Ohio. For seven years Judge Duncan was a partner in Jones, Day, Reavis & Pogue of Columbus, Ohio, and then returned to Ohio State as Vice President and General Counsel, and eventually secretary of the board of trustees. Judge Duncan served on two Presidential Commissions, including the Commission on White House Fellows (1970–74) and the Commission for the Observance of the Twenty-Fifth Anniversary of the United Nations. He has received many honors and awards, including an honorary degree from Capital University and the Dr. Frederick Douglas Patterson Award of the United Negro College Fund (1991).

RALPH KENNEDY FRASIER, a native of North Carolina, earned his bachelor's degree and J.D. from North Carolina Central University. Following law school, he entered the corporate world, serving for more than ten years with Winston Salem-based Wachovia Corporation. For twenty-two years he was general counsel and secretary of Huntington Bancshares Incorporated, based in Columbus, Ohio. In 1998 he entered the firm of Porter Wright Morris & Arthur LLP. This firm established a scholarship in his honor. Mr. Frasier was named the 2002 recipient of the Ritter Award, the highest recognition given by the Ohio State Bar Association for outstanding contributions to the administration of justice. Frasier is a Distinguished Lifetime Fellow of the Ohio State Bar Association, a Fellow of the Columbus Bar Association, a Life Member of the NAACP and of Alpha Phi Alpha Fraternity, Inc., as well as a Brawley Fellow of Sigma Pi Phi Fraternity, Inc.

CHARLES R. HANCOCK is currently professor and associate dean of the College of Education at The Ohio State University, where he has worked since 1986. He is past president of the American Council on the Teaching of Foreign Languages and has also served as project consultant to the Modern Language Association. His research and scholarship focus on the intersection of several disciplines, including teacher education, testing and assessment, multicultural education, and second-language education. Dr. Hancock is currently principal investigator for a five-year study, funded federally, that deals with raising student achievement by infusing culturally relevant pedagogy principles in the teaching of middle school mathematics and science for urban schools.

JANINE HANCOCK JONES is a labor and employment attorney at Baker & Hostetler LLP, where she regularly represents management clients in all aspects of the employment relationship, including litigation. She earned her B.A. from Spelman College and her J.D. from Howard University School of Law. She serves as co-chair of the Martin Luther King Jr. Committee of the Columbus Bar Association and as vice-president of the John Mercer Langston Bar Association. She is a member of the board of trustees of the Northside Child Development Center in Columbus. In 2005 Ms. Hancock Jones was named a "Rising Star" by *Ohio Super Lawyers* magazine, an honor bestowed on only 2 percent of Ohio lawyers. She was selected as a member of the Leadership Columbus Class of 2007.

ADIA M. HARVEY is an assistant professor of sociology at Georgia State University. Her research explores the intersections of race, class, and gender in the workplace and in occupations. She has published articles in the *Journal of Negro Education, Gender & Society,* and *Teachers College Record.* Currently Professor Harvey is working on a book-length exploration of the social and economic significance of entrepreneurship among working-class Black women in the hair industry.

WILLIAM B. HARVEY is vice-president and chief officer for diversity and equity at the University of Virginia, where he is also professor of education and African American Studies. Prior to assuming duties in Virginia, he was vice-president and director of the Center for the

Advancement of Racial and Ethnic Equity at the American Council on Education in Washington, D.C. He has also held faculty, administrative, and research positions as the University of Wisconsin–Milwaukee, North Carolina State University, Stony Brook, the University of Pennsylvania, and Earlham College. Dr. Harvey's research on the factors that impede progress of underserved groups, particularly in higher education, has been widely published in books, refereed journal articles, technical reports, and opinion pieces. He serves on the editorial boards of *Change,* the *Negro Educational Review,* and *Multicultural Learning and Teaching.*

MANNING MARABLE is a professor of public affairs, political science, history, and African American Studies at Columbia University. Professor Marable is also director of the Center for Contemporary Black History, and from 1993 to 2003 he was the founding director of the Institute for Research in African-American Studies at Columbia University. The author or editor of twenty-one books, Dr. Marable's most recent works include *Living Black History* (New York: Basic Civitas, 2006) and, edited with Myrlie Evers-Williams, *The Autobiography of Medger Evans* (New York: Basic Civitas, 2005). Since 1999, Professor Marable has been founding editor of *Souls: A Critical Journal of Black Politics, Culture and Society,* distributed by Taylor and Francis Publishers.

DEBORAH JONES MERRITT holds the John Deaver Drinko/Baker & Hostetler Chair in Law at The Ohio State University, where she is also adjunct professor of women's studies, sociology, and public affairs. She earned her B.A. at Harvard College and her J.D. at Columbia University. She received The Ohio State University's Distinguished Scholar Award in 2002 and its Distinguished Diversity Enhancement Award in 2004. She was selected as the University Commencement Speaker for autumn quarter 2004.

LESTER P. MONTS is the senior vice-provost for Academic Affairs and Arthur F. Thurnau Professor of Music at the University of Michigan. Since 2002, he has served as senior counselor to the president for arts, diversity, and undergraduate affairs. Dr. Monts holds degrees from Arkansas Tech University, the University of Nebraska, and the University of Minnesota. He has held teaching and administrative positions at The University of California, Santa Barbara, Case Western Reserve University, the University of Minnesota, and Edinboro University. He is an active researcher in the field of ethnomusicology and is considered one of the world's leading scholars on the music of the Guinea Coast region of West Africa. With Professor Ruth Stone of Indiana University, he is co-principal investigator for the Ethnomusicology Video for Instruction and Analysis—Digital Archive (EVIA), a Mellon Foundation-supported project to preserve and disseminate video data derived from the work of ethnographic fieldwork. He is a trustee of the College Board and active in numerous national academic and scholarly committees and projects. In 2004, he wrote an essay for the Martin Luther King Jr. commemoration at the University of Michigan (a revised version of which is chapter 5 in this volume).

Professor **john powell,** executive director of the Kirwan Institute for the Study of Race and Ethnicity at The Ohio State University, holds the Williams Chair in Civil Rights and Civil Liberties in the Moritz College of Law. He earned his undergraduate degree at Stanford University and the J.D. from the University of California at Berkeley. He also studied at the University of Minnesota on a postdoctoral fellowship. He was the founder and past director of the Institute on Race and Poverty at the University of Minnesota and has served as national legal director of the American Civil Liberties Union and director of legal services for the City of Miami, Florida. Professor powell is an internationally recognized authority in the areas of civil rights, civil liberties, and issues relating to race, ethnicity, poverty, and the law. He has taught at Columbia University, Harvard Law School, American University, the University of San Francisco School of Law, and the Law School at the University of Minnesota.

CHARLES ULLMAN SMITH is emeritus Distinguished Professor of Sociology and Graduate Dean at Florida A&M University, and immediate past managing editor of *The Negro Educational Review.* He completed his undergraduate studies at Tuskegee University, and earned his Master's degree from Fisk University. He was the first African American to earn the Ph.D. from Washington State University, and he completed post-doctoral studies at the University of Michigan. His career publications include seventy-five articles in scholarly journals, and he is the author, co-author, or editor of fourteen books and eight monographs. The first African American to teach at Florida State University, the University of Florida, and the University of Miami, he received more than $4 million in federal, state, and private foundation grants in support of his research. Dr. Smith is past president of the Association of Social and Behavioral

Scientists, Inc., the Southern Sociological Society's Florida Conference of Sociologists, and founder and past president of the Florida Council for Graduate Studies.

MAC A. STEWART is special assistant to the president for Diversity and vice-provost for Minority Affairs at The Ohio State University, where he served as dean of University College from 1991 to 2001. He earned his undergraduate degree in sociology from Morehouse College, an M.A. in counseling from Atlanta University (now Clark Atlanta), and a Ph.D. in higher education administration from The Ohio State University. Following the doctorate he had additional education at Harvard University and the University of Bonn, West Germany. Dr. Stewart is associate professor and member of the graduate faculty in both the College of Human Ecology and the College of Education at Ohio State. He has been a member of the editorial board of *The Negro Educational Review* since 1983 and served as editor in chief from 1999 to 2006, when he became chairman of the editorial board. He is a member of the board of trustees of the International Foundation for Education and Self-Help, an organization founded by the late Reverend Leon H. Sullivan, and has worked closely with its Teachers for Africa program. He has served on many other boards, including those of the Ohio Historical Society, the Mount Carmel School of Nursing, the Columbus Urban League, the Columbus Academy, and Boys and Girls Clubs of Columbus.

VINCENE VERDUN is associate professor in the Moritz College of Law at The Ohio State University. Her research has focused on critical race theory, including reparations to African Americans. Following graduation from law school, she served as corporate counsel for the Bendix Corporation and joined the faculty of the College of Law at the University of Detroit in 1980. She has also taught at the Capital University Law School. She is the advisor to the Black Law Student Association, participates in the project Leadership for Institutional Change, is member at large in the leadership of The Ohio State University chapter of the American Association of University Professors, and is a director of the Midwest People of Color Legal Scholarship Conference. Professor Verdun is founder of READ (Read Columbus Read, Inc.), a nonprofit organization that provides academic assistance, reading incentives, and access to computers to low-income children in the housing projects of Columbus, and she serves on the board of directors of the Dr. Martin Luther King, Jr., Arts Complex, an art and cultural center.

CHARLES V. WILLIE is the Charles William Eliot Professor of Education Emeritus at the Graduate School of Education, Harvard University. He earned his B.A. from Morehouse College, his M.A. from Atlanta University (now Clark Atlanta University), and a Ph.D. in sociology from Syracuse University. Prior to Harvard, Professor Willie served as professor and later chair of sociology, and Vice-President of Student Affairs at Syracuse University. Professor Willie is former vice-president of the American Sociological Association, former president of the Eastern Sociological Association, and a member of the Association of Black Sociologists. He has been appointed as master, consultant, or expert witness in several court cases and in several communities for the purpose of designing, implementing, or evaluating public school desegregation plans. Among his books are *Black Students in White Colleges* (1972), *Black/Brown/White Relations* (1977), *Black Colleges in America* (1978), *The Ivory and Ebony Towers* (1981), *African-Americans and the Doctoral Experience* (with Michael Gradfy and Richard Hope, 1991), and *The Black College Mystique* (with Richard Reddick and Ronald Brown, 2006).